ALBEST

ALBEST

UNTOLD STORIES FROM THE CORRESPONDENTS
FOR THE LEGENDARY TIME-LIFE NEWS SERVICE

EDITED BY JOHN F. STACKS

To order additional copies of this book, contact:
Xlibris Corporation
1-888-795-4274
www.Xlibris.com
Orders@Xlibris.com
114777

CONTENTS

Contributors

(In order of appearance)

Karen Tumulty
Larry Barrett
Joe Kane
Jay Branegan
Suzanne Davis
Ed Goodpaster
Chris Ogden
Barrett Seaman
Larry Malkin
Dick Duncan
Rick Hornik
Elaine Dutka
Eileen Shields-West
Eileen Harkin
David Aikman
Stan Cloud
Cathy Booth
Thomas
Chris Porterfield
Charles Eisendrath
Bill Marmon
Sam Allis
Bruce Nelan
Jan Simpson
Jamie Graff
David Jackson
Henry Muller
George Taber

Jeremy Main
Mary Wormley
John Stacks
Massimo Calabresi
Richard Behar
Roger Stone
Marlin Levin
Robert Goldstein
Jaime Florcruz
Mia Turner
George Russell
Dick Thompson
Strobe Talbott
Martha Smilgis
Andrew Purvis
Mark Thompson
Camille Cassata
Sanabria
Brian Doyle
Mia Turner
Barbara Ungeheuer
Eugene Linden
Ed Barnes
Joelle Attinger
Chris Redman
Johanna McGeary
Marguersite
Michaels

David Beckwith
Anita Pretap
Gerald Schecter
Joe Boyce
Margot Roosevelt
Phil Taubman
Nina Burleigh
Laverne Prager
Peter Ross Range
Ron Stodghill
Alex Smith
Ned Desmond
Sylvester Monroe
Michael Duffy
Jack E. White
Clair Senard
Roy Rowan
James K. Willwerth
Michael Kramer
Jonathan Beaty
Jess Cook
Lans Lamont
Leo Janos
Lisa Beyer
Roberto Suro
Paul Witteman
Frank McCulloch
Katie McNevin

Introduction

My adventures in that character (a newspaper reporter) . . . had their moments—in fact, they were made up, subjectively, of one continuous, unrelenting, almost delirious moment—and when I revive them now it is mainly to remind myself and inform historians that a newspaper reporter, in those remote days, had a grand and gaudy time of it, and no call to envy any man. . . . I believed then and believe today, that it was the maddest, gladdest, damndest existence ever enjoyed by mortal youth. **H.L. Mencken**

For most of us, for most of the time we were correspondents for the Time-Life News Service, that is a sound description of the way we lived and worked. We traveled the world at the company's considerable expense, we had access to the leaders of the political world and the luminaries of the academy and the arts. We were able to see human suffering in ways no one should want to see, but also to see human kindness and the occasional triumph of good over evil that helped balance the emotional scales.

In some ways, what we did was like attending school while being paid to do so. We were paid to learn and then to transmit what we learned to the readers of Time Magazine. Almost every week, almost every year, it was a feast of learning about the way the world worked and about how the human race functioned. It was at turns glorious and horrifying.

The News Service itself should be dated from 1962 when the U.S, Canadian and international news gathering operations were merged into one organization headed by Richard Clurman (whose photo is on the cover of this book.) At its largest, the news service had 135 staff correspondents stationed around the world and another 300 reporters not on staff but who served as part-time stringers for the magazines. The official history of the company between 1960 and 1980 (written by Curt Prendergast and Geoffrey Colvin) says that another 150 others were employed in support positions. The budget for the news service alone nearly equaled the cost of the rest of Time's editorial operations.

Obviously, this could not last and it didn't. The volume of reported material the news service produced every week dwarfed the amount of space available in the pages of the magazine. These files were sent by Western Union in the very old days and then by telex. The price of transmission was computed by characters in the files, thus abbreviations were employed. *Albest* was the typical sign-off at the end of a file and is an elision of "all the best". It persisted into the computer age.

Someone guessed that the news service produced the word equivalent of *War and Peace* every week. Partly because of the sheer excess of reportage but also because of the political slant the New York editors wanted to put on the story, being a correspondent was often very frustrating. Before Henry Grunwald became editor of the magazine in 1968, the correspondents never saw the final story until they picked up the magazine on Monday. We called it "apology day" because many of us would call our sources to try to explain why none of what they had told us appeared in the magazine. This also produced a certain tension between the correspondents and the editors.

By the dawn of the 21st Century, with the internet increasingly offering news for free, the pressure on all print organizations increased and the need to reduce costs rose. An obvious target at Time was the News Service. Who needed *War and Peace* every week when you could Google anything?

Still, it was a great run. When all the parts were working together—the news service reporting every scrap of information they could find, the editors and writers and designers all humming away--Time could produce amazing magazines, often on very tight deadlines. Former correspondent and managing editor Henry Muller has a description for those weeks when the place worked like a high priced piece of machinery. "It's like driving a Ferrari," he said.

The stories in this book are the ones the correspondents tell each other and their journalistic colleagues. They paint a vivid picture of what it was like to work for what was one of the great news gathering organizations in the world.

JFS

Border Power

I had read Time Magazine for as long as I could remember, even signed up for my own subscription when I was in college. So when I went to work here more than 15 years ago, I thought I had an appreciation for the power of that red border. But as it turned out, Newt Gingrich was the one who first impressed upon me what it really meant to be working for this extraordinary magazine.

It was October, 1994, the month that I joined TIME from the Los Angeles Times to cover Congress. It was also only a few weeks before what was looking like a potential earthquake of a midterm election. My new editors told me they wanted a *story* on the firebrand Republican congressman who was the face of the voter anger that suddenly seemed to be coming from everywhere.

There was a problem, though. Gingrich was barnstorming every conservative corner of America in an eight-seater airplane. Keeping up with him was impossible, as pretty much every political reporter in the country was discovering. At one point, I even went so far as to charter my own plane with a reporter from the Washington Post to get to a rally in Tullahoma, Tennessee. (Yes, younger colleagues, there was a time when a reporter could put a plane on the expense account . . .)

But it still wasn't working. The logistics were killing me. I couldn't get the kind of close-up view of the guy that I needed to tell this story right. Until I mentioned to someone on his staff that a Time *cover* might be in the works. Suddenly, one of those eight seats belonged to me.

As I buckled myself in, I pressed Newt as to why he had relented and let me aboard. He looked at me like I was a little thick for even asking that question. It was the fact that what he was doing had been deemed worthy of the red border. The future Speaker (and presidential candidate) told me, off the top of his head, that Richard Nixon had been on 55 TIME covers. That figure, it turns out, had made an impression on him when it had been cited at Nixon's funeral earlier that year. (Newt, of course, would go on to see himself there *several more* times, including as *Man of the Year* in 1995.)

Karen Tumulty

The Big Merger

Hedley Donovan in the mid-70's began the process of making TIME Edit and the News Service into something resembling one team rather than two antagonists. That plan was one reason a few writers and one senior editor—moi—reversed the usual flow pattern. The theory had something to do with cross-pollenization. A few footnotes to the history of that long & checkered effort.

Ring-Ring. Anyone there?

It isn't a huge stretch to imagine that I was the only member of the News Service—ever—to join the outfit while not on speaking terms with the chief of correspondents. Not long before Henry Grunwald informed Murray Gart that I would be New York Bureau Chief, Gart and I had conducted a rather uncivil phone conversation. It ended with Murray providing unwelcome anatomical advice and hanging up.

Why? Well, young radicals had blown up a Greenwich Village townhouse, with some loss of life. I was acting as Nation editor that week and Grunwald wanted a crash cover story. The NY bureau wasn't being as responsive as we thought it should be. So instead of writing a new query and sending it via the news desk, I picked up the phone. This was a clear violation of protocol. Before long, Gart was on the horn to remonstrate. A frosty silence between us ensued.

Grunwald was aware of all this. He and Gart disliked each other (to put it mildly), so the fact that Grunwald—with Donovan's backing—could foist me on Gart was an obvious rubbing-it-in exercise. But Gart rose above this foolishness. He took the initiative in patching things up and gave me a lot of leeway as the bureau dealt with major stories—including the New York fiscal crisis, the worst power outage in the city's history, Son of Sam, and primaries that decided the Democratic 1976 presidential nomination.

It was Gart, not Grunwald, who bestowed the first bonuses and stock options that fell into my Xmas stocking. In fact, of the many interesting slots I filled over three decades-plus with Time, my three-year stint running the New York bureau was probably the most enjoyable.

-0-

The 1980 campaign for the GOP nomination was really puzzling to establishment types in the Bos-Wash axis. How could the old Borax pitchman be doing so well? After George Bush took Ronald Reagan down a notch in the Iowa caucuses, it appeared to these folks that Republicans were regaining sanity.

In that era, there was a 6-week hiatus between Iowa and New Hampshire, so all attention focused on the cold, snowy Granite State. I was TIME's guy on the Reagan beat, and reporting that—despite some organizational problems—the old guy was doing pretty well. About two weeks before the primary, the several correspondents covering the large field of candidates got a rocket from New York. We were told that an essay was in preparation that would explain why the

Republicans, having learned their lesson in 1964, would not nominate an arch conservative. The magazine was about to predict that Reagan was toast. With only one exception (who shall remain nameless here), our political crew energetically opposed this notion. The editors on this occasion paid attention, and the essay was dropped.

-0-

In that case, keeping a bad item out of print was as satisfying as getting a good piece in.

A year later, covering that old guy in the White House, I learned that during the general election campaign the Reagan team had acquired material that the Carter folks were using to prep Jimmy Carter for the sole debate the candidates had. These pilfered papers were used by David Stockman, who played the Carter role in mock debates.

It was February, 1981, and the new administration was generating a large volume of initiatives and keeping us very busy. Still, the bit about the purloined briefing papers was interesting. A story was suggested, written, edited—and deferred because of space. The temporary Nation editor at that time (who also shall remain nameless here) said we'd do it the following week. For a couple of weeks thereafter, the same thing happened. Then everyone seemed to lose interest.

I tucked the item away, thinking it might be worth a few lines in the book I was planning. When Gambling with History appeared in 1983, what the newspapers called "briefing-gate" became a summer sensation. The FBI called, a House subcommittee staged an investigation and a variety of Democrats talked up the ostensible crime.

In this case, failing to get a good piece in had a strangely happy ending for the once-frustrated correspondent.

Larry Barrett

The Redneck Beat

Perhaps a neo-redneck theme of characters is appropriate.

George Wallace, Jesse Helms, Jimmy Carter and Howard Jarvis.

You knew Wallace was in trouble when Detroit partisans started winging chairs around Cobo Hall . . . before the band played the National Anthem. In a Laurel shopping center a few days later the shots rang out and the next thing I knew he was on the ground. His security guard, also shot, fell on my foot. But I had a secret (neither Newsweek nor the NYT were on this trip) and had to tell somebody. So I dashed across the parking lot, called Dick Duncan and went back to the scene where Wallace lay in the chaos and all I can remember was he wore white boxer shorts.

-0-

I was enlisted from the L.A. bureau for the cover on Jesse Helms.

Apparently I was the designated red neck. When flying to the historic Guilford County Courthouse, we chatted and suddenly Helms pulls out a pack of cigarettes. He did not smoke and it showed. He licked that cigarette until it fell apart. Never lit it and then gave it up as a bad promotion of North Carolina's industry.

-0-

We shoudda known Jimmy Carter's presidency was bound to be an embarrassment. While working on the cover of then-governor, myself and a cover artist showed up at the newly built mansion. Don't remember the artist but while I was talking with Carter, the artist spilled a blob of dark blue paint onto the new gold rug, Jimmy would never recover. Even as we took a funicular up Stone Mountain on Easter morning to be, apparently, nearer to his God.

-0-

Not quite southern but Howard Jarvis was a southern California redneck nonetheless. He had long been a pain in the ass to the Los Angeles City Council showing up regularly with one beef or another including Proposition 13, the tax issue. Like Wallace, Jarvis had no compunction about showing his fleshy self. Explaining why he did not feel all that well that day, he dropped his pants to show me a huge bruise. I guess I looked away as I did with Wallace when I interviewed him in his shorts.

Joseph Kane

Take Me to the Coup

I'd only been in Hong Kong a few weeks, my initial foreign assignment, when a major coup erupted against Cory Aquino in the Philippines. I was called in the middle of the night, and caught the first plane out of Kai Tak to the airport in Manila—where a band was happily playing in the arrival area. I took a car to the Manila

Hotel, and tried in those pre-cell phone days to reach our stringer Nelly Sindayen or our photographers, but they were out covering the counter-assault against Gringo Honasan and his coupsters. I'd never covered a coup, knew nothing about the city, and the Manila Hotel had grounded all its cars. Summoning all the reportorial skills I'd gained in Chicago and Washington, I went out to the street, hopped in a cab and said, "Take me to the coup!" Which, of course, the driver did, and I ended up with my first Time International cover story.

-0-

My last big story in Europe was actually helping to cover Princess Diana's funeral, an all-hands-on-deck affair for which TIME flew me over from Brussels. It had already been announced that I was heading back to Washington to cover the Clinton White House. At one point, Barry Hillenbrand, who by then had done a lot of royals' coverage, including the affairs, the divorce, etc., remarked to me, "I guess covering the White House is a lot like covering the Royal Family. You rarely get to talk to the principals themselves, you only deal with aides and public appearances." Then he added, counter-prophetically, "At least you won't have to spend all your time writing about Clinton's sexual peccadilloes." The Monica Lewinsky story broke two months after I got back to D.C.

-0-

When I was covering the Clinton White House, I attended one state dinner and sat at President Clinton's table, along with some politicians, a big donor, and others. It was just as the bombing of Kosovo was winding down, Clinton's gamble had clearly paid off, so the mood was upbeat. I was sitting between Martha Stewart (who caused a mini-scandale by showing up in Capri pants and flats) and Susan Sontag, the noted liberal writer (now deceased), who had been a vocal backer of the war, probably the only conflict she supported since WWII. That evening in New York at the U.N., they were finishing up delicate negotiations on terms to end the war. At one point during the entertainment (by Judy Collins, who serenaded the President and First Lady with "Chelsea Morning", for which Bill's and Hill's daughter was named), Sandy Berger, the national security advisor, knelt down next to Clinton and whispered into his ear for several minutes, delivering, we assumed, the news from the U.N. Eventually, Clinton flashed a thumbs up sign to us, who were all staring anxiously to gauge his reaction. Well, almost all of us. When Berger left, Martha Stewart asked, "Who was that?"

Jay Branegan

Our Hero

I was sitting in my office next to the Chief of Correspondents when he received a call from security. A deranged correspondent, who had been fired the day before, was in the building, had a gun and was on the way to the Chief's office to settle the score. On his way out the door to head for the hills, the Chief shouted "SD I know you can handle this!" (Editor's note: The Chief was John Stacks)

Suzanne Davis

Eddie, Who's the Queen?

In the rather tight confines of the Time-Life Washington bureau on Connecticut Avenue in the 1960s and early '70s, privacy was hard to come by. Sometimes you couldn't get it at all.

One afternoon I was in the home stretch of giving a young man who desperately wanted to be a trainee in the bureau the painful news that he was not going to make it. Why? he insisted on knowing. Well, I said, your horizon is still a bit narrow; you have to be more knowing of the world. Time correspondents, I said, are seasoned generalists who have to be able to deal with a truly wide range of subjects. Get some more experience and try again.

Just then the voice of White House correspondent Hugh Sidey, who was writing in his office next door, came rolling through my open door and started this high-volume exchange:

"Eddie (his favorite name for me)."

"Yes, Hugh."

"What's the name of the queen?"

"What queen, Hugh, what queen?"

"The queen of England."

"Elizabeth, Hugh, Elizabeth."

I looked up from the eyes-averted position I had taken about midway through the interruption. The young man had a wide smile on his face and was nodding without speaking. I mumbled some conciliatory words and ushered him down the hall toward the door.

Ed Goodpaster

Deng's Loogie

Great Hall of the People, Beijing, 1977. Just months after Mao Zedong's death, the fresh-in-office Carter administration dispatched Secretary of State Cyrus Vance to initiate contact with China's new leadership, primarily Hua Guofung, hand-picked by Mao as his successor as Communist party chairman. Hua was a moon-faced bureaucrat, notable mostly for his unusual six foot height. He meandered into the arrival area to meet Vance and ignored the entreaties of the Secretary's traveling press to come closer and take a question. He stood awkwardly and silent until Vance arrived and handshakes were exchanged. They headed into a private room to talk. We tried to follow. Security shooed us back. End of press op.

Next day we're back in the Great Hall for a Vance meeting with a second Chinese official. This one, about four and a half feet tall, strode in and plunged into the waiting group of about 30 reporters, sound and camera folks. He's pumping hands, asking—through his interpreter—each, one by one, where we're from, whom we work for. He's about a third of the way through the group when he sees Vance arrive. Normally, an official would break off and greet the dignitary. Not this guy.

He ignores Vance and keeps working the press group. Vance waits, shifts foot to foot, forces a smile. Minutes pass. The small Vance entourage looks baffled. Finally, the official finishes with us, the handshake takes place and it's off to the private room. We go to follow, security moves in, the Chinese official turns, barks a command, security falls away, he motions us to come along. Inside, they settle into overstuffed chairs, the interpreters mount their perches. We start firing questions and taking photos. The Chinese official does not reply, but breaks into a wet cough. Hawking up what appears to be a baseball-size piece of lung, he launches the loogie straight across

Vance's knees into a brass spittoon with a splat that sounds like Mike Tyson landing a round-house. A startled Vance, the most Brahmin and buttoned down of diplomats, launches himself backwards out of his chair nearly landing in the lap of his interpreter. As Vance tries to regain his composure, Deng Xiaoping calmly lights a cigarette, announces, "Now we can get down to business," and motions us out, the demonstration of just who's in charge in China complete. Within months, designated successor Hua is gone, never to be heard from again and the history-making Deng era is underway.

Chris Ogden

This Item Cannot be Cleared

July 1980. I was bureau chief in Detroit when the Republicans held their national convention there that summer. As such, I played a peripheral role in logistical preparation for Time's coverage—most importantly finding a suitable workspace for the hordes of correspondents, writers and editors who would descend on Motown for the week of the convention. At that, I succeeded, landing a little known social space belonging to the United Auto Workers in a building adjacent to Cobo Hall, site of the convention. It was a large room adjoined by a glassed-in balcony that overlooked the Detroit River—utilitarian enough to serve as a workspace and comfortable enough to entertain in (there was an upright piano tucked into one corner). In those days, work and entertainment were never far apart at Time.

The closest thing to public credit I received for finding this little oasis came in the form of a quote in the following week's publetter—from

Midwest Bureau Chief Ben Cate, who called the room "The best convention set-up I've seen."

The room was certainly well used that week. All the big bass from the Washington bureau set up shop there. "Chief of Correspondents Richard Duncan swiftly redeployed his forces, including Washington Bureau Chief Robert Ajemian, Congressional Correspondent Neil MacNeil, Senior Correspondent Laurence Barrett and National Political Correspondent John Stacks," gushed the publetter. "A series of TIME breakfasts and lunches (reserved, by the way, under my membership at the Detroit Athletic Club) with ranking Republicans had provided an informed commentary on the dynamics of the convention."

It was at night, however, that the rented room overlooking the river best reflected the true News Service culture. The visiting correspondents set out their Trash 80 computers and took turns sharing the handful of phone lines to transmit files to New York. We installed a bar in the center of the room. Naturally, it was well attended. By Friday night's closing, Ed ("I almost dropped my Bel Paese") Jackson had set up an ersatz news desk at a table in the corner from which he dispensed a flurry of checking queries to the assembled masses. Smoke filled the air above Atlanta Bureau Chief Joe Boyce who, with less than a central role in the action, set himself down and played jazz on the upright piano. I vaguely recall a fight almost breaking out, though I can't recall the prospective combatants.

Aside from filing a few graphs of local color (of which there was precious little in Detroit in those days), I had no reporting duties during the convention. So I wandered around the convention floor in Cobo Hall and drifted in and out of the hotels in town where the GOP biggies were housed. An old family friend from Long Island, a first cousin of George H.W. Bush, joined up with me for a tour of the convention on the evening of Ronald Reagan's acceptance speech. Just past midnight, relying on her Bush family connections, we took ourselves up to the newly anointed vice presidential candidate's block of rooms at the Pontchartrain Hotel. No sooner had we exited the elevator than a somewhat disheveled man of about my age lurched around the corner in cowboy boots, swinging a glass of something that appeared to be whiskey.

"Hello, George," said his father's cousin, who turned from her and squinted at me. "I know you from somewhere," he said. "Where do I know you from? Yale?"

"No, George," I replied. "It was Andover."

"Yeah!" he bellowed, pointing a finger at me as if he feared he might otherwise lose sight of me. "That's right!"

My companion, clearly embarrassed by her relative's condition, quickly turned and guided me back into the elevator bank. I didn't think much of the incident at the time. There was, after all, nothing to suggest that my erstwhile over-served schoolmate would in time lose the booze, find religion and two decades hence become the 43rd President of the United States. P.S. This item cannot be cleared.

Barrett Seaman

Afghanistan Before Osama

Most people forget that Afghanistan first emerged on front pages in April of 1978 with a coup by some leftist politicians in a country that was then known mainly as a hippie heaven. When I arrived with the New Delhi foreign press corps aboard the first commercial plane permitted to land at Kabul Airport, we presented ourselves as tourists and quickly fanned out to find a city virtually on holiday. Downtown markets were in full cry under the shadow of tanks whose tracks had chewed up the streets. But the question on everyone's mind was whether Moscow had somehow opened a new front in the Cold War. I made my way to the Foreign Ministry. At the gate, a pleasant, English-speaking voice came on the entry phone. I identified myself as Time's New Delhi Bureau Chief and informed him that correspondents for major American and British publications had arrived that morning.

"At the airport?" He was clearly startled.

"At the airport. We have come to verify that all is calm and the new government is in control."

"You can see that it is."

I replied that we could only be sure after we had spoken with the new president, Nur Mohammed Taraki, leader of the Khalq (Masses) party. Could he arrange that? I could hear the uncertainty in his voice as he hung up, promising nothing and saying politely, "Thank you for letting me know."

Then I called on the Indian ambassador, S.K. Singh, a compact Rajput aristocrat with a high, urgent voice and a museum-quality collection of Indian art. He told me that the Soviet Ambassador, Aleksander Puzanov, rode around in a huge armored limousine and by virtue of longevity was the dean of the diplomatic corps and was known behind his back as "The Tsar." I also heard that he was a barely recovered alcoholic and had been trout fishing at the time of the coup. Meanwhile Singh, whose interest was to keep Afghanistan a classic buffer state, took it upon himself to urge the foreign ministry to put Taraki on display to demonstrate he was a harmless third-world leftist. American diplomats in Kabul agreed with Singh that the explosion had probably not been touched off by Moscow, and so did United Nations officials, the foreigners who were closest to the Afghans. The feuding local Communists numbered no more than several thousand, and while Taraki's people called it the "glorious Saur (April) revolution," Tass judiciously referred to it as "a military coup."

At the telegraph office, I found correspondents from Cuba and East Germany, who had originally come to cover some non-aligned jamboree, which was the only reason the telegraph office in that normally sleepy place was open at all. Both expressed extreme skepticism that the Russians were involved at the start. I chatted with the Cuban correspondent in Spanish, and he said: "They have been burning the lights all week at the Soviet embassy. They don't know what to do next." The dour East German said (in English): "The 'friends' have been taken utterly by surprise." He seemed pleased by their discomfort. All of this amounted to fairly conclusive evidence that Moscow had been taken by surprise. That's what I filed, and that's what appeared in the weekly newsmagazine.

During the summer of 1978, Soviet advisers arrived to help inexperienced ministers, such as the deputy health minister, a doctor just one year out of medical school. But there was something wrong with this picture. Pro-Soviet Communists were soon purged or exiled, and the foreign minister, Hafizullah Amin, began upstaging Taraki (whose assassination he was to order a year later). Amin, a man straight out of the Afghan political bazaar, also courted America for aid. When I interviewed him, he reminded me that he had attended Columbia Teachers College and, grasping my hand, assured me in surprisingly good English, "I admire America."

Enter the American Cold War establishment, the CIA, and the press. James Schlesinger, then Energy Secretary and formerly director of the CIA, returned from Beijing, where he found the Chinese fearful that Afghanistan was being converted into a Soviet satellite. He eagerly imparted this intelligence to a Time editors' lunch in New York. Then the New York Times ran an unsigned story on its front page from Kabul declaring that Afghanistan was "moving into the Soviet orbit." I was promptly ordered to Kabul with instructions to find out the precise relationship between Kabul and Moscow, whatever it was.

Before leaving, I conferred with the senior American career diplomat in New Delhi, an old Afghan hand named Archer K. Blood and showed him the even-handed query from New York. "I wish we got cables like that," Blood said. It was clear that Washington's mind was already made up. In Kabul, the American ambassador, Adolph (Spike) Dubs, an exemplary diplomat and a fine human being, was a career Soviet specialist and displayed a familiar mindset. The first thing he asked was whether Amin had revealed to me the composition of the "Afghan Politburo."

Kabul was eager to appease Moscow even to the point of giving Afghanistan a new red flag and exchanging recognition of South for North Korea. Taraki and Amin appealed for billions in Soviet aid and arms. In November, I sat on the steps of the Foreign Ministry in Kabul watching boxes of files being loaded into trucks for a presidential trip to Moscow seeking a treaty of mutual aid and economic integration. They came home with nothing but a barter deal and a vague pledge of military cooperation.

Contrary to the official line, my story argued that a regime of incompetent radical politicians was losing support in the conservative countryside, now aflame with rebellion at enforced social change. Against Soviet advice, they abolished dowries, which happened to be the foundation of agricultural credit. The Afghan politicians were trying to show themselves more Communist than Moscow. The Pakistani ambassador, a Pathan from just across the border in Peshawar, warned me presciently that "the Afghans want to limit the Russians' options, just the way the regimes did with you Americans in Vietnam by forcing you to become prisoners of their rhetoric." As far as I know, this was the first published comparison between Afghanistan and Vietnam.

By then Washington was listening only to its own rhetoric. I began to notice curious insertions in stories strongly hinting that the original coup had been directed, manipulated, or at least inspired by Moscow. One editor, Burt Pines, refused to tell me the basis for this judgment. From what happened later, I can only assume it was based at least in part on information from Strobe Talbott, then Time's national security correspondent in Washington, later the Tsar of the Clinton Administration's policies on Russia. He and I had traveled to Kabul together in September, but he quickly departed for Teheran to report on the troubles of the Shah.

In January of 1979, I traveled to Peshawar, which was regaining its Kiplingesque reputation as a center of Afghan intrigue. With Robert Trumbull, a distinguished *Times* war correspondent, I unearthed the first real, live Afghan guerrilla, one Khan Mohammed, a 26-year-old radio technician who had walked across the mountains to buy bullets at $2 each. His head swaddled in a tarboosh and his eyes red with fatigue, he read from a combat diary of ambushes escaped, villages razed, mullahs slaughtered, and a sighting of Soviet soldiers. There was no way to verify his story, but he seemed the genuine article. We had reported on our share of wars, and I had fought in one as an infantryman in Korea. The Washington Star, then owned by Time Inc., jumped on the story and printed it. It soon drew the attention of the CIA.

About a fortnight after my return from Peshawar my office telex in New Delhi clattered out a message from Dick Duncan, then the chief of correspondents. It began by stating archly that "representatives of best-known Washington company, expressing admiration for your reporting from Afghanistan," had sought permission to speak to

31

me. He held no view on that, but he reminded me that we didn't tell spies anything that wasn't publishable and "We don't run errands for anyone."

I found this sound advice but was astounded that the CIA felt that it had to ask permission to talk to me, especially since the station chief (identified on the diplomatic list as an "attaché") lived down the block behind a walled garden with a sentry box, the only house so adorned on our street, one of the loveliest in New Delhi. I deliberately avoided the agency because Indians suspect that all American journalists are CIA spies anyway. It was also not well informed and had not foreseen Indira Gandhi's electoral defeat in 1977 although Time had—alone among American publications.

Unfortunately, New York had vitiated its intentions about the CIA by literally telegraphing them on an open wire monitored by Indian intelligence. I did not want the Indians telling the Afghans I was talking to the CIA—and certainly not my best source in Kabul, the lively and well informed Indian ambassador. I sent a letter of explanation to Dick Duncan—we still used snail mail in those days—with a copy to Talbott. If the CIA wanted to talk to me, I said, its agents knew very well where to find me, but would they please approach me with some discretion, and why did they have to ask permission anyway? Meanwhile, I asked to be excluded from all further discussions with the spooks.

A few weeks after the inopportune telex, I received a call at home from a defense attaché at the U.S. Embassy. He said Washington wanted him to talk to me. Since the line was also tapped and the damage already done if anyone was listening, I asked him to come to the office, but please not in uniform. He arrived with a long cable and began reading off detailed questions about what Army field manuals used to call EEI, or essential elements of information—weapons used by the rebels and government troops, their uniforms and insignia, race, possible nationality, and so on. It seemed obvious they were looking for evidence of Soviet support. I checked my notebook and told him I did not have the answers—but who was asking these questions? "The Defense Intelligence Agency," he said, adding, "I might as well show you the cable, because it's not classified."

I scanned it and noticed that the cable said (incorrectly) that I "lived on the American compound," that the Pentagon officer who signed it expressed the hope that I would "cooperate," and that his request to interview me had been "authorized by Mr. Strobe Talbott." I asked my visitor if he realized that the Pentagon, by sending the cable en clair, had almost certainly let it fall into the hands of Indian intelligence. He said he did not, and I asked him to leave. I cabled Talbott to cease and desist and complained to the chief military attaché at the embassy, who apologized.

A month later, not without some trepidation that Indian intelligence had tipped off Kabul, I flew there to report on the assassination of the U.S. ambassador, Adolph Dubs, who had been kidnapped by terrorists. This only ratcheted up Washington's suspicions of Moscow's motives. When I went to discuss Dubs' assassination with Singh, he was flying the Indian flag at half-staff, defying Afghan government orders against any display of mourning for his fellow diplomat and friend. To clear the air, I told him the story of the CIA's ridiculous approaches and asked if he had heard anything about them from New Delhi. Not a word, he cackled with laughter. "It only shows," he said, "that our intelligence is just as inefficient as yours."

Over thirty years, a lot has changed—for the worse in Afghanistan for the worse, and for the better in the CIA. The Soviet empire has fallen of its own weight and arrogance, with a push from events in Afghanistan. If you doubt that, consider what I learned from Anatoly

Dobrynin, who retired as Soviet ambassador to Washington after a quarter-century and asked me to edit his memoirs. He was visiting Moscow when Soviet troops were ordered to seize Kabul in the final days of 1979, and Leonid Brezhnev confidently told him, "It'll be over in three to four weeks."

No one who visited Afghanistan before it fell victim to catastrophe will ever forget the place. It was a step backward to an age before people understood the serial nature of events and the concept of what we now call cause and effect. Society was conducted by rules of personal honor, family obligation, and group hierarchy, not by law. The cycles of punishment and revenge predated concepts of the law explored in Sophocles' Antigone. Beyond the tribe, a sense of the public good simply did not exist, and barely any sense of nationhood.

In times of peace, exposure to such a world could be an enchantment. The level of formal courtesy was exquisite, of personal loyalty invigorating. In time of war, such a society can be as brutal as it must have been anywhere the Crusaders cut through, driven by militant religion. From the very start it would have been better for everyone to have left the Afghans to their own bloodthirsty ways than for us to have exploited them on their own blasted heath, like wanton boys killing flies for sport.

-0-

There is nothing like a strong editor to help a correspondent stand up to a bully, especially a member of Richard Nixon's cabinet whose bold politics the president admired. I am thinking of John Connally, remembered by history as the governor of Texas who was riding with JFK when he was assassinated—and by me as the only American Secretary of the Treasury who declared bankruptcy.

Early in August, 1971, I got a call from Pierre Rinfret, an eccentric but well connected business economist in New York whose political gossip usually proved true. I was then the magazine's national economics correspondent in Washington; Rinfret told me that big changes were underway in the administration's economic policies after Connally had warned the president that "You're not going to get-re-elected president just for going to China." He added some details about "incomes policy"—jargon for controlling wages and prices. We were doing a cover on the economy that week, so I called the Treasury, relayed what I had heard without naming the source, told them we were doing a cover on the economy this week and asked to speak to Connally. (They of course wanted to know if their man would be on the cover; I said that decision was not in my hands. In fact the cover featured several of the administration's quarreling economic managers.)

That was Monday. No reply on Tuesday. On Wednesday afternoon, with files due soon, the phone rang. It was Hedley Donovan: "Larry, I just got a call from the Secretary of the Treasury. He says that this week Time magazine will be saying that he told Nixon his trip to China would not be enough to re-elect him, and that he had to change economic policy . . ." And so on. I replied: "That's interesting, Hedley. I've been trying to get an interview with him since Monday." The familiar voice, deep with authority, instructed me: "You just proceed with that interview." Then Donovan hung up.

Five minutes later the phone rang again; it was the Treasury PR man, Alan Wade. "The Secretary will see you at 4:30." The first thing Connally said was: "Who told you that?" A friend of yours, I replied. He knew perfectly well where it came from and launched into a diatribe of sorts, then segued into details of policy: "I tell you, there are going to be some changes around here." The result was a scoop on the wage and price controls that were imposed on Aug. 15, 1971, and on a newly aggressive stance against America's trading partners, although he did not mention the historic break between the dollar and gold, which was decided only at the last moment.

In the months that followed, Connally's tactics negotiating a devaluation of the dollar to improve the nation's trade balance became truly abrasive. I heard from a Republican on the Hill that when the Secretary wanted to pin an opponent, he would say, "Let's kick him in the nuts." I asked the Treasury's chief economist, a good friend, if he had ever heard Connally say anything like that. He replied cautiously, "Sounds like him." One day Jerry Schechter, who covered the White House, said he had a good Connally story for me: "You know what he says in strategy sessions when he wants to go after someone, 'Let's kick him in the nuts.'" I told Jerry: "He's in print."

I filed the remark as the lead on a story about trade negotiations and watched it move up the editorial ladder, expecting at each step that it would be knocked out. But the following Monday, there it was in the magazine. As day follows night, the phone rang; the mild-mannered PR man said, rather breathlessly this time, "The Secretary wants to see you." "I suppose he wants to kick me in nuts." He replied: "That's about right."

When I walked into Connally's Moussolini-sized office, he was standing behind his desk scanning a copy of the weekly newsmagazine. "You write that?" he asked in an angry drawl. Fortified by the memory of support from on high, I said, "You know I did, but it didn't come from Democrats; it came from your new Republican friends—in the White House and on the Hill." This utterly self-confident politician was nonplused in a way I had never seen him before.

"Do you deny you said it?"

"I know I curse too much, but I would never talk like that. It's like saying 'shit' in front of a woman."

"Than if you want to write a letter denying it, I can guarantee you we will print it."

"That's right, I deny it now." A pause. "Sit down, have a cup of coffee."

Then followed ten minutes of policy spin, useful in its own way. Needless to say, no letter was ever sent, nor did Connally soften his tactics. But I was still not 100 per cent sure that the quote was accurate. At least not for several months, when I was talking with Arthur Burns, chairman of the Fed, who was then taking heat from Connally to ease up on the money supply to juice the economy in time for the 1972 election campaign. I asked Burns if he had heard the offending phrase from Connally. "Let me tell you, Mr. Malkin, what he says is this: 'Let's pull his pants down, and *then* we'll kick him in the nuts.'"

Larry Malkin

Head-of-State Extravaganza

In 1979 Editor-in-Chief Hedley Donovan decided he wanted to make a trip through the Middle East before he retired. Interviews with Heads of State were the rage in journalism at the time, so Cairo Bureau Chief Wilton Wynn pulled a handful of his usual rabbits out of the hat, and the three of us set out, in January, across the region.

Our first stop was Aswan, where we sat in lawn chairs on the Presidential Palace lawn overlooking the Nile, while Anwar Sadat talked about peace. He was a Nobel Prize winner, a TIME MOY, a wise and spiritual man. Exuding confidence and tranquility, he talked freely into the tape recorder I had bought for the trip. As we left, he introduced us to a man in army uniform who had been sitting at the edge of the lawn. His name was Mubarak, and he would succeed Sadat two years later, when militant Muslims repaid the President for his peace efforts.

From Egypt we went to Amman, to interview the PLK (for "Plucky Little King"), Hussein's sardonic nickname in journalistic and diplomatic circles. We sat eating fruit around a marble table, tape recorder turning, while the PLK, in his elegant, sonorous English, said nothing new for more than two hours. Then we returned to the Amman Sheraton, where Wilton and I left Hedley in the bar teaching the bartender how to make martinis ("Good, Ali! Good! But not good enough . . .") and went upstairs to transcribe the interview. The brand new tape recorder was blank. None of the PLK's ponderous bromides remained.

Wilton and I quickly developed an emergency reconstruction plan. First, the tape recorder went sailing, frisbee-like, from my hotel balcony into the pool below. Then we combined the contents of our minibars, and met in Wilton's room. The approach was simple. Prompted by our sketchy notes, one of us would play Hedley, and read a question. The other, seated in a chair opposite, would, in appropriately plumy accents, imitate the king's response. It went like this: "Your Majesty, how do you feel about Congress' refusal to authorize the sale of warplanes to Jordan?" Pause for a sip of scotch. Then: "I must confess I do not understand the position of our good friends in the American Congress, but I am confident that as they . . .. ." Etc. We were finished by midnight.

The next morning the three of us, slightly the worse for wear, met in the lobby. In the conviction that no Head of State Interview was a HOS interview too many, I was to meet Managing Editor Ray Cave and Corporate Editor Henry Grunwald in Moscow for a very big HOS indeed: Leonid Brezhnev, General Secretary of the Communist Party. Moscow Bureau Chief Bruce Nelan and bureau stringer Felix Rosenthal, undoubtedly aided by the Soviet desire to have us forget they occupied Afghanistan, had pulled off a commitment for the GS' first interview ever with a "western" journalist. Meanwhile, Wilton was taking Hedley to Damascus to interview Hafez Assad, father of the current Assad, whose reputation as a thug had been somewhat diminished since he had a mostly friendly round of negotiations with Henry Kissinger after the '73 War. We three would meet in two days in Bagdad, Wilton having finally extracted a "maybe" after his repeated requests for an interview with Saddam Hussein.

But first, on the way to my Moscow flight, I had a crucial chore. I stopped by at the PLK's press office, and nervously presented his officious little press chief with our "transcript" of the meeting the previous afternoon. Neither Wilton nor I had been able to recall whether the King's staff had provided their own tape recorder. He went into his office, closed the door, and left me sipping coffee. And sipping . . . and sipping. Finally he emerged, beaming. "Very good," he said. I grabbed my luggage and a bag of Jordan Valley iceberg lettuce for Rose Nelan's kitchen, courtesy of our Amman stringer, and headed for Moscow.

I found the next day that there would be no spontaneity in the Kremlin, and we all knew who had the most tape recorders. Brezhnev gave every sign of having suffered a significant loss of brain cells, due perhaps to his age (72), vodka, and too many Politburo meetings. Despite Grunwald's and Cave's efforts to contrive provocative, even seductive questions, Brezhnev's handlers carefully fended off any unexpected sallies, and we stuck largely to the agenda of previously submitted questions. A media advisor would hoarsely whisper the answers into Brezhnev's right ear, and he would obediently repeat them to us. Only once did this Charlie McCarthy act falter. The handler suggested something that Brezhnev, who was evidently monitoring the conversation as it traveled from his ear to his mouth, disagreed with. He stopped, swung his head to his right, and bellowed into the staffer's face, "NYET." Pause. Then he turned back amiably to us, and continued the interview.

The next evening I dragged myself into the Baghdad hotel, after having spent an interminable afternoon in the Damascus airport enroute from Istanbul. Had I missed the Saddam interview? No such luck, muttered Wilton. "I know the sonofabitch will keep us waiting until the last minute, if he sees us at all." Our only contact with the regime was through our Foreign Ministry handler, a gangly junior officer with an effeminate manner and a boundless admiration for Liberace. He played well for us on the grand piano in the hotel lobby, lamenting the lack of a candelabra, but compensating with extravagant gestures. Hedley, delighted, grinned and clapped loudly after each number, and I knew there would be some worthwhile commentary later in the evening.

That night we dined with the American Ambassador. The next day we were almost promised a talk with Foreign Minister Tariq Aziz, but then the Pianist discovered that he was not in the country. At the Pianist's insistence, we visited Babylon and then ate alone, waiting for the word that never came. Would we perhaps come next week, asked the Pianist? No, we said firmly, our plane to Rome was in the morning. So just after six we stood outside the hotel, on a beautiful sunny morning, waiting for our car. Birds chirped in the palms, and I had a Pollyanna moment. This is an interesting country after all, I ventured, and I'd really like to come again. There was a moment of silence. Wilton studied the tops of the palms intently.

"So would I," said Hedley, with the big grin that was his most effective management tool. "In uniform."

He would not get his wish. He died in August, 1990, just a week after the Iraqi invasion of Kuwait that led to the first Gulf War. There wasn't enough time for him to volunteer.

Googling the TIME archives, I find that two of those interviews, Brezhnev's and Sadat's, were published. PLK and Assad were outspaced.

-0-

When the U.S. invaded the Dominican Republic in 1965, Ed Reingold had the two of us alternating coverage, each spending about half our time in Santo Domingo. My wife and I had two small children, one less than a year old, and there was stress on the homefront. When I was in New York I mentioned this to Dick Clurman, who began ticking off possible remedies: moving, live-in help, etc. None of this seemed to make much sense to me, so he paused, and looked directly at me for emphasis. "Look. If money's the problem, that's no problem."

-0-

A couple of years later I succeeded Ed as Bureau Chief in the Caribbean. On a trip to New York I went diligently to the business office and talked to Rose Epstein, found out what the bureau budget was and how it broke into major categories. When Clurman came to Miami on some other business, he took me out to dinner. I was ready. I told him the bureau would certainly come in on budget, and maybe save some money. He was irritated. "How'd you find out

your budget?" He wanted to know. "I don't want my bureau chiefs knowing their budgets. Forget it."
Dick Duncan

Two Newstours and MOY

I am probably the only bureau chief to have twice hosted a Newstour in the same year I was the lead correspondent on an MOY. Both cases demonstrated the vagaries of mixing business and journalism.

Lech Walesa

In 1981, as Eastern Europe bureau chief I spent much of that year trying to get permanent accreditation in Warsaw to cover Solidarity's struggle against Poland's communist rulers. Visas were tough to come by, but in April we told the government there that we would be bringing 30 Fortune 500 CEOs in October on a fact-finding mission. I was able to leverage that to get a series of two-week visas that were often extended.

The Newstour was a remarkable event, including landing our chartered 707 at the Gdansk airport and taking the participants to have Sunday lunch with farm families by loading them directly into Mercedes taxis parked on the tarmac without any passport formalities. It also included the first public appearance of Gen. Wojciech Jaruzelski, for a lunch and Q and A session, the day after he became the first active military officer to assume control of a Soviet Bloc government. By the time the Newstour had moved on to Moscow, the Polish government was convinced that it had done a great job of selling its side of the story—Solidarity was well-intentioned but anarchic and the country was on the verge of economic collapse and chaos.

A month later I got my accreditation—probably thanks to the Newstour (Newsweek didn't get one)—and a month after that Jaruzelski declared Martial Law and arrested Walesa and hundreds of other Solidarity officials and sympathizers. Ten days before the crackdown I had what turned out to be the last major interview with Walesa as part of our MOY package, in which I had six bylines.

The military regime, however, had also severed all communications links with the outside world, so it was impossible to get playbacks or checkpoints. I had smuggled out files describing the brutality of the crackdown, but I worried that on balance the editors would tilt toward the narrative presented by Jaruzelski and his minions in October.

On Dec 23, I flew to Paris on only the second commercial flight out of Warsaw since the crackdown. Even though I had a reentry visa, it was a huge risk, as the government had already told me that I would be 'punished' if we made Walesa MOY, and it would be much easier to refuse me reentry than to expel me. One of my colleagues in Europe thought my decision unprofessional and called Bill Mader to say that I had abandoned my post: 'That's what happens when you send a boy in to do a man's job.'

As it happens, the editors had taken Jaruzelski's side, but for once my CACs carried enough weight to shift the balance back to Solidarity's narrative. My wife, Sue, met me in Paris where we had a very somber Christmas before trying to get back into Warsaw before the magazine appeared. We flew to Berlin and then took a night train to Warsaw. In spite of our valid reentry visas, we were thrown off the train at the Polish border by military police at 2 AM and spent the next six hours in an unheated station while our documents were checked. Eventually we were allowed to proceed, arriving in Warsaw on the evening of Dec 27, just as the MOY was being announced.

My fellow foreign correspondents were elated to see us when we turned up at an early dinner party that night—the curfew was 9 PM—because I was the first accredited journalist to leave and reenter. As for 'punishment,' after a few unpleasant encounters with the secret police in the vicinity of my tiny office, nothing more was ever said about the cover. And when Walesa finally got out of detention, he autographed it for me.

Deng Xiaoping

Transporting 30 CEOs and another 20 or so Time Inc editors and executives around China 26 years ago was a logistical nightmare that involved everything from chartering an Airbus from China Airlines to fly from Beijing to Shanghai to Guangzhou, to figuring out how to walk them across the border between Shenzhen and Hong Kong. The program was not as dramatic as in Poland, but China was still pretty exotic back then. The real show stopper was that after months of cat and mouse games, Deng Xiaoping at the last minute agreed to a very rare public meeting with all of the participants.

The session itself was hardly remarkable, but Henry Grunwald, who conducted the conversation, was in seventh heaven because Deng was one of the few world leaders he had not interviewed. With the rest of the trip looming before me, I had little time to bask in the reflected glory, and frankly thought very little about it until 10 days later at the final dinner at the Oriental Hotel in Bangkok. That's when I heard from Dick Duncan that Henry was so excited about meeting Deng that he planned to override the choice of Ray Cave and every other editor to make Mikhail Gorbachev MOY and replace him with Deng.

Some years it's hard to pick an MOY. Some years it's easy. 1985 was a lead-pipe cinch for Gorbachev who had just launched perestroika and glasnost to global acclaim. What's more Deng had been MOY in 1978 for launching his economic reforms, and Jimi FlorCruz and I had done a cover in Sept of 85 on how those reforms were running out of steam and into some pretty serious contradictions, as a Marxist might say. Worse still, the Chinese had decided that since they'd already gotten what they wanted from Time—access to all those CEOs—they had no need to cooperate, so we got absolutely no access to Deng's comrades or family members.

Needless to say, the cover was flat at best, as the writers and editors did their best to produce one of the least timely MOYs of all time. The best indication of that came in a telex from Bill Mader to me on Dec 4:

THERE IS ONE REQUEST, WHICH CONCERNS A KEY CONTRIBUTION FROM YOU AS BEIJING BUREAU CHIEF. WOULD YOU BE KIND ENOUGH TO PUT TOGETHER ONE TAKE WHICH PLACES WHAT THE PARAMOUNT LEADER HAS DONE INTO HISTORICAL PERSPECTIVE, *OFFERS YOUR ANALYSIS AND EXPLANATION AS TO WHY HIS BEING THE CHOICE MAKES SENSE.*

The response I wanted to send was along the lines of that old Lone Ranger/Tonto joke: What you mean we, white man? After all, Deng may well have been the only MOY ever chosen who had not been nominated by the relevant bureau chief—or by anyone. (Don't take my word for this. Time allowed CNN to film the editorial process and the video is painful to watch, particularly when Henry overrides Jason's choice for the cover art.)

Instead I conjured up something along the lines of how Deng's economic reforms and his laying the groundwork for an orderly political succession might lead to the first extended period of stability in the Middle Kingdom in almost two centuries. In a fit of what had to have been editorial desperation, George Church basically adopted that view for the kicker.

And less than four years later, Deng gave the order to shoot at the unarmed civillians of Beijing. But that's a story that doesn't involve a News Tour.

Rick Hornik

Covering the Stars

—The magazine was flying me to Thailand to interview "Bright Lights, Big City" star Michael J. Fox on the set of his next film. My arm was sore from a round of shots. My dog was in the kennel. On the way to the airport, I stopped at the bureau to pick up my ticket. A colleague ran out to the cab. "The trip is off," he said—relieved to have caught me. "New York saw the movie and hated it."

—It was 1980. I stood with Tennessee Williams and his boyfriend on Chicago's Oak Street Beach. A Time photographer captured the moment. The playwright gave me good stuff. The experience soured a few days later, when drama critic Harold Clurman died. Williams denied bad-mouthing the man. I stood by my story. Dutka vs. Tennessee Williams. I can't recall who won.

—Sitting with Katharine Hepburn in her Turtle Bay home, we talked about David Lean. His "Passage to India" was being released and, if hard news cooperated, would make the cover of Time. Was the director a happy man, I asked. After all, he had six wives. "Happy?" the actress shot back. "Who's happy? Are you happy? Am I happy?" She was the Protestant ethic incarnate. I redeemed myself when I came up with the name of Lean's prop-master. Hepburn was mine, after that. She talked about "Spencer," life and love, tough choices she had made. "Nice hiking boots," I commented at the end of the session. I'd been looking for some. "Thin socks or thick?" she demanded, insisting I try hers on. "Take these home and walk in them" were the marching orders. "Return them when you're done."

Elaine Dutka

Dancing at the White House

In 1976, I was a correspondent in the New York Bureau and was asked to cover Queen Elizabeth's visit in July to Philadelphia on the occasion of our nation's Bicentennial. From Philly, the Queen was off to Washington, D.C., to visit The White House and Capitol Hill. I knew that when I got to Washington, Chris Ogden, who covered State at that point, would take over. I got to the bureau and told Chris the Queen was his. Chris asked me if I had anything to wear to a State Dinner. I couldn't believe my ears. I had packed a simple long dress and I thought, "Well, I guess it will pass muster." It was a big break for me at TIME. Chris was so gracious to bow out. It was his story to cover. But instead he let me record how the Queen and Prince Philip were serenaded by Captain & Tennille to the words of "Muskrat

Love" and how VP Nelson Rockefeller gave the Queen a slap on the back at lunch on the Hill. There was substance too, of course, but these were the fun parts. As a pool reporter, that night I danced at the White House, alongside the guests of President and Mrs. Ford, and kept pinching myself that this was for real.

Eileen Shields-West

At the Center of Things

The newsdesk was the font for outrageous calls. We received the best of the worst. Just post-Columbine tragedy, a woman called to tell us she knew why it happened. You see, she was the high priestess of her WICCA coven, and there was a vortex in the cafeteria. Thank you, we'll get right on that.

Those calls were fairly regular. So when I received a call in December of 2006 from a man in California, asking me to turn to a certain page in that week's issue, I rolled my eyes and prepared for the craziness.

The page he referred to was part of a photo essay on an earthquake in Pakistan. A tiny girl, missing a leg, was featured hobbling through the remains of her village. The caller said, "I'm Marty, I'm a Shriner, and we want to help this little girl. Can you find her?"

I certainly couldn't find her, but I COULD get the ball rolling. My super-boss, Howard Chua-Eoan and I set out on a mission. We contacted the photo department, who contacted the photographer, Yuri Kozyrev. Yuri tracked down Insha Afsar, 7, in a refuge camp in Kamsar, Pakistan with the help of his notebooks and contacts in various relief organizations. In a remarkable play about humanity crossing religious and cultural divides, everybody had a role. Bobby Ghosh came on board to translate the Urdu calls to Isha's community, the Shriners arranged for her free medical care, and the Heal the Children Foundation provided a host family for Insha and her father. Howard paid for her passage. I tried to keep everybody in contact with each other. (my Urdu sucks.)

Insha and her father arrived in the U.S. in January, 2007. She was fitted for a special prosthesis, which will be adjusted as she grows. I can't begin to describe the euphoria I felt when the lobby called to ask for ME and tell me Isha, and her father were here to meet us. I wasn't prepared for the wee child with massive brown eyes who hopped, literally, into the newsdesk office. She hadn't gotten her leg yet, but nothing was stopping her. As Bobby translated, I swung Insha around in my chair and we giggled over some cartoons I put on TV. I asked Bill Kalis to take a photo for me, and I went to sit on the floor. Insha moved to the side of my chair and tapped it to indicate she wanted me to sit next to her. We snuggled and I don't know when I've felt so satisfied with my job.

When it was over, she hopped down the hall faster than an editor late for story conference. See, they were going to see "Lion King" and she was beside herself with excitement. The next day I FedExed a packet of jungle animals to her at the host residence. I got a call, a small voice trilling, "Lion King! New York!"

A happy little girl, whose life was changed by a photo and a story. The power of journalism.

-0-

The primary function for the newsdesk was putting people situated in New York in touch with people in the field, often waking whole households up if a story needed to be closed. We faced some occasional grievances, but generally the household was accustomed. And sometimes that household wasn't even a spouse and children. Sometimes it was reporters, drivers, translators and bodyguards. Let me explain.

Weekend overnights were an essential for the newsdesk. Twenty-four/seven coverage until the magazine was heading toward the news stands on Sunday, keeping an eye on events, anything that would change a story, the slightest mistake. Up until the incident I'm about to describe, my biggest "find" was a mistake on a story about the "Friends" TV show finale. Our story ended with "Whether Rachel ends up with Ross or Chandler . . ."

Hang on!!! Rachel never went out with Chandler! She went out with Joey!! A quick call to Steve Koepp and the copydesk, and the situation was solved. I felt confident in my position as newsdesk editor. And celebrated with a doughnut.

In December of 2003, I worked a Saturday night 8pm- to 8am shift, and came upon a more significant newsdesk—worthy event. By Sunday morning, around 5am, one could expect that the magazine was closed, done, checked and was being transmitted. So I sat on the floor, in sweats, organizing family photos and keeping an eye on the wires and our 2 TVs. I looked up and saw a grizzled old man literally being plucked from an underground bunker. The headline read "Saddam Hussein has been found".

There isn't enough caffeine in the world to compare to the adrenaline that surged through me as I called the Baghdad bureau, then waiting for 30 loooooong seconds to get a confirmation. Next on to Howard Chua-Eoan, Jim Kelly, Michelle Stephenson, and before I could say, "Uday is a Slug", my colleague, John Flowers was at the desk answering phones.

From 6am until noon, John and I took dictation (my least favorite part of newsdesk duty, short of packages from prisoners). We were taking dictation from heroic reporters who were doing their best to get information at a ferocious time in Baghdad, with the support of their brave Iraqi comrades. My respect is enduring.

By noon, the cover of Time Magazine was changed from Jesus to Saddam. I witnessed editors, usually dapper and trimmed, now in sweat pants with bed head. No make-up. Men and women. People RUNNING thought the hall with pages. It was a virtual machine, with prime parts operating.

"Stop the Presses!!" I'm proud to say I was a part of the operation.

Eileen Harkin

Solzhenitzyn and Tainanmen Square, 1989

One of the odder and more exhilarating aspects to being a Time-Life News Service reporter was the juxtaposition of unconnected, but equally fascinating reporting experiences in a very compressed time period. Thus in the last ten days of May 1989, I had the opportunity to conduct a full-scale interview with Russian Nobel Laureate in Literature, Alexander Solzhenitsyn, then, with only a day to pack my bags, to fly out from Washington to Shanghai and Beijing for the tragic last 10 days of China's student democracy movement. It was a high-adrenaline dose of reporting excitement crammed into a ridiculously intense two weeks.

The publisher Farrar, Strauss had offered TIME an interview with the usually reclusive Russian writer in exile. Strobe Talbott, then bureau chief in Washington DC, had generously asked me whether I wanted to do it. Are you kidding? I'd cut my teeth learning Russian by reading One Day in the Life of Ivan Denisovich, and I'd been a "writer" in New York at the Time-Life Building when editors wanted to write up Solzhenitsyn's rather gloomy 1978 Harvard Commencement speech. I took a sly pleasure in "greening" out (editing out for space reasons) the commentary on that speech by Editor-in-Chief Henry Grunwald.

It took me about a millisecond for me to say yes to Strobe's offer but the Beijing excursion had been my idea. I'd lived in Beijing for two years as Time's bureau chief there in the early 1980's. Many years before that, I'd spent years in graduate school studying Chinese and Chinese history. I think I sensed exactly what was going to happen in China: the People's Liberation Army was going to crack down on the democracy protest mercilessly. Hundreds, perhaps thousands of people would be shot. I'd even predicted on a CNN discussion program in mid-May that this would happen. My fellow discussants, all of them also former China-hand reporters, shook their heads in disagreement.

But first, Solzhenitsyn. I'd met Solzhenitsyn's personal secretary on May 23 in the small convenience store in Cavendish, VT, which posted a stern warning to all and sundry: "No restrooms! No bare feet! No directions to the Solzhenitsyn's!" With this somewhat intimidating warning in mind, I half expected the great writer to be a cross between a grumpy provincial school-teacher and an Old Testament prophet. After all, he'd been unceremoniously bundled by the Soviet authorities onto a plane headed for Frankfurt in 1974, had spent two years in Zurich, and then had lived the previous 18 years holed up in a fenced-off estate in rural Vermont. But Solzhenitsyn couldn't have been more charming. The interview went on for several hours, and it was pleasantly interrupted by a delightful Russian meal with the entire Solzhenitsyn family in the capacious family kitchen. I was given the great honor of sitting on the writer's right.

It would take several weeks to complete the interview transcript, and a rather tense session of telephone negotiations with Natalya, the writer's wife, over what could and couldn't be included in the published text. But TIME devoted the space it deserved because of the rarity of Solzhenitsyn's interview in general: three pages. To this day, I can remember exactly what Solzhenitsyn was wearing.

The China reporting turned into a crescendo of progressively more intense encounters, beginning on May 26 with interviews with China-watchers in Hong Kong, then a sort of slow-motion survey of universities in the Shanghai region. The Shanghai authorities, at the first sign of student unrest in Beijing, and then of copy-cat demonstrations in Shanghai, had cannily sent all the university students home before the scheduled end of the spring semester. On Shanghai campuses there were almost no students left, but enough political "wall-posters" to fill several trash-cans. On the Bund, however, Shanghai's famous waterfront, a small group of students was reading aloud a sample letter of students to their parents: "Mama, Papa! I've come back! I've come to explain to you what we are struggling for, what our democratic and patriotic student move is about. We are not wrong. We have not retreated. We have not lost. We will be back to make our case after we have rested."

Hmm, I thought. I wonder.

I was eager to get to Beijing as soon as possible because it was obvious that when the crackdown which I anticipated took place, it would be most severe there. I caught a plane which arrived in Beijing Airport in mid-morning of June 3, 1989. Correspondent Sandra Burton (tragically to lose her life in a home invasion in Indonesia a few years later) was already in the Chinese capital, having flown in from Hong Kong. TIME's veteran China expert in the bureau, Jimmy Florcruz, was also busy reporting the changing events of the still-ongoing student protest.

I was met by Lao Zhao, the Time bureau driver at the airport. "Please take me straight to the square, not to the hotel or the bureau," I told him. I had a sense that the end of it all might be just hours away. Lao Zhao rather nervously stopped the car near the Great Hall of the People, Beijing's largest public building on one side of Tiananmen Square. I got out, quickly ran up the main steps to the front entrance of the building and then cast a panoramic glance over what was happening in the square. Rows of army tents stood side-by-side, the pennants of various universities all over China snapping in the brisk breeze. The open spaces on the square were all filled up by crowds of students with bullhorns, announcing this or that new democratic project. Behind me, ominously, the official loudspeakers of the Great Hall of the People were repeatedly warning that martial law was in effect and that the square should be cleared completely.

Sandra and I had decided to spell each other in our reporting. I'd cover events in the center of town in the afternoon, she'd take over in the evening, and I'd report events around the square from early morning onwards.

In the late afternoon I was outside the back of the Great Hall, watching the ebb and flow of confrontations between sullen-faced soldiers and students who want to block them from moving into the square. There are clashes between the two groups, and when a soldier takes off his heavy belt and swings it around, it strikes a student in the face. Blood pours out and he is taken away by other students. Medical students arrive to take care of any more injury victims. Around 6:40, students begin hurling abuse upwards towards the windows in the GHOP, "Li

Peng, Step Down!" By an hour later, stones have been thrown through the GHOP windows.

At around 10:00 p.m. there's still no shooting near the square, but it's certainly begun out west along Chang An Avenue, the main avenue that dissects Beijing. I catch a few hours sleep at the Palace Hotel, ironically owned by the People's Liberation Army and just a few blocks from Tiananmen Square.

At around 4:00 a.m. I cautiously move back to the square. I have to be careful, because there are PLA jeeps patrolling the streets and Chinese security services would probably arrest any foreigner they saw wandering around. There are tracer rounds flying in all direction in the dark, and the sounds of automatic weapons firing in at least eight different parts of the city as far as I can discern. The PLA has completely surrounded the square and is the process of retaking it. At 4:10 a.m. I hear a great shout from a group of students, "Fascists!" Others in the crowd are more specific: "Execute the criminal Li Peng!" Around 5:00 a.m. there is a fierce rattle of machine-gun fire close to the edge of Tiananmen Square. A grizzled old man comes up to me, looks intently into my eyes, and says, "You should tell the world to condemn what the Chinese government is doing to the Chinese people!" Another student spots me and says, "The American government should do something!" If only, I think.

Wounded civilians and students are being transported on flatbed bicycles away from the streets where there has been shooting. But by 6:00 a.m. it's clear that the army has complete control of the center of Beijing. A column of tanks rolls into the square from the East, followed by several trucks full of soldiers. The last few student and civilian observers of the whole scene gradually melt away.

Shooting occurs periodically until early afternoon. After this Beijing shudders into silence and for about four days seems entirely devoid of any normal urban activity, indeed any official presence—except the soldiers in the square—with buses and streetcars completely inoperative from the moment the crackdown started.

I stay a few days in the city, do as much reporting as I can for a book Time-Life reporters are going to produce (*Massacre in Beijing: China's Struggle for Democracy*, Warner Books, 1989).

Reporting on the tragic and crushing suppression of the brave Chinese student democracy movement was certainly my greatest reporting experience at Time-Life. And a close runner-up was the Solzhenitsyn interview. Quite an interesting two weeks.

David Aikman

The Siege at Prey Tutong

It was just after Christmas, 1970, about 5 in the morning in Phnom Penh. Someone was pounding on my hotel room door. I rolled out of bed and opened the door. There stood Denis Cameron, a friend and photographer with whom I frequently worked, dressed in a safari jacket, tan trousers and dirty white sneakers, a couple of cameras dangling from his shoulder.

"I hear they've broken the siege at Prey Totung." he said in his usual laconic way. "I have up a chopper. We can be the first ones in. Want to go?

Prey Totung, a little crossroads town of 6,000 people, about 50 miles as the crow flies north northeast of Phnom Penh, had been under attack by North Vietnamese troops for more than two weeks.

No journalists could get there, but the briefers in Phnom Penh had told us that some 400 heavily outnumbered Cambodian defenders had retreated into a schoolyard just off the main highway and had been holding out ever since. The commander was a colonel named Srey Yar, whom I knew slightly.

I brushed my teeth, threw on some clothes, grabbed a couple of pens and a notebook and hustled down to the hotel lobby where Denis was waiting. On the way to the airport, he explained that a friend in the Cambodian air force had made the helicopter available. We figured we'd fly in, get the story of how the siege was broken, fly out and be back in Phnom Penh to file by nightfall.

The morning was clear and sunny when we arrived over Prey Totung. From the air, things looked quiet. We could see the schoolyard below, a large empty field on one side, the town center on the other. As we descended into the field, dozens of wounded Cambodian soldiers came streaming out of the schoolyard. Some were limping on crude crutches, others had their heads, legs, arms and stumps swathed in dirty, bloody bandages. All had plainly had their fill of Prey Totung.

The chopper's skids hadn't even touched down before the first of them rushed to scramble aboard, ignoring Denis and me as we dismounted. The pilot, concerned for his suddenly overloaded helicopter's safety (as well, no doubt, as his own), executed an emergency ascent, leaving scores of wounded—plus Denis and me—behind.

I have no idea what became of the chopper after that, because no sooner had we set foot on the ground than we realized there was a firefight in progress. The soldiers inside the schoolyard were being pummeled again. The siege at Prey Totung had not been lifted.

Lowering our heads, we hightailed it for the wall around the schoolyard, hustling through an open gate and taking cover inside. Dennis was already shooting pictures, while I tried to take notes of what I was seeing. I no longer have those notes, and the rest of that afternoon is pretty much a blur. All I remember is gunfire and smoke and men yelling, and wounded and more wounded. Not till sunset did the fighting cease so that I could talk with Col. Srey Yar. He, Denis and I were sitting at a wooden table under a large tree in the schoolyard. He seemed relaxed and confident, despite what he and his men had been through for nearly three weeks. He even found a bottle of French wine somewhere and offered us a drink.

I asked him something inane, like what the siege had been like. "Most of the time," he said, "we could not even lift our heads." Was it over? "Soon, but not yet."

The colonel, asked if we wanted to share what meager dinner rations there were for dinner. We were hungry enough, but it didn't seem right to accept the offer. "We brought our own food," Denis said. When I asked later what food he was talking about. He pulled from his camera bag one small tin of army-issue fruit cocktail and one plastic spoon. "Half for you, half for me," he said.

Around nine or ten that evening, the North Vietnamese, invisible in the distant, total darkness, opened fire again. The Cambodian troops just hunkered down as best they could. Dennis and I followed a few of them into an empty schoolroom. Outside, the pop-pop-pop of automatic weapons was punctuated by incoming mortar explosions and machine-gun fire that raked the schoolyard and the buildings. One .50 caliber bullet penetrated the thick concrete wall of the building we were in. Then came the nerve-shattering explosion of an incoming 122 mm rockets, one of which toppled the 60-foot tree we had been sitting under earlier with Srey Yar.

New sights and new sounds followed—fiery, ear-splitting explosions nearby and the scream of jet engines. Air support? Not likely, but that's what it seemed to be. Whatever it was, it had the quick, dramatic and most welcome effect of ending the attack, except for the odd mortar round now and then. Sometime well after midnight, Denis and I found ourselves empty spots on the wooden floor of the schoolroom and, using our shirts for pillows and a couple of wooden desks for some measure of protection, tried to get some sleep.

By sunup, the shooting had stopped entirely. I asked Srey Yar what had happened. "American F-102s," the colonel said. "They've hit the communists hard." This was becoming a bigger story than we realized. The use of U.S. aircraft to support Cambodian ground troops was expressly forbidden by the Cooper-Church Amendment, which the U.S. Congress had passed the previous June. Personally, I was never in my life happier to witness a violation of federal law, but this violation was news all the same.

A little while later, I overheard a Cambodian soldier speaking by radiotelephone with an English-speaking pilot. Hoping to get some kind of useful quote, I asked if I could say something. The radioman handed me his handset. "American pilot, American pilot," I said, "This is American correspondent." After a very long, static-crackling pause, came the pilot's reply: "Put the Cambodian back on."

Around noon that day, Denis and I saw a few town residents, who apparently had fled when the fighting began, trudging past the schoolyard, going back to see what was left of their homes. We decided to join them. As we started to leave the schoolyard, Srey Yar approached. "I wouldn't go yet," he said. "There are still some enemy stragglers around."

"Just to take a quick look," I said.

What we found was a town ruined by napalm and bombs and a wider area littered with bodies, civilian and military. Many of the military bodies were wearing the traditional "black pajamas" of North Vietnamese and Viet Cong fighters. One was near a melted machine gun and had both legs blown off just above the knee. Another was charred quite literally to a crisp.

After spending a half-hour or so looking around, Denis and I were returning to the schoolyard when we came under fire ourselves. We could hear the bullets zipping by and could see them digging up the ground 20 or 30 yards beyond us. We hit the dirt fast and were flat on our bellies as Srey Yar, a big smile on his face, peered down at us over the schoolyard wall, his chin resting on his arms. "I told you not to leave," he said. "There's a sniper over there, who's been bothering us." he pointed. "I don't think he can hit you on the ground. So stay down. I've already sent some men to get him." A few minutes later, while we still lying there, Srey Yar reappeared. "Okay," he said, "you can get up."

That afternoon several helicopters came in to carry the wounded—as well as Denis and me—back to Phnom Penh.

Once there, I filed a report to Time from the post and telegraph office. I made a point of the role played by U.S. warplanes. The story that appeared in the Jan. 4, 1971, issue included an "internal by-line" for me and a bit of my reporting. (The time difference and Cambodia's primitive telecommunications system, prevented my seeing a playback.) But the writer failed to include any mention of the F-102s and paraphrased a nameless "French journalist"—no affiliation given—as reporting that in Prey Totung he had seen "the bodies of North Vietnamese . . . chained to their machine guns . . ." Denis and I saw no such thing, and, whoever this "French journalist" was, he or she must have arrived well after the fighting.

In any case, the epic battle there turned out to be just another forgotten incident. The previous summer, Cambodia had, in effect, been forced into the Vietnam conflict after Richard Nixon authorized an American invasion. And a little less than five years after that, the Khmer Rouge marched into Phnom Penh and established one of the 20th century's more murderous regimes.

POSTSCRIPT: Twenty years after the battle of Prey Totung, I was back in Cambodia, on another Time assignment, and was a passenger in a car traveling along Route 7 from Kompong Cham to Phnom Penh. I was sound asleep when I awoke with a start and looked out the window. Now, I am not much given to mysticism, but what caused me to wake at that instant I'll never know. What I do know is that I looked out the window and saw a sign that read "Prey Totung." I hadn't even known the town was on our route. "Stop the car!" I cried. I got out and walked around for a few minutes. The town had been rebuilt, but the schoolyard looked just as I remembered it, right down to the bullet holes in the wall.

As I inspected them, I was reminded again of how futile it all had been.

Stan Cloud

Dinner with El Jefe

Fidel, the devil in the blue suit, is out to wow 47 American executives. "Dear friends," he says as an opening. Somehow, miraculously, the TIME Newstour has made it to Havana. We are in the Supreme Court room of the Palacio de la Revolucion with its pre-Revolutionary heavy burgundy curtains, burgundy leather seats and fine wood. The atmosphere is as sterile and humorless as a good Communist. Fidel is wearing his double-breasted Dutch designer suit by Merel van't Wout—a gesture to his visitors. He is standing. He will stand for hours flattering and lecturing them. His visitors will nap. It's all a joke to him. "If you find something luxurious here, it's not my fault," he says, smiling and attempting some humor. No one laughs. "We are in a courtroom. In this case, you are the magistrates and we are the defendants." That gets a few chuckles. The old man's charisma has them hanging on his every word, for about 30 minutes. But it goes on for hours—three? four? five? We lose track. By 10:30 p.m., the Japanese businessman behind me is napping. Fidel, 69, is still on his feet, talking. "Those who are sleeping, go to sleep, take a nap!" he says jovially. He performs, expounds on the fall of the Soviet Union, the rise of the Chinese communists, the 33-year-old U.S. embargo. He is an old man wistful about the Revolution. "Perhaps we're at fault, too," he says. "We had our dreams of a better world." The businessmen fidget. Long after midnight (Could it really be nearly 1 a.m.?) he sends us off to dinner. "Eat as much as you want. We are already broke. It could not be any worse," he says, a tad sourly. But first, it's time for cocktails and trading gifts. Gerald Levin presents Fidel with a glass Steuben eagle along with a speech I'd written about the broken eagle on the USS Maine Monument and how this may come to represent repaired relations between our two countries, meaningless diplomatic gibberish. Reg Brack—who's become a favorite of Fidel's from the past two dinners we've had in Havana—speaks, then Charles Schwab gives Fidel a signed baseball and a jacket. It is after midnight, the martinis and mojitos are flowing and dinner is a standup affair. Everyone is pooped. It has been a long day, starting with the briefings in Washington. The older execs are sitting on the sidelines of the dining room like girls waiting to be asked to dance. Beverly Sills, clocking in at 300 pounds or so, asks if she can leave. The first group of capitalists since the Revolution to be entertained by Fidel and they want to leave. Sills grouses something about Fidel getting to sleep all afternoon. She should have seen my week . . . The Cubans never got the Newstour concept. Until Thursday night, they thought these guys were really in Cuba to discuss business. First, we had an argument over where the meeting would take place. They wanted to use the pug-ugly concrete Palacio de Convenciones, built in the '70s. I begged them to think of history and use the Palacio de la Revolucion for its symbolism. (Heh heh, it was built in the '50s and Facist inspired.) Eventually they agreed, presenting the whole thing as Fidel's idea. Then we couldn't agree about dinner arrangements, who would sit next to Fidel. They wanted tables of 8 or 9 or 10, but when they found out Reg, their favorite, would not be sitting with Fidel (a position Reg had ceded to Norm Pearlstine, whom the Cubans didn't like), they agreed to a buffet. At first, they wanted a Q&A with National Assembly president Ricardo Alarcon and economic czar Carlos Lage, but the two men have never much liked each other and besides, Fidel hates competition, so they agreed to a Fidel Q&A. Then we argued over the bus route for the Saturday tour of Havana. They hated the idea of us going to a farmer's market; Fidel actually mused out loud during dinner whose idea that was. (Thank you, deputy chief of correspondents, Rick Hornik.) I added the dollar stores, which upset them, too. Anyway, they kept going over my head to Rick and Reg. Luckily, both backed me up. Then at the last minute, there was an issue over the presentation of the American eagle, a "symbol of capitalism," they protested. But the Cubans worked that out with us, too. The really big blowup on Thursday was over lunch Saturday at La Bodeguita del Medio, the Hemingway hangout in old

Havana. We had invited the dissidents and, of course, not told the Cubans. My poor Minrex minder, Homero Saker, pulls me aside in the afternoon and asks me if I want to tell him about Saturday lunch. Somehow they had gotten hold of my invite to Martha Beatriz Roque, the dissident economist. I had delivered most of the invites by hand, including one to Elizardo Sanchez, but I had left Martha's under her door. Dumb. (I later learned she had gone to stay with her sister because the Cubans were harassing her, making her phone ring 24 hours a day.) So mush-mellow-man Homero, who's never raised his voice to me, is furious. We're standing in the hallway of the Hotel Nacional and I explain about Newstours, how we meet with all sectors of society in the countries we go to, etc. That night, I get a call from Roberto Dominguez, the big gun at the Ministry of Foreign Affairs, and we're soon screaming over the phone at each other. I'm worried about New York; he's worried about Fidel—and his neck. Like a petulant little boy, he says he's going to call Felipe Perez Roque (Fidel's young chief of staff) to complain and take me off the dinner list. I'm beat. I'm screaming back. I lose it. Totally. I am out of control, tired, angry. Roberto's screaming, What kind of business can these guys talk about with dissidents? I'm screaming back that under U.S. law, they can't talk real business anyway. And he's telling me not to be stupid. Anyway, finally, he gets beaten down and says, "OK, OK, OK." But Friday, when we meet, the smiles are pretty frigid all around. Felipe, who never liked me because I called him a Yummy, an upwardly mobile Communist, in a TIME article, is positively gelid. So the idea that we're now having dinner at the Palacio de la Revolucion, smiles (and yawns) all around, is something of a miracle. Fidel has really laid on the buffet: lobster medallions, giant shrimp cocktails, oysters served in a glass, roast pork (the tortured head staring out from its shrunken body), bacalao with potatoes and onions, rum, mojitos, cigars, cigars and more cigars. The capitalist boys are so taken with the cigars and the occasion, they are forgetting to talk to Fidel, who is sipping his dry martini alone with Juanita, his translator. So I go up to him and he is bemoaning the fact that no one is eating his oysters. I laugh and tell him that's because we can't eat them in the U.S. right now because they are bad so he sends me off to encourage people to eat. Fidel isn't eating at all, just sipping his martini. Slowly. His famous beard has gone all wispy and he has a wicked case of shingles or eczema on his face, especially around the moustache. Jef McAllister asks him if he wants to die with his boots on in the job. Fidel laughs and says yes, but adds mournfully, that his job just isn't what it "used to be"—that 10 people do what he used to do alone. Slowly the crowd grows around him. Last I see, there is a covey of executives smoking Cohiba cigars all clustered around Fidel, who has had to give up cigars. Steve Green, the CEO of Samsonite, told me later that he asked Fidel if the smoke bothered him and Fidel just laughed and hugged him. The morning after, they are all talking about how they admire the man, but they ridicule his "theology." Our Saturday lunch drama is not yet over, alas. As I'm leaving the bus for our tour of Old Havana, the economic dissident Martha Beatriz Roque, a former professor at the University of Havana, calls me and tells me she won't go with any taxi driver we send because the government has been sending drivers, too, claiming to be from TIME. She has been under increasing harassment since she started talking to me and Chris Marquis from The Miami Herald. That morning, she says, a death threat was placed under her door. It was signed by the Cuban American National Foundation (an anti-Fidel group in the states which would clearly have no interest in threatening her). It read, "We know who you are. We are constantly checking on where you go. Your time is coming." I can hear the fear in her voice and she's not a woman who frightens easily. She says a man has come to her door recently waving a gun. (While on the Old Havana tour, I am followed by a Minrex minder until we get to Bodeguita, where a bevy of these pumped-up "minders" from the ministry is hanging around. Most everyone in Cuba can barely put food on the table so these guys really stick out now.) On Sunday morning, I go check up on Martha. She's in her usual hole-y yellow and white stripe cotton shift. The phone is ringing constantly in the background. Since our interview a month before, the Cubans have subjected her to this: A computer dials her number and the phone rings 11 times, then it hangs up and redials. 24 hours a day, 7 days a week. She won't disconnect her phone for fear of being out of contact. (Cuban phones, which date to prehistory, don't have our new-fangled gizmos for temporary disconnection.) Once, she says, she got 65 rings in a row. She picks up the phone and no one is there. Trying sleeping through that. She stayed with her sister for a while, but her sister was going crazy, she says, then the police visited her sister at work. No one in the family can work legally now. Martha has no food, not even coffee to offer visitors. When I call to check on her later, there is a jackhammering noise covering my voice. I can faintly hear her saying, "oigo, oigo," in the background. Then nothing. The Newstour goes on its way with its weary executives. I think of Fidel laughing about how Cuba will be a "madhouse" when American tourists and businessmen return. I remember him saying oh-so-sincerely, "If anybody has a book with solutions to the world's problems, please forward them by fax, the sooner the better." Martha Beatriz Roque had some ideas, economic ones. Two years after the Newstour left, the Cubans sent her to prison for that.

Cathy Booth Thomas

Saturday Duty . . . at the Earthquake

The News Service was an exciting place to work. Vivid experiences overtook me even as a trainee in the Washington bureau, before I became a correspondent (and before I started on the job, if you count my unnerving introduction to Henry Luce at a bureau dinner on the night before I reported for duty).

In February 1964, for example, I covered the Beatles' first U.S. tour—still one of the most gratifying assignments of my career. (I've described that adventure on Time's website: *http://www.time.com/ time/arts/article/0,8599,587795,00.html*) A month later, I landed in a more dramatic situation. I covered the Alaska earthquake of 1964, a cataclysmic, 9.2-magnitude tremor that killed 131 and caused more than $2 billion worth of damage in today's dollars. How did a 26-year-old Washington trainee end up covering such a big story more than 3,000 miles away?

It was like this. I had drawn the Saturday duty in the bureau that week. The responsibilities consisted mostly of calling correspondents at home, reading them incoming queries and checkpoints, then relaying at least the polite portions of their responses back to New York. The wires were teeming with news of the quake, which had struck the day before, but I assumed it was of remote concern to me.

Wrong. A call came from the Air Force. It was sending a plane to Alaska in an hour and a half, carrying federal officials and members of the Alaska Congressional delegation. Seats were available for the press. Did Time want one?

I called correspondent after correspondent. None were able—or willing—to go. Finally, time running out, I made my first executive decision as a Time Incer. I assigned myself. Grabbing my unlined raincoat, I took $100 from petty cash in the wire room and raced to Andrews Air Force base.

I guess I had some naïve notion that the plane would stop briefly in Alaska and then fly us back. In fact more than a week would pass before I saw Washington again.

We landed at Elmendorf Air Force base outside Anchorage and were put up there overnight. Aftershocks jolted my barracks room. I remember watching a floor lamp rocking back and forth and wondering whether it or I would topple over first. (It did.)

Such was the devastation in downtown Anchorage that a hotel room was out of the question, so the next day I took shelter in the home of Time's Alaska stringer, a rotund former state trooper and bush pilot named Joe Rychetnik. Joe and his wife and kids were among the lucky Anchorage residents who still had water and electricity. San Francisco bureau chief Roger Stone, who had arrived a day ahead of me, was already ensconced and had claimed Joe's living room couch. I got the floor.

For the next week, I divvied up the reporting with Roger and Joe, surveying damage and interviewing officials, victims and survivors—all the while buying toiletries and underwear wherever I could. Joe loaned me a warm jacket. The newsdesk refreshed my money supply. What more could I ask?

In those days correspondents on the road sent their files to New York by Western Union. In our case, we may have relied on Air Force telegraphers, since even after five years of statehood the Air Force ran the communications grid in Alaska. Anyway, we criss-crossed the disaster area, got our files in somehow, and enjoyed many late, liquid nights in Joe's living room, listening to his tales of the Alaskan bush.

The aftershocks continued, but the only time I felt real danger my feet weren't even on the ground. A handful of other reporters and I were being ferried in a single-engine Air Force plane to inspect Seward, one of the coastal towns that had been virtually leveled by tsunamis. We swooped in over Resurrection Bay on our approach to Seward's little airstrip, ringed on three sides by mountains. Once over the runway, we hovered agonizingly, and kept on hovering. With the end of the runway flashing beneath us, suspense turned to terror as the engine groaned and we lurched into a sickeningly steep, banking climb. All I could see ahead was a wall of mountains. I was pretty sure I was about to meet my maker. But no, we skirted the slopes, circled out over the bay and came in for a routine landing.

The pilot, besieged by his shaken passengers the moment he stepped out of the cockpit, casually explained that he'd wanted to check the length of the runway for damage before touching down. "I probably should've warned you about that," he said cheerily.

For Time, the earthquake was a two-week wonder. After its second round of stories the magazine moved on. Roger and I made our way home, this time by commercial flights, which had been restored to some extent. During our stopover in Seattle, remembering that Joe and his wife had complained of being unable to find fresh vegetables in Anchorage, Roger bought a case of asparagus and shipped it to them. When I had lunch with Joe in New York 30 years later he was still marveling over those asparagus.

Roger, having relished the moose meat he ate in Alaska, had packed a frozen slab of it in his luggage. Unfortunately it thawed before he got home and his suitcase was a bloody mess.

My homecoming was happier. My wife had joined my parents on a vacation in Florida, but she'd left me a tiny box containing a miniature doll. Wrapped around the doll was a note that said only, "Late November." She was pregnant with our first child.

Chris Porterfield

Clurman, the Magnificent 1

In those days, the Company took care of you and mentors in the News Service showed you how to live. Note that I didn't say "told" you. I met Richard M. Clurman in his office, where he was getting a shoe shine and offered the same to me. Nobody had ever done either in my entire, two-and-a-half year journalism career at the St. Louis Post-Dispatch and the Baltimore Evening Sun.

John Steele had sent me to New York after interviews in his bureau chief's office across from the Mayflower Hotel in Washington. Things hadn't gone all that smoothly. When he told me he would recommend me "to New York," I'd said how happy I was to be joining Life. "This is Time," he snapped. "Life is up the hall." In fact, until that very moment, I had indeed been interviewing for a job at Life, but I was learning fast, including that "New York" could mean one human, in this case also singular in being falcon-like and improbably blond. "Washington says I should take you," said New York, a cigarette artfully squeezed between long fingers. "You'll be working for me. Do you know what that means?" I had no idea. "It means that when we give you an assignment, we will also give you anything you say you need for it. You. If you need to learn a language, learn the language and send us the bill. If you need to charter a plane or a ship, do it." By this time it was my Cordovans that were being shined. ". . . Which also means something . . . Namely, that if after learning the language and chartering the plane your version of some particular story isn't the best in the world, we will all know whose problem that is . . ." He cocked his head significantly. "Won't we?" I had lost track of my shoes. I'd lost track of everything except that nobody had ever talked to me like that.

Two fast forwards:

—Miami Beach about 4pm August 8, 1968, a story conference of the Company's Republican National Convention team. One hundred strong, it is run like a warship, complete with a "purser" who stuffs my pockets with $1's, $5's and $10's, explaining "so when your car—you will have a car and driver—pulls up somewhere with everyone else, the doormen know which car to let through first." I was six months into my TLNS career. "New York" was now "Dick" to me and he was furious with the United States of America for permitting one of its major political parties to nominate "this nonentity" for vice president of his country. "Has anyone ever met Spiro T. Agnew?" Clearly, anybody who so confessed would be admitting links to the unworthy. Only my hand went up. While the Evening Sun's real political reporters golfed on Saturdays, I was occasionally sent to Annapolis for Governor Agnew's vapid press conferences, called on weekends because no important reporters attended. To general astonishment, Dick gave me the assignment, a crash cover. He wanted to know whether I had ever written a short book over a weekend but didn't seem interested in my answer.

—Post-election, a late November meeting in Dick's office, where again shoes were being shined. This time I wasn't alone. Fellow ex-Washington trainee John Stacks had been summoned too. Stacks had been assigned as my opposite number with the Democratic vice presidential race.

"Gentlemen," we were told, "We like your work equally well. What would you like to do next in any part of the world?" To that astonishing and inspiring question, we both gave the wrong answer: 'Paris.' What a disappointment. Didn't we know as young reporters that "the action now is all in the third world?" How about Africa?

Asia? South America? 'Paris,' we repeated. Dick asked for no explanation. Instead, he produced a quarter and said "one of you gets what you want and one gets when you want." I lost. Stacks got Paris and began taking French, planning to arrive in the spring of 1969. He didn't get there, however. Clurman was kicked upstairs and Murray Gart, his successor, rescinded all Clurman assignments. Stacks stayed home and after a stint as George McGovern's press secretary, returned and became chief of correspondents. That elevated him to being "New York" to the entire TLNS empire. Just as well. I didn't want up, I wanted away. Right then. Any country that could elect Spiro Agnew was a country to exit for a while. As in so many walks of my life, however, Vietnam blocked the path, in this case to London, Dick's idea of a consolation prize. Continuing to avoid Vietnam meant somehow moving there without compromising my most valuable possession—a secure draft-dodge position in the Army National Guard of Maryland. The alternatives were not good: Going AWOL, (unacceptable), or being assigned to a unit abroad in a branch of the military with no units abroad. Dick was not interested in the details. "Do whatever needs doing down there," he said, meaning the Pentagon. For a full month I did nothing else and accomplished nothing . . . until TLNS's military and Capitol Hill correspondents deployed wondrous out-of-channels firepower. Suddenly my way to the London bureau lay open. Everyone was vague about how that happened.

To a full generation of graduate students and mid-career journalism fellows at the University of Michigan, I have applied my lessons from TLNS. The words themselves weren't important. It was how their effect made you grow: To get what you want, give

72

people everything they say they need because guilt and terror make the ultimate motivational cocktail. If asked to do the impossible, say okay. If you can get when you want, don't wait for what.

Charles R. Eisendrath

Clurman the Magnificent 2

An early and strong Time memory is meeting Dick Clurman for the first time and getting a very special job offer. It was 1964. I was a college senior and had been the campus stringer at Princeton. I had come to the Time Life building for an interview for full time job. I already had an offer to teach in Northern Greece for a year. an opportunity which I would have to give up, according to other staffers who interviewed me. I came into Clurman's office. He was sitting behind that huge marble desk with an even larger map of the world behind it with red push pins in Bureau cities. In course of our conversation I mentioned that I had the offer to teach for a year in Thessaloniki. Without hesitation on his part or further elaboration from me, Clurman said: "Go to Greece for a year and the Time job is yours when you return. You will be a better correspondent for us after a year in Greece." What a classy guy. I still get emotional shivers when I remember this very special, Clurmanesque job offer.

Another strong memory is crossing the Suez Canal with the Israelis in the October 1973 Yom Kippur war. I had driven down to the canal in my own car and was then escorted across the canal to join a tank brigade commanded by a crazy Israeli general, known as "Pinko", who had a mutilated hand, partially blown away and burned in an earlier war. No one spoke to me as I arrived. I was clearly unwelcome baggage. I spent the night sleeping in my clothes outside the armored personnel carrier and was awakened before dawn by activity all around me with tanks starting up and rumbling into position. I was motioned inside the personnel carrier and was asked in some wonderment by one of the soldiers, "Why are you here?" A few minutes later I knew why. Pinko had been shouting into his radio in rapid Hebrew and the tanks were forming into an assault line across the dessert. Pinko then turned and in his first words to me said: "Now you will see Jews fight." He then gave the command in Hebrew into the radio and the line of tanks roared and belched forward. They stopped, reluctantly, 20 miles from Cairo.

Bill Marmon

Police Academy . . . in Arabic

One of my favorite memories in the News Service was the time I spent watching Police Academy 4 in Arabic on TV at the Damascus Sheraton with Roberto Suro. "Watch" is the wrong word. We were glued to the screen, transfixed by Steve Guttenberg's command of the language. We were in Damascus to cover the PLO funeral of Abu Jihad, taken from this life by the Mossad. True to form, it was packed with a terrifying number of crazy, zany folks ready to suffocate in the narrow streets of the big refugee camp there for the fallen Abu. I'm tempted to say you haven't lived until you've covered a PLO funeral, but the truth is, you haven't lived until you've watched Police Academy 4 in Arabic.

Also, it would be wrong of me not to mention the sweethearts from New York on a playback. To wit: "You say 7 miles from the border and the Times says 5. Which is it?"
Sam Allis

The Worst Week of my Time Years.

It was the summer of 1972 and I had arrived at my new post as Bonn bureau chief too late to sign up for credentials for the Olympic Games in Munich. I was at the annual trade fair in Leipzig, East Germany, when I heard on the radio that Palestinians from the terrorist organization Black September had killed two Israeli athletes and taken hostage nine more. I climbed into my rented car but because of East Germany's peculiar rules had to go back through Berlin rather than drive straight to Munich. I arrived in Berlin to find newspaper headlines announcing (because of a false statement issued by West German officials) that the hostages had been rescued. But after landing in Munich I found that all the hostages and most of the Palestinians had been killed in a storm of gunfire and grenades.

It was a profoundly sad and depressing week of reporting in Munich. These were Jewish athletes and they had been killed on German soil. Everyone concerned was feeling terrible and so was I. As we closed the cover that Friday night, I felt weak, dizzy and sick. Back home in Bonn, I found out that I had whooping cough, a gift from my 2-year-old son, Terence, who was just recovering.

-0-

In January 1979, landing an interview with Soviet President Leonid Brezhnev was a very big deal. He hadn't seen a western reporter for years and had been variously reported to have cancer, liver disease, or lymphoma. I had submitted an interview request as soon as I arrived in Moscow the year before, and was amazed when we got word that it had been accepted.

Henry Grunwald, Ray Cave and Dick Duncan flew in and we gathered to await the summons. Eventually the limos came and swept us through the Kremlin gates and up to the Supreme Soviet headquarters where Brezhnev had his office. We passed through several layers of antechambers and guards and then came face to face with Brezhnev. He was dressed in a heavy-silk, black suit with two rows of medals. He looked to me just like Mayor Richard Daley and had some of the mannerisms of the Chicago boss as well. He shook hands with us and turned us to face a photographer (the picture appeared on the front pages of the next day's Pravda and Izvestia).

But so far Brezhnev hadn't said anything. He sat us down at the long conference table and then took a very long time to autograph a copy of his autobiography for each of us. Then he handed over a set of written answers to questions I had been ordered to submit in advance. His handlers obviously hoped to halt things right there but Henry Grunwald would have none of that. He began asking questions and that marvelous interpreter Viktor Sukhodrev put them into Russian. The Soviets looked at one another, wondering what to do. Then Brezhnev began to speak, slowly and with much slurring of words. At a couple of points, Leonid Zamyatin, the party secretary sitting beside him, tried to whisper answers in his ear. Brezhnev turned to him with a withering glare, said a loud "Nyet," and gave his own answer. This was clearly a sick man, but a man very much in charge.

At our celebratory lunch, the New York bosses fancied the caviar and blini. But the Moscow-dwellers, who hadn't seen a green vegetable since September, gorged on the bags of lettuce Grunwald and Duncan had brought with them.
Bruce Nelan

Rabin's Assassination

My head was in a washbowl at my hairdressers when my cell phone went off on the Saturday morning of Nov. 4, 1995. It was the newsdesk calling. Yitzhak Rabin had just been killed. Before I could ask any questions, my phone died too. I had only started carrying one everywhere I went since becoming the Deputy Chief of Correspondents that July and, still a newbie, I had forgotten to charge the battery. I looked around. A woman sitting across from me was chatting on her phone. "I need your phone," I demanded. "The prime minister of Israel has just been shot. I work for Time Magazine and I've got to organize our coverage of it." She blinked. But she gave me the phone. I needn't have worried since Johanna McGeary had returned to the Jerusalem bureau to fill in while Lisa Beyer was away. Johanna had already begun deploying the troops on the ground and we turned around what became a cover story in 12 hours, just making the close.

-0-

Frank Rizzo's notorious treatment of the Black Panthers, the MOVE Organization and other members of Philadelphia's black community when he served as the city's police commissioner and later mayor had made him a bad guy in my eyes. Rizzo had been out of office for four years when the magazine scheduled a major takeout on the efforts to reign in the excesses of big city cops, but I still felt I should talk to him. So I asked for an interview. And he said yes, that I should come out to his house and talk to him there. I wasn't sure how he'd react when he opened the door and saw a black woman standing there. And he was wary at first. But something happened as the interview went on, the conversation grew warmer and warmer. On both sides. He told me stories; I asked for more. He told me jokes; I laughed. He cooked pasta for me and I ate it. I was supposed to stay an hour but ended up spending the whole afternoon with him, mainly in the kitchen. There had been rumors that he was going to run for mayor again but he refused to confirm them. Still, as he walked me to a waiting cab, I tried one last time, saying something like, "Mr. Mayor, do me a favor if you decide to run, call me and tell me." Which, to my surprise, he did, allowing us to be the first national publication to break the news.

-0-

Norman Mailer was turning 60 and "Ancient Evenings," his fifth novel—the first in 18 years—was coming out and so the magazine decided to do a cover story. Paul Gray was assigned to write it and I to report it, which meant spending a week with Mailer. That week turned out to be one when he was a guest writer in residence at the University of Pennsylvania and was scheduled to testify on behalf of the defendant in a murder trial in Portland, Maine.

The trial was particularly controversial because Mailer had recently supported the parole of Jack Abbott, a convicted murder who had spent nearly half of his life in jail and written a book about his time in prison called "In the Belly of the Beast." Six weeks after his release, Abbott got into an argument and stabbed a man at a downtown restaurant.

My time with Mailer had been catch-as-catch can between his engagements at Penn. He didn't seem all that happy to have me there and he sure as hell wasn't forthcoming about anything. But then, we had to make the trip to Portland. That meant getting up at some ungodly hour and schlepping to the airport. We flew from Philly to Boston, changed planes and went on to Portland, getting to the courthouse just before the hearing began around 10 a.m.

Misery can bring people together. Mailer and I bonded over the early travel, the bad airplane coffee and his weird reception in Portland: the judge called a recess right after Mailer's testimony and asked him to accompany him to his chambers, where he asked Mailer for an autograph; meanwhile, local reporters interrupted their press conference on the steps of the courthouse to do the same.

We had a long liquid lunch. Then we set off for the airport to make the return trip in time for a cocktail party the University had planned that evening and we drank on the plane too. By the time we arrived in Philly, we were giddy. There had been several questions I'd wanted to ask Mailer and high on the list was why he had infamously stabbed his second wife during an early-morning argument in 1960. So, as we lolled in the back of a cab, I just blurted out the question. He looked at me for a second and then sighed. It was, he said, just a crime of passion. And then we both started laughing at the inanity of the answer and couldn't stop.

The rest of the week, including visits with most of his nine kids and at least two of his six ex-wives, plus a formal interview at his apartment in Brooklyn Heights, went terrifically. But Ancient

Evenings was nearly unreadable and so the magazine cancelled the cover story. Paul wrote a section lede instead. Mailer called me to find out what happened. I don't remember what I told him. But I do know that he didn't hold a grudge because he invited me to the party he was having to celebrate the 100th anniversary of the Brooklyn Bridge. I went. And I had a terrific time.

Jan Simpson

An Expense Denied!

In Sarajevo in the mid-1990s, Time had the coolest armored vehicle in Bosnia, hands down: a giant white Chevrolet Silverado pickup truck that photographer Chris Morris had gotten shipped in. The beast had been armored in Texas, so it had Texas plates (it still does; you can see it, impressively worse for wear, on exhibit at the Newseum in Washington). Once when I was driving it to Pale, the depressing mountain redoubt where Radovan Karadzic spewed his poison, we encountered at the checkpoint a Serb militiaman with a real thing for Texas; he claimed to have a brother-in-law there. While his partner hassled me and photographer Filip Horvat for our papers, he was on his knees with a screwdriver, liberating a treasured American souvenir. It took two cartons of Marlboro reds to buy him off. That truck was also responsible for the only expense I recall ever having been denied by the endlessly understanding Camille Sanabria. It had to be parked in the basement of the Holiday Inn, and some days you had to really gun it in the approach to avoid snipers. When you got down the ramp, the space was badly suited for maneuvering a huge American pickup. Once I managed to nick the bumper of an old Mercedes, and was quickly surrounded by four serious dudes who dictated restitution of 200 deutschmarks on the spot. The receipt I submitted was deemed unacceptable.

Jamie Graff

Could Time Correspondents Really Charter a Plane?

In October 1982, I was sent to Beirut to help relieve Bill Stewart and Roberto Suro, who were long overdue for some R&R after covering the Israeli invasion of Lebanon and the massacres at Sabra and Shatilla. Flights to Beirut in those days were infrequent and hard to get on—if you missed your Middle East Airlines (MEA) flight from Athens, you could be waiting for days for the next one—but I managed to get a reservation that would coincide with Roberto's departure.

With my flight confirmation in hand, I decided to fly to Athens a few days early so I could spend some time in the Greek islands before proceeding to Beirut. In Mykonos, where I ended up, the weather in mid-October was already turning cool and windy, which made finding a nice hotel easy because most of the tourists had left. After a couple of days, however, I noticed that hotels and restaurants were starting to shut down for the winter so I asked my hotel about the ferry schedule back to Athens. That's when I found out I was trapped, and I wasn't the only one. A young American woman and an Australian couple staying at my hotel were also frantically trying to get reservations, but ferry service and flights had not only become sporadic, but everything was fully booked. Tourist season was over.

What I had assumed would be a leisurely side-trip through the Cyclades was now looking like a mad dash to the airport. I had to make that flight to Beirut, because if I didn't, it could be a week before I could get on another one.

What to do?

Charter a plane!

I called Olympic Air and they said that if the weather allowed, they could try to send a plane to pick us up in Mykonos (my fellow travelers said they'd be glad to pitch in on the cost), but the winds had already cancelled a number of flights and things weren't looking good. Well, I told them, I'm with Time magazine, and I've got to make that flight to Beirut.

A few hours later, the wind sock on the tiny air strip at Mykonos was horizontal when the small plane finally bounced down and its lone pilot descended the stairs in hat and full uniform to hurry us on board. The weather delay meant it was going to be close for me, and I asked the pilot if he could radio ahead to alert the MEA flight. Then I settled back and buckled in.

During the flight back we were blown around like a leaf as our pilot shoehorned our prop plane in between the international jumbo jets that were lined up for landing at Athens. Except for a few hair-raising flights in Chicago during thunderstorms, I've never been thrown around more, or more relieved to finally touch ground.

The best, however, was still to come. Our pilot barely slowed after landing as we veered off the runway and continued taxiing for several minutes toward the far end of the tarmac. Soon we saw his destination: An MEA jet sat waiting, a flight attendant peering out from the top of the portable stairway.

Our pilot steered our plane to a stop a few feet from the foot of the stairs, then jumped up, put his hat on, and opened the door for me. "Welcome to Athens," he said proudly.

I made the flight.

David Jackson

Encounters with the Truly Bizarre

It's tempting when reminiscing over a 30-year career at Time to focus on the encounters with world statesmen and other major enchiladas. Actually, what often remains most firmly embedded in the memory is time spent in the company of truly bizarre people.

At the top of my list is Mengistu Haile Mariam, the army sergeant who brought mayhem to Ethiopia after the fall of Emperor Haile Selassie. It was 1986 and I had just become chief of correspondents. Playing a card familiar to every correspondent, the unforgettable James Wilde, then Nairobi bureau chief, told the Ethiopians that a boss with a long title wanted to revisit the country he had known as a Peace Corps volunteer and, of course, interview the esteemed head of state. The scenario unfolded as it always does with third-world despots. First, hurry up and come to our capital. Then, hurry up and wait. James and I spent almost a week travelling around the country at the government's expense as we waited for the Very Busy Leader to make time for us. We visited centuries-old Coptic monasteries on Lake Tana, refugee camps near the Sudanese border and even my old village.

Finally, we were summoned. François Mitterrand would receive visitors in a gilded salon, Helmut Kohl in the ultramodern chancellery along the Rhine in Bonn, Mikhail Gorbachev around an intimate conference table in the Kremlin, and Chinese leaders in stuffed armchairs with doilies. Mengistu opted for a hall large enough to hold the U.N. General Assembly. After a perfunctory handshake and a cold dismissal of my attempt to proffer a greeting in Amharic, he positioned himself on the dais and we took our places at a table so far away that we could barely see him. Not far enough, though, to conceal the fact that he was reading from prepared texts instead of responding to any of our questions.

At the end of the second hour of this set piece, it was clear that we weren't going to get much substance. But the bottled water James and I drank as we became increasingly bored and frustrated was beginning to have an effect on our bladders. Now, Mengistu was known to have fed prisoners to the deposed emperor's lions for offenses less serious than getting up as he spoke, so we sat still, trying not to focus on our discomfort. At the end of the third hour, Mengistu was still reading from his sheaf. We tried every now and then to signal our intentions. "Well, thank you Mr. President, you've been very generous with your time . . ." Nothing doing. Only after a full four hours had elapsed did Mengistu abruptly end the meeting. There was no handshake. I've rarely been so relieved.

-0-

In a completely different key of strangeness there was William Casey, Ronald Reagan's CIA director. Bruce van Voorst gets the points for landing us an interview with him just as the Iran-contra fiasco was blowing up. The day after Casey's dreadful performance before a congressional committee, he welcomed us to his inner sanctum on the top floor of CIA headquarters in Langley. We didn't find it particularly strange that he slurred his words; he was known to do this, and journalists generally suspected it was a well-honed ploy to evade pointed questions. Even so, Bruce and I were surprised—gleeful, actually—that Casey was spilling more beans than anyone in his predicament should. Once the interview was over, we stopped at a gas station to use a pay phone (remember those?) to call New York with news of our scoop. We still didn't know just how we'd scored. The next day Casey collapsed and required emergency surgery to remove a brain tumor. He never returned to the office, and died a few months later. Bob Woodward later claimed to have obtained a few nods and winks from Casey in a four-minute deathbed encounter, but in truth Casey's words in Time were his last for the public record.

So much for the odd ducks. For me no Time memory is complete without mention of Gorbachev. It's hard to convey today just what a mysterious, cloistered place the Kremlin was during the Cold War. Time was the first American publication to penetrate those thick walls when it interviewed Leonid Brezhnev in 1979. When the young, dynamic Gorbachev came to power nearly a decade later, we immediately started lobbying for similar access, and thanks to the unrelenting efforts of John Kohan and Felix Rosenthal we eventually succeeded. It was such a breakthrough that Nick Nicholas, co-CEO of the newly merged Time Warner, lent us a company Gulfstream for the flight over. Editor-in-chief Jason McManus came along, as did chief of correspondents John Stacks, Washington bureau chief Strobe Talbott and photographer David Burnett.

In Moscow we were put up in a guesthouse usually reserved for Communist VIPs, and at the appointed hour we were driven to the Kremlin in a ZIL, a Soviet-built dinosaur of a vehicle that looked and rode like a Cadillac from the fifties. Intoxicated by the importance of his mission, our driver took us on a high-speed ride down the middle lane reserved for Party brass, making sure that the car's manifestly bald tires squealed at every turn. Shaken but giddy as we emerged from the ZIL, we were ushered down endless hallways until we finally reached the power center of what Ronald Reagan had called the Evil Empire. First there was a bit of small talk during which Gorbachev displayed the easy charm that would win him fans outside his home country. Then he invited us to sit elbow to elbow at a small conference table. The leader's flacks had predictably asked us to respect his tight schedule and we, just as predictably, were determined to overstay our welcome. It wasn't hard. Gorbachev enjoyed bantering with Kohan and Talbott in Russian. His answers were direct, if long-winded. And as we stood around chatting after the formal part of the interview, he didn't hesitate to answer personal questions. Gorbachev allowed Burnett to take pictures the whole time we were with him—including the group portrait that Nick Nicholas later framed and hung in his office.

I saw Gorbachev on several occasions subsequently, in public and private. He never failed to recall Time's interview, underscoring its importance to the process of perestroika that would ultimately dissolve the Soviet Union and lose him his job.

Henry Muller

Judgment of Paris

The biggest story of my career in journalism was a wine tasting.

In 1976, when I was a correspondent in Paris, an Englishman named Steven Spurrier owned a wine shop and wine school in Paris.

He had the slightly nutty idea of staging a blind tasting of some of the most famous French Cabernet Sauvignon and Chardonnay wines (Château Mouton Rothschild *et al.)* against their California counterparts. He was well respected in the local wine community and lined up nine eminent French judges.

Spurrier, who used to stage events like that to drum up business and become better known, sent out invitations to all the French, British, and American journalists in town. But a few days before the event at the InterContinental Hotel just off the Rue de Rivoli, no journalist planned to attend. It was obviously going to be a non-event, and no publication would print a story on famous French wines beating unknown California ones in Paris. I had also turned it down. But then he remembered that I had taken a course at his wine school, and so he picked up the phone to ask me to reconsider. Trying to let him down gently, I told him that I might come if I didn't have anything else to do. I offered the story to the Modern Living section, and it was scheduled. I didn't have illusions, though, of anything getting into the magazine.

It turned out I was the only reporter present that day, and the results were surprising. A California wine won in both the red and white categories: Stag's Leap Wine Cellars and Chateau Montelena. The story in the magazine was only four paragraphs long and was a filler after the main one about a new theme park in Atlanta.

When it was published in the June 7, 1976 issue, the *Time* story shook the wine world. The wine-and-food critic Anthony Dias Blue called it the most important wine tasting of the 20th century, and it put Napa Valley on the map. Frank Prial, the wine writer of the *New York Times*, devoted his column for the next two weeks to the event that became known as the Judgment of Paris, the headline on the *Time* story.

In 2005, Scribner published my book *Judgment of Paris*, which has now sold more than 100,000 copies and been translated into Chinese, Japanese, Korean, Portuguese, Croatian, and delightfully French. It was also the basis of the 2008 movie *Bottle Shock*. In the movie there's a weird-looking *Time* correspondent named George Taber.

Woody Allen said that 80% of success is showing up. I showed up.

George Taber

The Grandest Times of Our Lives

A Time correspondent 50 years ago had a life and a lifestyle that might be unimaginable to correspondents who came on the scene much later. We didn't spend much time in places such as Kabul or Baghdad. We were more likely to find ourselves settled comfortably in Rio or Paris (well, there was Moscow). We were lavishly supported. And Time was at the zenith of its influence and affluence.

In my case I found myself in Paris in 1961, having already had assignments in Washington, Mexico City, Madrid, Berlin as well as Tokyo and Korea (the latter for Stars & Stripes). Paris was, of course, a gorgeous city to experience. It was also a major source of news—honestly—there was de Gaulle, a constant nuisance; Algeria, fighting for independence while the French Army fought both the Algerians and its own government; the Common Market, which was finding itself; the French nuclear force (whatever happened to it?). and NATO, preparing for a Soviet attack. As well as France, we covered Benelux, Switzerland, Spain, Portugal, and North Africa.

To do justice to this rich stew of news, Time-Life ran a bureau consisting of more than two dozen people. I can't remember today the exact count, but we had five or six Time staff correspondents and a bureau chief, a Life bureau of three or four correspondents and two or three staff photographers (Life covered a much larger area of the globe from Paris than we did in the Time bureau). Because much of what Time correspondents filed from many parts of the world were relayed through Paris, we had about five people in the wire room running the telex machines. We had two chauffeurs (one of whom was frequently dangerously drunk) to drive our Mercedeses. We had our own in-house travel agent, and two librarians. We had excellent stringers in Brussels, Amsterdam, Geneva, the South of France, and Spain. There was also, of course, a sizable business office for the publishing, advertising, and circulation side.

We were generously supported by the company. In my case, our delightful house in the Villa Montmorency was subsidized and the company paid for our childrens' schools. We traveled first class. When our turn for home leave came up—after two years—we went first-class on the "France," with our car in the hold, and a special dining room for the children. The French authorities were also generous, if unconsciensely so. France has an income tax, just as we do, so after I had been there a few months I asked our company lawyer what I had to do to pay my taxes. She looked at me curiously, and asked, "Has anyone asked you to pay?" They hadn't. "Wait until they ask," she said. By the time we got back to New York four years later, nobody had asked.

Paris was a grand city in which to enjoy a generous expense account. The visit of a senior editor or the chief of correspondents, or almost any excuse, for that matter, became the occasion for a splendid meal in one of the great restaurants in Paris. One of my proudest moments came when, in the absence of the bureau chief, I received a command from Clare Boothe Luce to arrange a dinner with two English-speaking, influential, bachelor Frenchmen right away. It was left unsaid that they should be attractive. We needed two because Clare was traveling with a lady friend. Within hours we rounded up two gentlemen who fitted the requirements perfectly—the editor of Realites and the head of the French equivalent of the Gallup Poll, both fluent in English, charming, intelligent and handsome. We had a splendid dinner at the Grand Vefour with good conversation and I think Clare was satisfied. (Her friend fell asleep.)

What also made the Paris assignment special were the people in the bureau. The chief, Curt Prendergast, was the best boss I ever had—smart, hard-working, generous and encouraging. We became close friends as did our wives. Some of the other Time and Life people became great friends: Jud Gooding, Friedel Ungeheuer, Lee Hall, Bob Ajemian, Jim Wilde to name a few. We shared a love of Paris and excitement about the news we covered. Curt infected us all with his enthusiasm. When a query came in from the "people" section late one Saturday after we had just closed a cover story, asking for the color of some damned actresses hair, Curt leaped into action as if he had had nothing to do all week. We had our share of excitement too—bombs went off in Paris from time to time (one just next to the Prendergast's house), the streets often filled with gendarmes, generals were arrested and tried, Algeria won its independence.

It was the grandest time of our lives.

Jeremy Main

The First Cell Phone

One newsdesk anecdote that popped into my head is the story of how how Westedit got its very first cell phone:

In November 1993, a massive, fast-burning fire swept from Topanga Canyon to Malibu. Pat Cole was on the scene reporting and called in for Newsdesk updates. At one point we were talking and he said something like, "Um, Mary, I've got to go now. The house I'm calling from is on fire and the firefighters want me to get out." Pat escaped safely from the fire—and with amazing reporting, of course. After that the bureau got a cell phone, and every weekend duty person thereafter probably was grateful for having a phone, even though it was one of those brick sized things with its own shoulder holster.

Mary Wormley

The Chief's Fly is Down

In 1973. Time had a very rare scoop on a Supreme Court decision and it was a major decision indeed. The case was Roe v. Wade and we had the court's decision in the magazine the Monday it was announced.

This infuriated the chief justice, Warren Burger, who demanded a meeting with the top editorial management of the magazine. A dinner was arranged at the bureau and Hedley Donovan and Henry Grunwald and Murray Gart (I think) all flew down for the occasion. I was the very new bureau news editor and expected the New Yorkers to grovel before the august presence of the Chief Justice of the United States.

Burger showed up with a burly security man. He was carrying a green loose-leafed binder with a small type-written label that said "David Beckwith." Burger proceeded to berate the magazine and Beckwith for having penetrated the court's usually impenetrable security. Burger assumed that the scoop had come from one or another of the justice's clerks. This, he argued absurdly, was tantamount to tapping the justices' phones.

By the end of the meal, Hedley had had enough of Burger's silly argument. "Mr. Chief Justice," Hedley growled, "I find your arguments quite unpersuasive. I thank you for coming to dinner but in the future if we can scoop the court, we will."

Adding to Hedley's dismissive attitude toward Burger may have been the fact that each time Burger referred to the notes in his binder, he rocked back in his chair, put his foot on the dining room table, whereupon it was obvious to all of us that his fly was down.

-0-

It was a quiet Sunday morning in 1974, with the magazine safely closed and the weekly swirl of Watergate scoops and revelations over until the next week. The phone rang at home. It was a copy boy calling from the Washington bureau. He said he had stopped by to pick up some books for school, read something on the telex and that Hugh Sidey told him to call me. Nixon, the lad said, had fired Haldeman and Ehrlichman and Ron Zeigler. I thought Wow! because this was months before the group did finally resign. I immediately called the New York switchboard, asked to speak to Grunwald urgently, and was connected quickly. I explained the news I had heard. Henry said that he was stopping the presses.

I quickly reached out for Dean Fischer, our White House correspondent who was in Florida with Nixon. It was Fischer's file that had been read to Sidey. Oddly, I couldn't find Fischer. There was no one in the White House press room in Key Biscayne. How were we going to get going on the new and sensational cover story? I was close to panic, and maybe I was in the early stages of panic. What to do? Time was wasting. Grunwald was spending tens and tens of thousands of dollars to redo the magazine.

Phone rings again. It was Kim Eisler, then also a copy boy in the bureau. He wanted to read me the Fischer file. The title: "A Florida Fantasy." It was an item Fischer had sent for the Monday Washington memo, describing what Nixon needed to do to get out of the Watergate mess.

I called New York and was patched into Grunwald. I explained. Grunwald said, "Oh" and hung up. He never mentioned the incident to me.

-0-

I was in South Africa to interview Nelson Mandela as he assumed the presidency of South Africa. It was the second interview I had had with Mandela, the first coming just after he was released from jail after 23 years. Each time, it was an awe-inspiring experience. I never really understood how he absorbed the loss of most of his adult life without bitterness or any apparent desire for revenge.

The day before the swearing in, Mandela and Desmond Tutu and others appeared at a rally in a soccer stadium in Soweto. Carol and I attended and left a bit early to watch the mostly black audience leave, waving their new paper South African flags. We each bought one and stood watching with huge smiles as the happy audience came streaming past. Suddenly, a black woman ran up to me and have me a huge hug. She was smiling and weeping. Then another woman, and another. Men hugged Carol. They clearly thought we were white South Africans who supported their liberation.

Anyone who had been in the old South Africa and talked with hard men like PW Botha and his loathsome information minister Pic Botha, could not have dreamed of this outcome for South Africa. Tears ran down my own cheeks as we stood outside the soccer stadium in Soweto being hugged by the black citizens of a new country.

John Stacks

Balkan Driving Lessons

When Joelle Attinger sent me to cover Central Europe and the Balkans in 1995, I had heard stories about parties at Vienna's Café Central, bureau-financed business ventures and living large off the expense account. It was probably a mark of my inexperience that most of the money I ended up wasting as bureau chief went to vehicles—and not the luxury kind.

When I arrived in Vienna I learned that edit shared 50% of an armored Chevy Silverado pick-up truck with photo. I managed to use it for a few trips to besieged Sarajevo before Time's ace photographer Chris Morris took it into a fire-fight where a sniper round shattered the windshield's bullet-proof glass on the passenger side and shrapnel tore up the body.

The truck still ran well, though, and I used it to cover the aftermath of the war. During one nighttime reporting excursion a local driving a Yugo pulled into the blind spot created by the sniper round's starburst on the windshield and I hit him. Angry at the substantial damage to his car, he pulled a grenade and, with his finger in the pin, threatened to blow up me, my translator, and the truck. I laid 100 Deutsche Mark bills on the hood until he put the grenade away. The divine Camille Sanabria never questioned the receipt, delivered in my handwriting on notepaper: "$500 for the angry man with the grenade in Sarajevo."

Some tax-deduction-seeking bean counter in New York (Stacks? Hornik?) decided the truck should be given as a donation to the Newseum in Washington, DC, where it is on display now. (Editor's note: both gentlemen deny this libelous allegation) This turned out to be a costly mistake. I was left using rental cars for my trips to the Balkans, like the one I was driving in the middle of the night on the highway outside Belgrade when I hit a stray dog and then the guardrail. The rental company accepted $700 in cash for new panels.

As the war in Kosovo approached, I argued to the New York-based bean counters that we needed another armored car. Domestic (Stacks? Hornik?)(Editor's note: both gentlemen say it must have been someone else) said no, but International generously approved the purchase for 20,000 DM from the Jewish Community in Sarajevo of their Land Rover, which had been fitted all over with 1/4" steel plates. Driving it back from Croatia where I had purchased black market papers, I underestimated the truck's enormous weight and slammed into a stopped car in front of me. I was rear-ended by the car belonging to the head of Sarajevo's anti-terrorism squad (no idea why he was tailing me). Total damages: $1,500.

I drove the new/used armored truck to Belgrade and gave it to our stringer to drive down to Kosovo. He parked it outside the converted brothel we used as a hotel in Pristina and it was stolen the first night he was there. It was later seen in use by Serb forces.

Massimo Calabresi

A Whore with a Baby

A few months after joining *Time* (1989), I was steamed that I couldn't get some exclusive investigative pieces into the mag. One day I charged into John Stacks's office to bitch that the Monday story meetings in the NY Bureau featured some reporters carting in clippings from the previous day's NY Times as *their* hot ideas for articles. Taking a deep draw off his cigar, John explained the situation as delicately as he could. "It's long been said that *Time* with a scoop is like a hooker with a baby," he said. "It's really cute, but what the hell do you do with it?" And that, he added, is what he and Henry Muller were determined to change.

They surely did—at least for as long as they could. Case in point for me: the Scientology cover, which sailed off the newsstands and, if memory serves, broke a record for letters to the editor (over 1,100)—all of which I still have pack-ratted in boxes. The church responded with full-page ads in *USA Today* denouncing me and *Time* with a daily litany of ludicrous and vicious allegations—which that newspaper was happy to print. (I was told that these endless ads, plus a 14-page full-color Sunday insert titled "The Story *Time* Wouldn't Tell"—lifted McPaper out of the red that quarter).

A decade of litigation followed, costing Time Inc. millions. The church had declined to answer any questions pre-publication, but our legal system somehow permitted their puke-drooling lawyers to depose me for 28 days (or one day for every 260 words we'd printed). Questions ranged from my experiences as a "fetus" to when was the last time I'd seen my mother. Stacks, Steve Koepp and others were also deposed (sorry, all). Ten years later, Floyd Abrams phoned to say that the Supreme Court refused to hear the church's appeal.

"You won," said Floyd. "It's over."

"Really?" I responded. "What exactly did I win?"

"The right to be left alone," he said.

My most surreal moments were spent, not with the church's lawyers, but with their gormless private eyes—often round-the-clock, and sometimes a dozen at a time. It was my apartment building's super who had tipped me off to the gumshoes. I should have noticed myself, as I lived back then in the gritty, punkie, East Village—where middle-aged men in trench coats leaning against graffiti-crusted walls while (no kidding) reading the *Daily News* tended to stand out like sore pigs.

I popped in to see Jim Tierney, the head of security for Time4 Inc. "Ahh, so it's *you*," he said. "There are strange men standing by the elevator banks all week spying on someone, and we haven't been able to figure out who." We did a test—with me scampering across the lobby to various elevator banks. "It's you, alright," said Jim. "Every time they see you, their radar goes through the roof."

Time, Inc. brought in its own PI team—a Spy vs Spy crusade that was great fun, but often confusing—as it was hard for me to tell the good guys from the bad guys. En route one morning to Nation editor Terry Zintl's funeral, and suddenly spotting a bagel shop, I veered sharply into a parking lot—nearly causing a four-car smash-up. (Turns out my motorcade included **two** vehicles filled with the evil sherlocks, with my agents in a car behind **them**.) Through it all, I tried to keep a sense of humor—at one point roller-skating up to the car window of a startled sleuth and challenging him to a race. "Okay, let's go!" I said—and then skated up Second Avenue against the traffic, losing the tail instantly.

At times, I only *thought* I was being shadowed. Like the time an old Forbes colleague, Tom Jaffe, and his girlfriend (a former stripper) invited me to dinner. Tom's date then suggested we visit the Vault, an R-rated celeb-packed S&M club on 14th Street. We spent an hour there (only *observing*, I swear under oath)—and the next morning I shared the hilarious visuals with a Time colleague. At some point, he dropped the *Post* on my desk and flipped to Page Six. **"LIKES TO WATCH,"** screamed a headline. **"Time Magazine editors would have heartburn if they knew that one of their top scribes was at the Vault on Saturday night—and he wasn't there reporting** ... **In fact, he was with the prettiest transvestite in the club."** [I paraphrase, but I think I'm 90% correct."]

Did church PIs follow me that night, and did they plant the story?! I joyously yakked it up with colleagues, until one of them said, "Idiot. That's not you. It's *Bernstein*. The clue is 'heartburn' (the title of his ex-wife's book)." I walked down the hall, stuck my head into Carl's office, and asked if he was at the Vault on Saturday. Yes, he said very sheepishly.

I'll end with a few goose-bumpy moments—ones that I suspect couldn't happen today (but I'll forever hope they can).

It was always said that the only way to see a smile on Reg Brack's face was to hang him upside down. So I expected the worst when I was seated next to him at (what else?) an annual libel defense dinner. The company's chief bean-counter and budget-hacker turned and said, "Aren't you the guy who wrote the Scientology story?" After I confessed, Reg said," It's cost us millions, but I'm glad we published it. If we don't do those kinds of stories, who will? BTW, I was not drunk or dreaming. That really happened.

Similarly, I remember sitting in a conference room with Jason McManus, Jim Gaines, and Robin Bierstedt. We were wondering whether we should publish a hot but very controversial story I'd reported about Tyson Foods and Bill Clinton. "What are the odds of us getting sued by Tyson on this?" Jim asked Robin. "Very high," she responded," adding that under the relevant law, we'd likely lose the case. "But it's a great story," she said, "and a terrible law that ought to be changed." A long and tense moment of silence, with all eyes on Gaines. "We're running it," he announced.

Richard Behar

A Sherpa for Henry Luce

In 1962, I was the shavetail bureau chief for TLNS in San Francisco, responsible for reporting on a splendid territory that encompassed the Pacific Northwest, Alaska, and Hawaii as well as northern California. Out of the blue, I was told one day that Henry R. Luce was planning to attend the World's Fair that took place in Seattle that year, and bring a young grandson along. Marching orders were to go up there, my wife too, to show the Luce party around. I had never met Mr. Luce but of course had heard the tales of his relentless quest for information and sad stories about what became of people who worked for him but could not answer his staccato questions. With little prior warning Flo and I worked with the World's Fair staff and others to lay on elaborate plans for the visit, to begin the morning after the Luces' mid-afternoon arrival. We met their plane and, assuming the Luces would be tired after the long flight from New York, bundled them into a limo to take them to the hotel for what we had planned as a quiet dinner and early bedtime.

"What are we doing now?" Luce asked, and I explained. "No, let's go the fair now. I want to see the heart." "What heart?" I was forced to ask while mine sank. "You know," Luce said in stentorian tones. "The heart. The heart." So we diverted the limo to the fairgrounds, where I managed to arrange some of the tour (including a heart surgery exhibit)) that had been scheduled for the following morning. The next days we returned to the fair and moved briskly through it and paid the obligatory visit to the Space Needle. For variety on the final day of the visit I had chartered a large power boat for a cruise on Lake Washington and had invited 40-50 of the region's power elite, from Boeing brass to the symphony conductor, to join us for lunch aboard. Approaching the pier, Mr. Luce grew anxious. "How long do I have to stay on that thing?" he asked. So I shortened the planned time. But before disembarking Mr. Luce got wind of the fact that Boeing was building the first 707's at a waterfront plant at the other end of the lake, and suggested (demanded, more like it) that we go there and have a look. More frantic consultations, and a moment of stark terror when our yacht ran hard aground a few hundred yards offshore. But with help from a Boeing flotilla of little boats we made it into the plant and toured while our yacht was towed off into deeper water.

That night the four of us gathered for a final dinner before the Luce party's departure early the next morning. Mr. Luce, somehow relaxed and enthused by what he had seen and heard, with Flo guilelessly leading him on, was reduced to giggles and reminiscences about his teenage years. Roaring with laughter, perhaps prompted by a glass or two of wine, he demonstrated how at boarding school he would place a pat of butter on one end of a spoon, bang on the other end, and launch the butter on a brief arc to a crash landing on another table.

It was a fitting end to what had turned out to be a memorable, warm, and wonderful encounter, the only time we ever met the great man. For some reason I was not subsequently relieved of duty, and went on to many more great TLNS experiences at home and abroad.
Roger D. Stone

The Nuclear Molar

I was editing some copy in my office in Jerusalem a number of years ago when a man of about 35 walked in. He was an American and he wanted to give TIME the story of the year. That always touches off alarm bells but I tried to look interested.

He had come to Israel because he was trying to get away from THEM. "They" were after him. "They", he said in answer to my question, were the CIA. It was all a case of mistaken identity but they had grilled him night and day for weeks. Finally, they took him to a clinic and there is where they did it.

Did what? I asked,

He came close to me, opened his mouth and pointed to an upper molar.

"Do you see that molar? They implanted a miniature nuclear bomb in there."

I pushed him out of my office, told him to keep going and warned him to keep his mouth open till he got far out of town.

Lunatics are sent over to Israel by their families in America who think that the country and especially the Army will straighten them out.

-0-

I had barely recovered from the man with the nuclear molar when I received an anonymous telephone call one Friday afternoon. He had a heavy Brooklyn accent and he was whispering as though he did not want anyone else to hear.

He asked me whether I was aware that Patty Hearst was in Israel. The entire world was looking for her at the time and in fact there had been a rumor running around that she had fled with one of her kidnapers to Israel. In those days people running away thought mistakenly that Israel was a haven.

If you want to meet her, he said, be at the Alaska Cafe tomorrow night after the Sabbath and she will be there to talk to you. You can bring a camera. This will be an exclusive. He hung up before I could question him.

What do you do? You are 99% sure it is a hoax. You have two tickets to a fantastic concert. But there is that one percent chance. So you go to the Cafe and wait. At the appointed hour, you see the Newsweek correspondent coming in with a copy of Newsweek, the Times correspondent coming in with a copy of the Times, a few photographers and a wire service man sitting at different tables trying to act nonchalant and drinking enormous amounts of coffee.

Half hour after the scheduled hour each of us slinks out, not saying a word, knowing that we had been had.

-0-

And then there is the reader who gave us some comic relief. It happened during a particularly difficult period in 1977 when one of our editors, in a story on Israel injudiciously and without conscious malice, rhymed the name of Prime Minister Begin with Fagin. Fagin, being an anti-Semitic character in Dickens' novel "Oliver Twist", it resulted in a great deal of reader criticism and reader cancellation.

I was in the Jerusalem bureau at the height of this crisis when the phone rang on my desk. The caller was an Israeli resident of Tel Aviv. He said he was a faithful reader of TIME and he was angry over all the fuss that had been made over this Fagin business. Fagin, he said, was not anti-Semitic.

"I'm glad to hear that from a TIME reader," I said. "What is your name?"

"My name is Fagin."

The sequel to the story is that sometime after that I spoke to Mrs. Begin and asked her whether her husband was angry over our faux pas.

"Well," she said, "he would have preferred that you rhyme his name with Regan. It would have been more correct. His name is not pronounced 'Baygin' but 'Behgin'."

Marlin Levin

Adventures in LaLa Land

In 1978, while Education editor in New York, I was asked by Murray Gart if I'd be interested in a vacant spot in the L.A. Bureau. Soon enough, I was checking into The Chateau Marmont on Sunset Boulevard and experiencing my first taste of Hollywood: as I schlepped all my bags onto a cart and approached the front desk, Joe Cocker, the rock and roll icon, stumbled into view ahead of me.

On this lovely spring afternoon, Cocker, in baggy pajamas and reeking of gin, seemed stuck at 4 A.M. He held a half of a hundred dollar bill in each of his shaking hands. He pleaded with the clerk to fix the bill, stammered his thanks after a piece of tape did the trick and exited elevator left. The desk clerk beamed: "Well, then, now lets get you into that Bianca Jagger suite." So began what has now become my 33-year visit to California.

Memories of the office are as fleeting as a one-exit freeway hop. Bureau Chief Bill Radamaekers led a productive, easy-going crew, among them, Joe Kane, Jeff Melvoin, Mike Moritz, Jim Willwerth, and Jeanne Vallely. Before my three-year stint was up, Ben Cate would replace Bill.

As Willwerth's showbiz back up, I got to meet some interesting celebs. In the middle of that first summer, on an 85-degree day, actress Diane Cannon insisted I make a fire in her Malibu bedroom; that was after showing me her primal scream room where she led me in a moment of silent reflection. Funny, you could almost hear the screams.

When Diane Lane's taxi-driver/manager dad told me to bring a bathing suit to my interview with her for an ingénue cover we were doing, little did I know how helpful it would be. Diane was extremely awkward and shy, so after 20 minutes or so of mostly unproductive chatting, her dad cut in to tell us to go for a swim. We did, in the Chateau Marmont's little tile pool, and as I basically stood there, she darted about and dove in and out of sight like some dolphin. Marco Polo!

At one point, she dove down and came up right in front of me. "I'm sorry," she said, dripping sincerity, "I don't mean to be a difficult interview. I just don't know what the hell I am doing. "I told her, welcome to the club, and the rest of the interview was all fun and relaxed—and full of holes. Accordingly, my file was like "making chicken salad from chicken shit," as Kane used to put it, or should I say tuna salad in this case, but Diane still made the cover.

One of my Hollywood interviews came back into the news years later—with a bang. On the morning of February 4, 2003, I heard a radio news story that wasn't entirely surprising. Legendary Rock Producer Phil Spector had shot and killed a guest at his home, a woman he had met that same night at a Hollywood club.

It finally happened, I thought, along with likely many others. In 1980, when Spector was on a comeback rise, he was chosen by the Ramones to produce a new album, *End of the Century*. Time Music

Editor Jay Cocks wanted to do a piece on the album and the creative pairing, and queried L.A. to do an interview with Spector, who then lived in an old Spanish Hollywood Hills home.

I went with the late Time-Life Photographer Tony Costa and spent almost two hours covering all the points we needed for the story. In the large foyer, as Tony was packing up his gear, I turned his way for a moment and then turned back to . . . whoa! . . . I was looking down the barrel of a rather large handgun. I stood frozen as Spector told me he thought it wasn't time for us to leave yet. He walked us back into the living room, where we sat down and I took out my pad; he kept the gun cradled in his hand.

I wasn't completely surprised by Spector's behavior. Jay had already shared his reporting on the Ramones with us, which included a vignette of Spector brandishing a gun to keep a recording session going. Can't remember precisely how the situation cooled, but Time chose not to pursue any action afterword. (Since then, *Rolling Stone* reported that Spector once actually discharged a gun during a session with John Lennon. "Kill me if you want," Lennon reportedly said, "but stop messing with my ears.")

At one point in the pre-trial legal proceedings when I heard that Spector's defense was arguing that the woman had committed suicide (!) and the prosecution theory was that this was a case of misogyny run amok (!), I contacted the prosecution. The DA's office wasn't interested in my story or my assessment that this manifest case of involuntary manslaughter could be another instance of misguided LA celebrity justice in the making. Embarrassed by losing OJ and Robert Blake, the DA was looking for maximum mileage out of Spector, and the ego-deranged defense obliged by never arguing for involuntary manslaughter. Spector, 72, is now serving 19 years-to-life for second-degree murder; he will be eligible for parole in 16 years.

L.A. was a traditional jumping off point for several correspondents before me, and in 1981, my interest in partnering with a local film producer to do a sequel to a very successful movie he had just co-produced was far greater than considering Dick Duncan's suggestion for me to move on to another domestic bureau. So I took my severance and thanked Dick for the gentle push.

And thank you Time and the Time-Life News Service for the good friends and fine memories, some of the latter of which may actually still be accurate.

Robert Goldstein

The Accidental Correspondent

I am an accidental foreign correspondent in China. I happened to be in the right place (Beijing) at the right time (post-Mao China). TIME had just opened a bureau in Beijing, one of a dozen U.S. media groups to open one here after China and the US established diplomatic relations in 1979.

I was then a senior at Peking University majoring in Chinese history. In 1980, Newsweek hired me as a news assistant and stringer, doing research and reporting in my spare-time. Among my many assignments, I reported on the trial of Jiang Qing (Mao's widow) and her "Gang of Four" co-accused. It turned out to be my break-out story for Newsweek. In the spring of 1982, after I graduated from Peking University, TIME hired me.

TIME took a chance on me by bringing me on board from Newsweek. I had no Ivy League degree, no impressive resume, no job references. English was not my native language. But I was proficient in Mandarin Chinese and knew China inside out. (By then, I had lived and worked in China for eight years.) And I shared a passion for journalism and story-telling. For 18 years I reported on China for TLNS as a stringer, reporter and later as Beijing bureau chief.

China then was a remote, hardship post. Sources were scarce and scared to talk on the record. Officials were typically stiff and talked in hackneyed slogans and gobbledygook. Still, China was a nice gig. The People's Republic was a sprawling, opaque and inscrutable nation in a state of flux. Stories were hard to get but whenever we got some, they proved compelling.

Our biggest "scoop"? Our Beijing team broke the news of Jiang Qing's suicide. Reliable sources told our team that Jiang Qing had indeed committed suicide, but should we report it? Could we? Unless and until Chinese officials announced it themselves, it did not happen. Officials could dismiss it as mere "rumor". If we reported it, we could get into trouble with the officialdom. We could be accused of "spreading malicious rumors" or, worse, of "leaking state secrets".

After consultations with New York editors, we decided to "break" the news with a one paragraph item in the magazine's Grapevine section. A day after the magazine hit the newstands, journos in Beijing and New York phoned TIME to seek confirmation. They also asked Chinese officials, who declined to comment. No comment but no denial either. A week later, the official Xinhua News Agency, reported the suicide story. Of course, Xinhua made no reference to our earlier "scoop".

Over the years in the 1980s and '90s, editors kept us busy with commissioned stories. A spate of them invariably came whenever top editors visited China.

I remember when Henry Grunwald returned from his triumphant visit and exclusive interview with Deng Xiaoping, China's modern day emperor who clearly impressed our own. Henry promptly commissioned a cover story on Deng. After an exercise in "democratic centralism", he selected Deng as that year's Man of the Year.

Before we could start our reporting, however, New York had a request: could we possibly send them a list of reasons why TIME had selected Deng the MOY?

Our stories were not solely about hard politics.

One of the most inspired stories I had done for TLNS from Beijing was the one commissioned by People Magazine.

Assignment: cover the visit of Nancy Reagan's favorite hair-dresser. Based in Washington DC, the chap was invited to visit China as a sort of cultural ambassador.

My well-meaning comrade and bureau chief Richard Hornik unselfishly passed the unique assignment to me.

I followed the hairdresser in Beijing and Shanghai, visiting state-run barbershops and parlors, department stores, tea-houses and tourist spots. I watched him "exchange experiences" with his Chinese counterparts, swapping insights and skills on how best to cut and coif the people's hair. Perming hair then was uncommon in China, in part viewed as a bourgeois luxury.

For the expatriate community, Beijing was a hardship post. We spoke of "Pamper runs" to Hong Kong, the designated R and R destination. We would leave Beijing with two half-empty suitcases and, days later, return with them packed with fresh supplies of cheese, coffee beans, chocolate, wine and, yes, Pampers.

I thank TLNS for inviting me on board. It was a crazy, fun ride

Jaime (Jimi) FlorCruz

Better Than Fiction

In July, 1979, I was living in the Gran Hotel Costa Rica in downtown San Jose. That had not been my intention when I got on a flight to La Paz three weeks earlier to cover an infrequent and mostly unheeded Bolivian presidential election. There was a message waiting at my La Paz hotel from Dick Duncan telling me to call, which I did. Dick told me I was not supposed to be in Bolivia. I was supposed to be in San Jose, covering the last days of the Nicaraguan revolution from the diplomatic side. A day and a half later, after a lumpy nap in the Lima airport, I was in semi-tropical Costa Rica, which was a big improvement, except for the cold-weather clothing that was all I had with me.

The diplomatic side of revolutions, I found, can be boring. In this case, it was made doubly so by the convolutions of U.S. diplomacy. The fighting in Nicaragua between Anastasio Somoza Debayle's National Guard and the revolutionary Sandinistas was mostly a standoff. (Whatever happened there, veteran correspondent Bernie Diederich had well in hand.) Meantime, a five-member Junta of National Reconstruction, made up of businessmen, intellectuals and other civilians was holed up in a San Jose villa, holding clandestine meetings with a gaggle of Latin American diplomats. A U.S. State Department contingent, led by an Assistant Secretary of State named William Garton Bowdler, hung out elsewhere, bargaining via the mediating Latin gaggle. The idea was to make it look like the U.S. was not involved.

So Bowdler would talk to the Latins, the Latins would talk to the junta, at night the junta would get on the radio with the Sandinistas back in the jungle to pass on various aspects of the deal. Then the junta would hold a press conference and denounce the U.S. for some perfidy or other. Wash, rinse, repeat.

This all took time. It also took a while to realize that a deal was being cut to pull the plug on Somoza. None of the participants were anxious to let that fact out of the bag. Thus it was hard to find something to file for a weekly report. But this was also the first year of Time Inc's ownership of the Washington Star, and Stan Cloud was a very assiduous foreign editor. Productivity was the watchword. Sometimes, the watchword was just "Murray [Gart] wants this."

In terms of coverage, this meant a lot of time spent in the hotel lobby, where a vast amount of coffee was served, shaking down every diplomat who came through the door. It also meant a certain amount of time lurking in front of the junta's villa. The horde of visiting reporters there teamed up with each other for efficiency's sake and also to build bargaining power of their own.

My team-mate was debonair New York Timesman Warren Hoge, who was a bachelor—I was not—and determined to make a big impression on the emancipated women of Costa Rica. This meant more than my share of time for me at the junta villa, where, with Diederich's help, I met Miguel d'Escoto Brockmann, the group's foreign affairs spokesman, and later Foreign Minister. D'Escoto was a charming, vitriolically anti-American Maryknoll priest, who proved to be a great source. He promised me quietly that if he ever flew into Nicaragua at the finish, I would be on the plane with him.

I shouldn't have been surprised when d'Escoto double-crossed me, but there was Stan Cloud to consider, which made me nervous. D'Escoto slipped into Nicaragua in a tiny airplane by himself, to seal the final bits of the deal. He had the decency to call me after he landed and gave an exclusive first-person account of his arrival back on native soil. The next day the President of Mexico, Jose Lopez Portillo, sent his official plane down with an entourage to take the junta, the members' families, the Latin diplomats and Bowdler's State Department crew into Nicaragua as soon as Somoza and his henchmen left, in order to recognize the revolutionary government.

There were not going to be many journalists on that plane. Hoge and I made it damned clear that we were going to be the only U.S. representatives among them. Once again, I thought we had a deal.

Then, as we waited at the San Jose international airport for something to happen, another single-engine plane took off. The buzz went around that it was a junta representative, that the arrangement for Somoza's departure had fallen through. Double-crossed again!

Hoge and I looked at each other. Then we jumped into a red pickup truck with the local AP stringer and roared off toward a nearby commercial airstrip where we could rent a charter plane. If the junta could go in, we were going in.

Except it was a false alarm. We found that out by way of a short-wave radio call about the time we got to the other airport, 10 kilometers away. The call said the Mexican President's plane was leaving in five minutes.

I did not want to have to explain to Dick Duncan, or Stan Cloud, or Murray Gart how I failed to get the only scoop I had expressly been sent to get. Hoge and I pleaded with the AP stringer, the only one of us who spoke passable Spanish, to get on the radio with the international airport tower, and patch us through to the President's plane. We told Lopez Portillo's top aide, an American-educated whiz kid named Andres Rosental, that it was impossible to leave without the two most important journalists in the country on board. We probably wailed a bit.

For some reason, Rosental bought it. They held the plane for ten additional minutes while we roared onto the tarmac and raced up the plane stairway, sweating profusely, with suitcases in hand. Rosental was at the top of the ramp, muttering, "You guys are fucking lucky. So fucking lucky."

Hoge was ahead of me. He pelted up the stairway so quickly that his well-worn blue jeans split all the way down the backside.

And thus I came to know—as did the revolutionary government of Nicaragua, the U.S. State Department envoy, the special representative of the President of Mexico, the assembled Latin American diplomatic corps, and several extended Nicaraguan familes—that when in the field, the South American bureau chief of the New York Times did not believe in wearing underwear.

Hoge changed pants in the President's lavatory. The plane landed in Managua, the only flight incoming that day. Somoza was gone. The tarmac was littered with spent cartridge cases. Heavily armed campesinos were everywhere. Occasionally one of the exultant Sandinistas on the airport rooftop would fire an exuberant clip into the humid air; a few people would reflexively throw themselves onto the ground, but the war was over. The junta headed to a nearby airport hotel owned by one of their number, Alfonso Robelo, and began to greet *comandantes* in Castro-style fatigues who were filtering out of the bush.

Hoge had recovered his aplomb. He scavenged in the looted airport bar until he found a couple of beers, then showed me how to turn an ammo box into an instant cooler. We wandered back onto the center-line of the airport landing strip, kicked aside some cartridge cases, and sat down.

Huge purple lightning sheets flared across the darkening horizon, as a storm began to move in from the coast. We listened to the pop-pop-pop of small arms fire, and the occasional scream of victory, and watched floppy-hatted revolutionaries dance on the roof with their machine guns.

Graham Greene, we decided was not a novelist. He was a journalist who hit Central America on the right day.

George Russell

-0-

More Fun Than A Vacation

In the first five years I worked at Time, I don't remember ever taking a vacation. I could not think of anything that would be more fun than working for the magazine. In those years (1978 to 1983) in the San Francisco bureau, I reported on George Lucas and the special effects of the Star Wars movies; on Steve Jobs at Apple; on Edward Teller and his Star Wars missile shield; and on Bill Shuler who built nuclear bombs (including the smallest nuke ever detonated) at Livermore Labs.

I covered the emergence of the mysterious Gay Related Immune Deficiency, GRID, later renamed AIDS. I also covered the assassination of San Francisco Supervisor Harvey Milk and Mayor George Moscone; and the "White night riot" that followed the slap-on-the-wrist verdict given to killer Dan White. I reported on Jerry Brown in his first incarnation as California's governor. I spent one Thanksgiving inside Jim Jones's People's Temple, talking to the family members of people who had committed suicide by drinking poisoned Kool-Aid in Guyana.

There were brief assignments with the Black Panthers and Huey Newton, and I lost my professional cool in the press box when Dwight Clark made "The Catch" and locked up the NFC title for Joe Montana and the 49ers with 51 seconds left. I flew in the front seat of a biplane piloted by a 17-year-old kid who took me through the stunts he taught commercial pilots, I was pushed off a Coast Guard cutter into the Pacific to test an experimental survival suit, and I was sent to Grenada following the US invasion and had a mind-bending time with Hunter S. Thompson.

And our little outpost on the Left Coast was filled with some of the nicest people on the planet including Olivia Stewart, Long X. Long, Joe Boyce, John Austin, Gavin Scott, Mike Moritz, Bill Doerner, Eileen Shields and Paul Witteman. It was great.

Then I took an academic year at MIT for science journalists, and where I developed an interest in global environmental issues and molecular biology. After MIT, I was transferred to the DC bureau and organized a meeting (in Boulder, Colorado) to explore global environmental threats including ozone depletion, the burning of the Amazon and global warming. Al Gore gave a new talk about climate change. It was a powerful experience for some, and the issues became important for many of us in the science section.

DC was another wonderful bureau. It too was filled with lots of nice people (Hugh Sidey and Strobe and Lissa, Neang and many, many more)and quirky people (The Ranger was part of a small pack). I was lucky enough to find a good friend in Murray Gart who, I'm told, had mellowed in those years.

In 1993 I was assigned to take the lead reporting on Hillary Clinton's health reform effort. With the promise that nothing would appear inthe magazine until the plan was released, I reported from inside the Old Executive Office Building for months. But the plan was leaked one Wednesday afternoon, three days before my wedding. A decision was made to make it a cover and I worked through each of the following nights with Mike Duffy. On Saturday, I continued reporting the story at my wedding (at Chris Ogden's Georgetown home), closed the story from our DC hotel suite over Champagne and chocolate cake, but we had to cancel our Tuscany bicycling honeymoon to work on the following week's story.

The story of the wedding and the missed honeymoon were in the Pub Letter Ogden wrote, and one irate reader castigated Time for making people work like that, proclaiming that my marriage was doomed at the start. He wasn't quite right—from that day to this I've known that being married to Kristin makes me the luckiest dog on the planet.

My time in the DC Bureau was filled with adventures that rivaled the fun I had in San Francisco. I flew a small plane over the Amazon. I interviewed a cosmonaut from the USSR closed site at Star City as he passed overhead in his spacecraft. I reported on AIDS again and again.

I interviewed John Glenn as he prepared for his return to space, and was at Cape Canaveral (surprised to find tears in my eyes) when his shuttle lifted off. I reported from Kabul when it was under the siege of the Taliban in the mid-1990s, saw hospital rooms slick with the blood of children, and met heroes who were trying to save them from the mine field that Kabul was in those days.

I didn't do any of these things alone. I worked with amazing teams. Time's science section was a powerhouse of gifted writers, dogged researchers and bright editors who were all wonderful people. To be part of that team for many years was one of the most enriching experiences of my life.

I left Time in 2001, at the beginning of what turned out to be the great journalism diaspora, and I took with me the values that guided me through all those years. I found myself in a new environment, at the World Health Organization (WHO), and then running WHO's communication during SARS. I wanted WHO to be a good source, the kind of source I respected as a Time reporter. So I made sure WHO experts and I were available at all hours and always told the truth (even when the truth was "I don't know"). I went on to develop the global standard of "Outbreak Communication" which simply boiled down to: Tell the truth fast (or, to me, be a good source), and then I trained officials from 120 countries to be good sources.

So I ask you, who would want to miss one day of that?
Dick Thompson

Remembering Gaddafi

When Muammar Gaddafi went to his just reward in October, I found myself recalling the interviews I conducted with him for TIME. For the supremo of his country (even though the only title he used was "Colonel"), he was mighty elusive. On that occasion, in 1977 or 1978, I was supposed to see him in Tripoli. When I landed at the airport there, I was met by a foreign ministry handler who said the venue had been changed to Benghazi. When we got there, we were told that Gaddafi was now in Tabruk, near the Libyan-Egyptian border. Off we went, across the desert, and I was ushered into a 5-star tent. He'd summoned me there so that I could watch him watching Anwar Sadat's historic visit to Jerusalem for the signing of the Camp David Accords on Egyptian television. He put on quite a show, fulminating at what was happening on the screen. On another occasion, in 1986, once again I was supposed to see him in Tripoli and ended up being packed off into the Sahara, this time southward, to Sebha, where Gaddafi was overseeing Libya's intercession in the civil war in Chad. This time he was eerily relaxed, almost spaced out. He sipped orange soda while rambling about the inevitable disappearance of the Zionist entity and the triumph of Libya as a model for governance in the Arab world. Sic transit.

Strobe Talbott

Brooke Shields, Imelda Marcos and OJ

The most challenging, and yet least significant, cover I reported for Time was that on actress Brooke Shields when she attended the first—and last—Manila Film Festival. It was the brain-child of the one and only Imelda Marcos, before multiple-shoe fame. The last-minute post-haste cover assignment came from a Ray Cave-Martha Duffy decision to beat Newsweek, which meant Newsweek was already onboard the jet with Brooke heading to Manila.

Playing 30 minute catch-up, I boarded their jet at the LA Airport armed with only my passport and credit card. The celeb entourage consisted of Brooke, her alcoholic mother Teri Shields (the tyrant enforcer), relatives, Warren Cowen and his pr contingent, and Newsweek's photographer.

From the get-go, it was disaster. Unbeknownst to me, Time magazine had thrice rejected Teri Shields request for coverage of her daughter. There was nothing like a scorned alcoholic mother to make my task hell. Second hurdle was Imelda Marcos, every bit the uneducated back-alley beauty turned empress who was puffed up on her "Divine Right of Kings." Taking me under her wing, because I worked for Time magazine, she, again and again, explained her need to wear 4 carat diamond-studded butterfly sleeves to keep the poverty-stricken masses at the clinics we visited on their knees, singing her praises.

While Imeda, and Ferdinand Marcos (light-years brighter than Imelda and of Chinese descent) filled my ears with their domineering political power plays, the loopy and vindictive Teri Shields refused access to her precious daughter, miraculously studying for her college exams on the insane trip. "Blue Lagoon" by the way, was still the most popular film in the Philippines even though it had been out for years. If Teri Shields wasn't headache enough, a Palace Coup added to the ongoing drama. While following Ferdinand's black stretch limo in a motorcade, suddenly we all stopped. From nowhere came a phalanx of men, opening limo and SUV trunks, pulling out bazookas (looked like anyway). With guards atop the cars, we were rushed in the Palace Gates and ordered to stay in a lock-down.

The Palace Coup was all over the news of course, along with a photo of yours truly yakking at that night's banquet with Ferdinand. Apparently, that prompted our intrepid News Service honchos, unable to get a reporter or stringer into the Palace, with the exclamation "What is Martha Smilgis doing there?!?" Believe me, Martha Smilgis was counting the number of grapes Brooke was eating for dinner because Brooke next had to go on to Rome for a Valentino fashion show and was concerned about her weight. Fortunately, late into the night, Teri had caved and was a non-stop vendor of info about how she made her daughter's career.

The Palace Coup fizzled and after the one-movie Film Festival I continued on to Rome with the entourage. Unfortunately, I had to type (this was 1980 pre computer) and file in the middle of the night one weekend from an ancient building that housed archaic western union services, truly pre-Morse code. By the way, one week later, I finally bought another outfit in Rome.

-0-

The second most memorable Time assignment in the LA Bureau happened simply, at first.

Listening to the radio, early, on the morning of June 13, 1994 while getting ready for work, I heard a news report that OJ Simpson's ex-wife had been stabbed in Brentwood. The radio report went on to say OJ was in Chicago. I didn't think too much about it except OJ was "the juice", did car commercials and was a former USC star.

Following my usual routine, I drove to the bureau, then located on Barrington and Wilshire, arriving just in time for our scheduled story conference. Jeff Ressner came into the half-filled room complaining there had been a stabbing on Bundy around the corner from the house he had just bought on Dorothy. He was concerned about crime in the neighborhood bringing down property values. Turning the corner, he said he saw a covered body being wheeled out.

At that moment, the bureau's co-ordinator, Corliss Duncan came in listening to her radio, and informed us that Bundy was the location of the murder victim, OJ's ex wife. Our intrepid Bureau Chief Jordan Bonfonte, wearing one of his impeccable Saville Row suits, looked up from his assignment sheet, thought a moment, and said "Martha, you go over and find out what is going on." Then, he looked at Pat Cole who was working on a music story for back-of-the-book, paused, and said "Pat, you go." Eager to get away from our desks, we two took off, deciding to walk since the murder scene was just about three blocks from the bureau. I picked up a coffee on the way.

Pat figured we were assigned because OJ was show biz now with his commercials, which meant my beat, and I figured Pat was chosen because he was the handsomest guy in the bureau, and OJ was handsome. We didn't expect this would be a big story, but became very curious as we approached the yellow police tape. We could see, even step in, the drying blood on the sidewalk. We couldn't go up the condo's walkway, but on the sidewalk all along in front there were bloody paw prints going back and forth.

It was quiet, and fairly empy. No reporters, except an unidentified satellite truck pulling up. Police and plain clothes detectives milled about inside the tape, near the entry to the condo complex. The amount of blood, was overwhelming, it was a complete saturation of the walkway.

We just stood there staring at the scene. The cops weren't about to talk to us, and no one else was there. A neighbor did walk up and Pat went over to talk to him. To my right, coming down Bundy at a fast clip was a young guy, buff, about 25, in shorts, flip flops—very upset. He came right up to the tape, jumped at it, shook his head, jumped back. Of course, we cornered him and he muttered something . . . "it was Ron, OJ damn it.'" We extracted enough info to find out he was Ron's roommate, and he worked at Messaluna with Ron.

Even though we didn't get who Ron was, we made a bee line for Mesaluna restaurant a few blocks up Bundy. We were the first to talk to the manager who told us, off the record, the other victim was Ron, gave us his full name and then muttered—"everyone knew Nicole. I told Ron not to mess with her, but he didn't listen." I remember saying to him "but she was OJ's EX-WIFE," and I remember he just shrugged like that didn't matter.

Pat and I passed the murder scene again on the way back to the office. By then, Bundy was clogged with TV trucks, cars, reporters, photographers. Right then, we knew it was going to be a huge story. And I remember thinking, the power of football, then, if OJ is in Chicago, maybe he hired some one to kill her—and this Ron, but then why, if she was his EX.

Of course, the sensational story didn't stop for me with this introduction. I later became the best girlfriend of Faye Resnick and learned all about Nicole, Faye, their fast friends and the infamous "Brentwood Hello.' In yet another peculiar twist, days later, when I was driving down Sunset I heard on KNX radio that the white Ford Bronco chase was getting off the freeway right behind me. I remember pulling into a station, to call Jordan and ask him, on a pay phone, if I should cover it. He said yes, and I was sandwiched in the awful crush of TV trucks and police descending on Rockingham. OJ and AC Cowlings were taken into custody. What a nightmare, I climbed over a neighbor's fence to get away from the mob. I could see nothing, and was stuck in traffic for 6 hours trying to get out of the police zone. Rappers and gangsters from East LA had joined the fracas.

Two years later, during the civil trial in Santa Monica, I actually interviewed OJ when he was back home at Rockingham. He was polite, trying hard to make a good impression on me—on Time magazine. We were sitting at his bar, looking out at the pool, and on the bar was a big glass fishbowl filled with matchbooks from restaurants around town. What was so significant about that bowl was that Faye Resnick, early on, told me OJ had a big fishbowl on the bar of the house filled with uppers, downers, every drug you could imagine. Faye was a hottie, a one-time addict, and knew OJ well. But, to her credit, she told the truth.

F. Lee Bailey came sauntering in during the interview, and OJ became angry, visibly angry, when my attention was momentarily diverted. (Time correspondent Elaine Lafferty had been dining with Bailey often, she had become Bailey "best buddy", and I sent her greetings.) OJ's trigger-anger over such a minor incident stunned me. OJ hadn't said anything significant, just his usual self-puffery. Knowing all that I knew by then, two years after Nicole and Ron

Goldman's murder, it was a travesty of justice that he was a free man.

Martha Smilgis

Tales of Africa

Kikwit. The biggest story in the world to ourselves. Major outbreak of Ebola fever in central Congo, then Zaire. It was 1995, just after the release of the Dustin Hoffman film "Outbreak" and Richard Preston's "The Hot Zone", in which he described internal organs liquefying. A lot of fear in the air. The outbreak was in a remote part of central Zaire, a few hours flight over the rainforest from the capital Kinshasa. Journalists were flying into the capital from all over the world. But it was hard to travel. The army had cordoned off Kikwit, closing roads and the airstrip. But a group (about 30) of us managed to scrounge a plane anyway, a 'Casablanca'-era DC—3. We took off in high spirits. But as we approached Kikwit, and some journalists (inexplicably) donned surgical masks and rubber gloves, the pilots got spooked and told us plans had changed and they would only stay on the ground 3 hours. General panic . . . a group of photographers rushed into town to the main hospital and straight on into the isolation ward snapping away. Two hours later they were gone. Myself and one other reporter decided to stay behind. When we turned on a shortwave that night we learned that the whole crew—ALL the press corps—had been detained upon returning to Kinshasa airport by the military . . . not allowed to leave . . . most of them couldn't file . . . we (myself and an NPR reporter) had one of the biggest stories in the world to ourselves for six days . . . we relied on one satellite phone, run by the local mission, shared with the handful of doctors from WHO and CDC flown in to control the epidemic.

A moment when being a weekly worked in our favor. I stayed because we needed more than spot news; I wanted to have a closer look at what was behind the outbreak, specifically how it started and what was being done to trace its origins. I spent the week on a variety of stories, talking to nuns whose members came down with some of the first cases, walking hut to hut to find the first cases.

Mogadishu. $35,000 in cash. For the coverage of the US operation in Somalia, Operation Restore Hope, December 1992, we needed cash badly. I was in Mogadishu and spending $300 USD/day per person, most of it for 'security', (three khat-chewing gunmen). Our bureau arranged to fly in $35,000 USD from Nairobi in 100s. Clive Mutiso landed one morning in a small hired plane. The plane was immediately surrounded by gunmen from the clan that controlled the airport. I climbed aboard and peered out at these men as Clive discretely pushed towards me a small nylon gym bag stuffed with cash. I got off the plane and a young gunman immediately demanded the bag. He insisted. I handed it over. He carried it to my truck, with me following closely behind, and threw it in the back, none the wiser for its contents. At the time, a clan controlling the airport demanded 100 USD for access to the strip and as part of the service provided mandatory 'baggage handling'. Later: I had to leave the cash stuffed in the back of my sock drawer. There was no safe or anything like it where we were staying, an abandoned hotel that a bunch of journalists had arranged to re-open. One day, I came back from a long day reporting and the door was kicked in. It was a very long walk to the drawer with the cash in it. but it was still there. My roommate James

Wilde had kicked down the door, not wanting to go down and pick up the key from the front desk.)

In the end, despite carrying so much cash around, I had very little stolen. Mogadishu was completely lawless but thanks to a private army, my material goods were safe. Equally, having that 'security' force of three armed men at all times was not completely reassuring. My vehicle was more than once ambushed by men trying to steal the car, 'my' gunmen opened fire on the attackers with all their fire power but with little thought for the safety of their passengers in the front seat. Their job was to save the truck.

South Sudan. How we got stuck in the sand with rebels approaching. There was a big famine in S. Sudan, 1995, I believe. We flew in via World Food Programme Hercules and camped out for a few days. It was very isolated, just a few huts and a feeding center. This was near the place where South African photographer Kevin Carter shot the famous picture of a vulture stalking a baby. We finished reporting in three days and arranged, with a Reuters B/C, to have a plane fly in from northern Kenya to pick us up. There was not much time, as a rebel group was headed in our direction. The pilot was not experienced. He hit a sand pit while taxiing and got stuck. We got out and dug out the wheels. Started again. Hit another sand pit. Dug out again. This time, I watched propeller hit the sand and come up with its blades bent at right angles. The Dinka were laughing uproariously. Our pilot seemed to be worried that the service he was providing was not up to snuff. Meanwhile, radio reports of Nuer militiamen heading our way. We abandoned the plane and managed to catch a UN food flight. The village was overrun the next day and the plane stripped. It's probably still there.

Luckily, because of this detour, we ended up getting a strong interview with the rebel commander Riek Machar, who happened ot be in the town where the WFP flight landed on the way out of Sudan.

Rwanda Helmet. I had to scramble from an interview with Rwanda rebel leader Paul Kagame to a UN C-130 transport plane flying out of Kigali during the genocide in 1994. I strapped in next to a senior Canadian peacekeeper. I had scarfed down some peanut butter before getting on the plane and as we flew low over the mountains to avoid fire, the lunch returned. The general handed me his helmet, which I used as a sick bag, and handed it back to him as we landed in Nairobi.

Goma, Zaire. I remember staying up most of the night (Saturday, domestic cover) for CACs and running out of water. There was a cholera epidemic raging, and all water was contaminated. 50,000 people died. And we had run out of Fanta and everything else non-alcoholic to drink. All that was left was half liter bottles of warm Primus beer.

- Friday nights under African skies looking up at satellites waiting for playbacks. (via satellite telex, the beautiful little communications dishes of the day.)

- Crossing the 'green line' in Mogadishu, one gunman, about 16, high on qat, held a gun to my head but my security held his gun to this boy's head.

James stories! I think he left you with some of those? Vanishing for 2 weeks in Southern Kenya /Tanzania with Massai drinking blood. Congo. I miss him.

Andrew Purvis

Lessons Learned

The military always generates scouting reports so raw recruits rushed to the front lines will at least have some idea what's going on when they arrive. It was the same thing when I came to TIME.

Ace correspondent Bruce van Voorst: "After New York ignores one of your story sugs three times, forget about it," he confided. "It's D-E-A-D." Editing, another new colleague noted, could be rigorous for someone used to the rush of newspapers. "Never read your story," he advised, "in the magazine." Elaine Shannon, our longtime Justice and FBI correspondent, also offered sage advice my first week in the magazine's Washington bureau: "Our job—covering the military and law enforcement—is very simple. We're playing defense—like a hockey goalie. We're trying to keep stuff out of the magazine"—zany offerings by colleagues and freelancers with over-active imaginations—"not get it in."

How right she was. We fought valiantly together over the years, and sidelined lots of boneheaded reporting. But some stories, alas, seemed to have a tailwind of their own that pushed them onto TIME's pages. Yet our record of hits, misses and errors stands as a good one. Most weeks, working for the news service was akin, I imagine, to being a piston in a roaring, redlining V-8. And the ever-intrepid news desk was our own STP, the racer's edge.

Mark Thompson

Little Gifts

It was July, 1978 and my first day working for the TLNS. As I sat at my desk trying to get acclimated, I noticed several very distinguished men walking by the opening of our offices. Finally one brave soul walked in and asked for Katie McNevin. When I replied that she was on vacation, he looked a bit crestfallen—like someone who had come a long way and was very disappointed in the outcome. Knowing firsthand how special Katie could make people feel, I understood his disappointment. Composing himself quickly he stood and introduced himself. "I'm Marsh Clark from Johannesburg" he said. "Here for the Bureau Chief's meeting, and you are"? For a moment, all I could think was—Johannesburg, South Africa? Wow! Then, composing myself just as quickly, I extended my hand, and clumsily stated my name as he sat down in the ever-present visitor's chair aside everyone's desk. As we continued to make small talk about his life in Jo'burg, he put his hand inside his jacket pocket, produced a gift from South Africa and handed it to me. Instinctively, I knew it was meant for Katie, but I couldn't resist either his charm or generosity of spirit. That scene was repeated several times that day as each colorful correspondent Wilton Wynn (Rome), John Dunn (Melbourne), Gavin Scott (Rio) presented a small gift to me meant for Katie (sorry Katie) to me. It has been more than 30 years and I no longer remember what each token gift was, but the memory of that day as well as the magic of the TLNS remains as vivid as if it all happened yesterday.

Camille Cassata Sanabria

Jonas Savimbi: No George Washington

In the early 1980's shortly after the Reagan administration came to power in Washington, Jonas Savimbi (resplendent with a heavy beard, wearing combat fatigues and black beret) who was the leader of the western armed faction in Angola (UNITA) came to Washington to lobby the new administration for more aide mostly in the form of money and arms to keep fighting the Soviet backed faction (MPLF) which had taken over when the Portuguese government had ceded to the Angolans the former colony. I cannot fully remember but I believe David Aikman through a source helped arrange an off the record luncheon at the suite that TIME had at the Hay-Adams Hotel. The luncheon was on a Saturday and I had asked to go as I had an interest in what was happening in Angola especially with the involvement of the Cubans who had sent troops to support the MPLF in their fight against UNITA. The gathering included a good number of editors from New York along with the a number of correspondents from the D.C. Bureau. Also invited was Murray Gart, our former boss, who by that time, had left TIME and was over at the Johns Hopkins Foreign Service School. The nearly three hour lunch ended with Savimbi extolling everyone with his plans to not be involved in any future political activities once Angola was free of the Soviet backed MPLA. His only purpose, he said, was to free his country for democracy" everyone went their way. I then offered Murray a ride home. On the way I asked Murray, "so what did you think of the guy?" Murray replied calmly, "well I don't think we were looking at George Washington."

-0-

On numerous occasions I have had what I call "Adventures in Visa Land," and dealing with the old Soviet consulate here in Washington was always a true adventure. There was one instance when I attempted to get a visa for Henry Grunwald to visit Russia and interview the

Soviet Premier (I cannot recall who was in power then). The Soviet consulate at that time was way the heck up 16th street from the TIME bureau at 16th and I streets. So I call the consulate and they tell me amazingly that the visa is "ready." This was an unusual occurrence as the Soviets usually made you sweat to the very last second. I told Emily Friedrich that amazingly they had the visa ready and I went to Joan Connelly to get cab fare to ride up to the consulate to get the visa. When I arrived, a very short and stocky Soviet apparatchik by the name of Victor Volkov (I can't believe I still remember his name) comes out to meet me and tells me that he "cannot" authorize the visa. When I inquired why he told me that Grunwald's assistant had sent his old passport number and it could not be used. At this point I asked Volkov if I could use his phone and call New York to see if somehow we could straighten this out. He initially said no as there could be no long distance charges to his phone. I finally convinced him that there would be no charges and if so TIME magazine would certainly pay for any costs. By this point it was around three-thirty in the afternoon and Grunwalds' flight was leaving JFK that evening. So I called the Bureau and had Millie Mackey patch me through to Grunwald's office but no one answered (there was no voicemail at that point). I finally after many tries (it seemed interminable at the time) with Volkov looking over my shoulder reached Grunwald's assistant who the gave me the proper number. Again, it took a considerable bit of persuasion on my part including throwing in free magazines to Volkov when the interview with the Premier appeared in the magazine to get him to stamp and authorize the visa. We parted with a smiling handshake. The problem then was the cab which took me up to the consulate had long disappeared and did not wait for me. I had very little money on my person. So I walked to 16th street (the consulate was on a side street off of 16th) and tried vainly to find a cab. After waiting a good half hour and no cab in sight I hopped on a Metro bus and for a quarter (shows you how long ago this was) I rode the bus straight down 16th street to the bureau where I then put the visa in the capable hands of Waits L. May who was waiting in the lobby to go to National Airport to fly the Eastern Airlines Shuttle to NYC to rush to the building to give Grunwald the visa. Suffice to say it was a close call but Henry made his flight with the visa.

In another instance of dealing with the Soviets and visas, there was the time that Michael Kramer was going to Russia to cover (if my memory serves me) the first fledgling democratic presidential election. The problem was because Kramer was in NYC the visa had to be processed via the consulate in New York and he was leaving the next day. So Rick Hornik called me and said to get the visa. I called the Russian consulate in NYC and had a discussion with Mr. Ivanov who said to me, "are you prepared to pay $400 dollars in cash for special processing of the visa?" I said," yes of course" and told Mr. Ivanov I would have Michael Kramer's young assistant (he would be the one to go and take Kramer's passport to be stamped and to pick up the visa) to ask specifically for Ivanov at the appointed hour which we jointly agreed would be eleven o'clock the following morning. I then called Kamer's assistant give him Ivanov's name and what time he was to go over etc. At that point, having dealt with the Russian Consulate in Washington I had a bit of knowledge as to how their consulate folks worked and I knew there could not be much difference in how the NYC consulate worked. I told Kramer's assistant to not take $400 dollars in cash with him but $500 dollars in cash. My instincts were right because as soon as the young fellow went over and met Mr. Ivanov he said he was "mistaken" and that it would be $500 dollars cash. We got the visa and the rest was history.

It also paid off to develop a relationship with the Soviet consulate's personnel despite their obnoxious style in jerking you around as to when authorization of visas occurred. Once I had to get another Russian visa for Strobe Talbott to go to Russia to report a story for the Special Russian edition we did in the early 1980's. Of course, they were once again jerking us around (plus they still did not like Strobe for translating Khrushchev's memoirs). I had gotten to know one of the consulate's people (All I can remember is his name was Ivan) through the course of my dealing with him. I did learn that he had two children.

Apollo-Soyuz was the first joint space venture between the two super powers. As with previous American space missions a special patch was created for this historic flight. I had asked Jerry Hannifin who covered the space program for TIME to buy in the museum shop at Cape Kennedy a couple of those patches and to send them up to me. I smartly took two of them with me that day when Ivan—being the dutiful apparatchik he was—told me, "No the approval cable had not arrived for Mr. Strobty (it was the way he pronounced Strobe's name)Talbott" I started to walk away. I then remembered he had two sons and pulled the two patches I had on me and said, "Ivan, this is a little something for your boys." I started to leave and Ivan shouted from behind his little glass window, "Stop. Let me check once more to see if by chance the cable had arrived." Well, lo and behold it was there—as it had been all along. I thought the patches were a worthwhile investment.

In many ways getting visa from the Arab states was at times as difficult as getting visa from the Soviets. In this instance Murray Gart needed six visas, all from Arab states (Saudi Arabia, Syria, Qatar, United Arab Emirates, Bahrain and Kuwait), and he was leaving in five days which meant I had to have all the visas by Friday so he could leave on Saturday. I got this little assignment on Monday morning and astonishingly, as the week moved on I had been able to get all the visas except the Kuwaiti visa by Thursday. I did have to endure the verbal dressing down by the Syrian consulate official for not going to him directly as Murray had instructed me to contact the Ambassador's office directly due to the fact they were personal friends. After listening to this guy berate me for about five minutes I informed him that I surely will next time Mr. Gart spoke with the Ambassador I would have him tell the Ambassador just that. That shut him up in short order. As it was, things were going way too smoothly. But, I had been assured by the Kuwaiti Embassy visa office that the visa for Murray would be ready Friday at 2:00PM. I called at one thirty Friday to make sure everything was on track and there was no answer. In fact, the consular visa office had left for the day. In a panic, I started to dial random numbers using the prefix of the embassy's main phone number. Amazingly, the Ambassador himself picked up one of my blind dialings into the embassy. I explained the situation to him and he said to me, "can you come over to the embassy?" I told him I could be there in 15 minutes and he informed me that he would have someone meet me at the front door of the embassy. This was the last week of July and the temperature in D.C. was in the 90's and the humidity was off the charts. So I get lucky and end up in the only taxi with a non working air conditioner and we hit every red light possible on the way over. I arrive looking like a wet dog and at the front door of the Kuwaiti Embassy is one of the largest and blackest men I have ever seen. In a very Barry White basso profundo voice he says to me, "follow me." We enter the embassy and walk over beautiful white marble floors covered by gorgeous Arabian rugs which God only knows cost how much. We then proceeded down two flights of stairs where three very tiny (we all were in relation to the big guy) fellows were attempting to unscrew this beautiful Teak desk (again, only God knows how much it cost) with the Ambassador himself watching them attempt to open the desk and get Murray's passport. After a few minutes of the failure of these three fellows to open the desk, the Ambassador turned to the large black man and said, "open it." He proceeded to step forward and put his hand on his the desk and his other hand on the drawer the three fellows were attempting to open and ripped the drawer out of the desk shredding the teak wood everywhere. The Ambassador turned to one of the three gentlemen and said, "fix it." The Ambassador then turned to me and asked me to personally apologize to Murray for the inconvenience of all of this and I assured him there was no need of an apology as Mr. Gart would fully understand. While we were talking the sound of a visa being pounded with an official stamp in Murray's passport was resounding in the background. The Ambassador then offered to see me out and I told him there was no bother of that as his man (Giant) could show me the way. So once I get out of the embassy—the cab as in the other situation with the Russian visa—had disappeared even though I asked him to wait. The Kuwaiti Embassy is located way down towards Rock Creek Park off of Connecticut Avenue. So I started to walk up towards Connecticut in the hope that somehow a taxi might be coming up or down the road and I could hail it. No such luck, of course. I reached Connecticut Avenue in roughly five minutes (all uphill I might add) and hailed a cab. I returned to the Bureau and went in looking worse than a wet dog and asked where Murray was and was told by Millie Mackey that he was next door at the Hay-Adams having a drink and that I should go there to give him the last visa. I found them in the bar and he said to me to sit down and have a drink. I handed him the passport with all six of the visas and he said to me, "I hope it wasn't too much trouble getting them." That's our Murray.

Lastly there was the time Mark Thompson was scheduled to go on a trip with the Secretary of Defense to Russia and many of the "Stan" countries (Turkmenistan, Pakistan, Kirghizstan, Kazakhstan, and Russia for meetings with their various defense ministers. I was asked by Mark if I could get those visas because for some reason or another the DOD was not handling them for this trip. I was able to get them fairly easily including the Kirghizstan visa. As it turned out, the trip to that country was cancelled at the last minute just before Mark and the Secretary and other DOD reporters left on the trip. During the flight from Pakistan to Kazakhstan the Secretary's plane had to make an emergency landing in Kirghizstan because of bad weather ahead. And, because Mark was the ONLY DOD reporter to have a visa for that country he was the only one allowed off the plane with the Secretary. All the other reporters had to stay on the plane overnight and they were all pissed.

Brian Doyle

TIME in China

The sources were good and the news was historic but there was always the tingling doubt that something could go wrong. It was the feeling Jimi FlorCruz and I had when we broke the story of Jiang Qing's suicide in May 1991.

Mao Zedong's widow was convicted of the horrors of the Cultural Revolution in 1981 after a high-profile trial that marked the end of the Mao era. At the end of the trial, Jiang was dragged from the courtroom screaming and shouting revolutionary slogans. She was never seen again in public. Tagged as a ring leader of the Gang of Four, a group of left-leaning politicians and ideologues, China's former First Lady was given a suspended death sentence later commuted to life imprisonment.

"I was Chairman Mao's dog. Whomever he told me to bite, I bit," she said in her own defense at her trial. That's all we knew of her later life. Not surprising in a country that prides itself for the secrecy that surrounds all its leaders, past and present.

Ten years later the news of her death arrived in my small kitchen in Beijing while I was cooking for a dinner party. The kitchen was hot, the food almost cooked when the news was told. It came out casually at first—almost like chitchat—but with an intent to convey a strong message.

I was wrapped up in being a cook but the news turned me very quickly back into a journalist.

Jimi's long experience in China was put to work to gauge the reliability of the sources and the information. While it was a surprise for us to hear anything about her, it was more of a surprise to hear she had committed suicide. Her strength of character clearly did not hold up to the bitter end. That is, if the story was true. But was it?

We rummaged around to recall the last news of her. Rumor had it that she was under house arrest on the outskirts of Beijing. Others said she suffered from throat cancer.

Our sources said she tried to commit suicide in the past and so the walls of her rooms were covered with thick rubber to prevent her from smashing herself against them. But despite the protection, she managed to hang herself on May 14, 1991.

She was a sensitive point for the Chinese government which was trying to move away from the havoc wreaked by the Cultural Revolution and the uncertainties following the Tiananmen Square massacre in Beijing in 1989.

We knew that because her death had not been reported officially, we had to make a judgment call like many journalists: we could print the story but it could be denied. Or we could be accused of just adding to the rumors and possibly get us into serious trouble. But the sources were good so we ran with it.

When TIME came out that week in the Grapevine section with the news of her death, the phones rang off the hook. Colleagues wanted a confirmation of our story. We hung on the trust in the sources and didn't deny it. But still the Chinese media kept silent.

We were too tense to leave the office that night. Jimi and I stayed up late working but largely waiting. Would we be asked to leave the country for rumor-mongering? Anything was possible in China two years following the events of Tiananmen on June 4, 1989.

And then after midnight the Le Monde correspondent, Francis Deron, called. I could almost hear his chuckle. He knew what we were waiting for. "Mia, you're safe," he said, "Xinhua has reported the story." And they reported it just as we had written it. No small compliment in a world as secretive as the world of Jiang Qing.

Mia Turner and Jimi Florcruz

A "Stringer" in Vienna

Friedel and I arrived in Vienna in August, 1968, exhausted after a tour of duty in Biafra. We had had a mere half day in Paris to pick up suitable clothes and were in Vienna to fill in for the vacationing Eastern Europe bureau chief Peter Forbath. We were totally unaware that the student revolution of 1968 had begun that evening. Our sleep in the hotel was deep until the telephone rang at 2 a.m. Dick

Clurman told Friedel to leave for Prague immediately. Soviet forces had invaded Czechoslovakia several hours earlier. Friedel initially refused to take me along on his new, possibly dangerous assignment. I fought hard and won. He chose the most northern border crossing from Austria to Czechoslovakia, hoping the Russian tanks hadn't yet arrived there. When we got to the crossing in our white office Mercedes just before 7 a.m., the border guards at a small station were weeping while refugees had begun trickling through, headed in the opposite direction to ours. The guards' refusal to let us through was couched in regret but, they assured us, final. After urging them to help the free press cover the heinous invasion, Friedel convinced them to take a vote. When they withdrew to their chief's office, we watched television coverage of tanks firing from their turrets as they advanced into Wenceslas Square. The guards' verdict was a study in Czech caginess: Friedel would not be admitted but I could enter if I still wanted to. I was 26 years old. Should they be called to account later, my passport that listed me as a student might protect them from trouble. No doubt they believed their artful gesture would end the matter because I wouldn't want to go alone even if my husband would let me. But off I drove in the grand white Mercedes while he made his way back to Vienna. Prague was about two and a half hours away. As I drove closer, I found dirt roads to hide in whenever I heard the rumblings of approaching tanks. But how to enter the city and find the journalists' headquarters, the Alcron Hotel with its parking garage? I'd been in tense situations before, but this one stretched my nerves more than a little. Entering a country not a word of whose language I knew and with no papers or contacts might have been okay if an army weren't invading: the *Russian* army at that! Not that my fear excluded youthful vanity: I kept wondering how long I'd be able to survive in a Siberian labor camp without washing my hair. Wondering and wondering until the luck of the blind arrived in the person of a young hitchhiker on the highway. He was friendly and strangely excited for the adventure lying ahead. He knew not only how to avoid the Russian tanks in order to gain access to the city center but also its every back ally that would take me to my temporary safe haven. A bird of paradise colored my first vision of the Alkron's lobby. Shirley Temple Black, to be the American ambassador to Czechoslovakia two decades later, was showering attention on herself in yellow patent leather boots with a gigantic yellow bow stuck on her head. Leaping to and fro beside an endless line to the telex room, she was telling everyone she must send immediate messages to President Johnson and to her husband. The contrast with Heinrich Böll, who was looking amused while quietly smoking at a table, was close to total. More luck: on my way to very nearby Wenceslas Square, I ran into Tad Sculz of the *New York Times*, who was one of only three American correspondents in Czechoslovakia during the holiday month. Knowing I was a German national and that Germany had no embassy in Prague, and learning that I had no hotel room, he urged me to make my way to the American embassy across the river before curfew. He promised to ask Ambassador Jacob Beam to give sanctuary to "the kid stringer." During the next six hours, I roamed the city, absorbing sights of aggression and futile attempts to fight it. Climbing on Russian tanks, Czech youths cursed young Soviet soldiers, many of whom truly didn't know where they were, let alone what they were doing to the Czechs. As the day wore on, the danger of massacre lessened. Graffiti appeared everywhere. I was lucky yet again, now in finding East German students who translated curses in Czech and Russian, together with epitaphs and historical bon mots. "One day the affairs of this country will be given back to its people," read one of the latter, which I quickly copied. The quote from Jan Hus became the first sentence of that week's *Time* cover story. Shortly before curfew began, the embassy admitted me, *whew!* Ambassador Beam gave the three American correspondents and me permission to use the State Department's secure telex machine: 30 minutes to file a report for each of us. After Tad Sculz's breath down my neck helped my limited English to fly from me totally, I switched to German, knowing that Friedel in Vienna would improve my text while translating. After being fed some sandwiches, we slept on the carpet of the visitors lounge. The next day went to more sightseeing and interviewing; also to hoping Friedel would somehow join me. The story had begun to move to political developments, about which I knew I couldn't deliver. When both he and Peter Forbath appeared on the third day, any cliché would have been suitable to describe my relief and joy. And when that week's pub letter praised them both, I was happy for the three of us until a cable addressed to me arrived from Henry A. Grunwald. "Barbara—thanks for your help. But in the future, we shouldn't make a practice of Time wives getting involved in their husband's job." I became a foreign correspondent for *Die Zeit* not long afterward.

Barbara Ungeheuer

The Eyes of Hate

My first big piece was an investigation of fragging in Vietnam published by the Saturday Review in Jan. 1972. I was in their offices writing some notes on the edit as the art department and the editors discussed the cover art. They wanted a picture of a fragging note (soldiers usually wrote a warning before actually trying to blow up their officers) with a hand grenade on top of it, and I heard one man say they needed handwriting that really looked psychopathic. Then I noticed that they had stopped talking. I turned around and they were all staring at my handwriting. "Just keep writing," one of them told me. I wrote the note: "You are one dead REMF."

Fast-forward 24 years. TIME was doing a cover on militias—"How Dangerous Are They?" I had nothing to do with that cover, but as the piece was closing an emissary from the art department showed up at my door. She explained that they were looking for someone's eyes to shoot for the cover. I think she may have said, "The eyes of hate," or some such. Apparently, it's not just my handwriting that looks psychopathic.

-0-

I did a cover on "The Rape of Siberia" in the late 1990s and travelled for a stretch of the reporting with Tony Suau. Getting around was rough and over the weeks I/we chartered a run-down helicopter to get to a stretch of forest in the Russian Far East, trucks, and even a Soviet era pilot boat with a crew of about 20 to get to the remains of a prison camp on the Arctic Ocean. The trip ended up in Kamchatka, and after some trips around that spectacular landscape, my reporting was done.

Tony, however, wanted to charter a helicopter to do some shooting in an area of hot springs—Russia's Yellowstone. He wanted to split expenses. "But Tony," I said, "I'm done."

"Sure," he said, "but without a cover shot you don't have a cover." We split the cost, but there were more surprises to come. The chopper Tony found was a giant bird, the Soviet knock-off of the Chinook. Having paid a few thousand dollars, we expected to be flying up ourselves, but when we boarded there were about twenty-five

Russians on the plane. The pilot, a Soviet-era airman, had a pretty good business going.

Tony did his shooting while I wandered around taking in the spectacular scenery, but as the day wore on fog and clouds began to close in. The pilot signaled us urgently to board. Even as we were getting seated, fog was shutting down visibility to zero. The pilot took off immediately and did a spectacular maneuver in which he gunned the helicopter down the side of a ravine to gain some airspeed and then corkscrewed in an extremely tight circle straight up. Once we cleared the surrounding ridges, he carefully brought the copter down until it was below the fog and just above the tree tops, which is where we flew the entire trip back to Petroplavosk. Tony's panoramic image made for a spectacular cover.

One last thought. That trip sometimes verged on the slapstick. In order to get to meet tiger poachers, Tony and I assumed a false identity. Here's the first paragraph of the box that accompanied the story:

"I am sitting in the sparsely furnished house of an Udege house in southeastern Siberia while the owner tries to sell me a tiger skin and bones. My cover is that I am part of a group of American businessmen here for a week of bird watching. The other "bird watchers" consist of Steven Galster, an environmental investigator, Anthony Suau, a TIME photographer, and Sergei Shaitarov, a Russian environmentalist who works with Galster. My ludicrously rudimentary disguise consists of a borrowed pair of binoculars. If the tiger trader asks me to name one species of local bird, we are sunk."

-0-

When I did the reporting for "Lost Tribes Lost Knowledge" back in the early 1990's, I helped defray the enormous expense of a global story by splitting expenses with National Geographic, for whom I was doing a story on "Apes and Humans." It was a fine synergy since many of the tribes I was reporting on in Africa and Asia lived in areas also inhabited by great apes. At one point I had to get from Bangui, the capital of the Central African Republic to Bayanga on the Sangha river at the western border of the country. I got a lift from Andrea Turkelo, who was studying gorillas and who had a truck. The trip was aobut 530 kilometers, but she promised that she knew a "short cut." through a logging concession. The trip turned out to be a nightmare of road blocks, rutted, almost un-drivable, and mired tracks, and a farcical ferry crossing, during which the drunken ferry crew tried to extort money from us at every turn.

While in Bayanga, I met a peace corps volunteer who told me about a western-trained native named Bernard N'donazi, who was trying to use traditional medicines to provide care in Bouar where people could neither afford, nor obtain western medicines. I filed this in the back of my mind as something I might investigate further at some point, while I made plans to get out of there after I did my reporting on the gorillas in the area.

As luck would have it, I was visiting Dzanga Bai (a gathering spot for wildlife) one day when we encountered a group of paratroopers from the French Foreign Legion who were visiting the bai for some R&R during a break from exercises back in Bangui. Bangui? Only in Africa would a reporter ask for a lift from a cadre of paratroopers, and only in Africa would their commander say, "pourquoi pas?"

Before he could change his mind, I dashed back to get my kit, and then showed up at the airstrip. Once there, however, the captain informed me that he'd gotten new orders. Instead of going back to

Bangui, they were heading north to Bouar. Bouar! Even better. The captain was somewhat mystified that I want to go Bouar, but I knew there were good roads connecting Bouar to Bangui, and I'd get to interview N'donazi to boot.

N'donazi turned out to be a wonderful interview and we featured him in one of the boxes accompanying the article. In this case, the photographer, William Coupon, had the leisure of putting together his own itinerary once I had done a draft of the article. When it came time to shoot N'donazi, Coupon took the expedient of chartering a plane to fly directly to Bouar

Bad move. Africans tended to be extremely wary of photographers in the first place, and to show up in a plane convinced N'donazi's relatives, who were not as saintly as N'donazi, that money was to be made from this photo shoot. Essentially, they held him for ransom until a substantial fee was forwarded from New York.

Eugene Linden

"Get the Fuck Out of My Country"

There was never a good day covering the war in Bosnia but this one really sucked.

As my photographer, Tom Haley, and I straggled back one evening to the Hotel Bosna in Doboj we were barely talking. It was my first story for Time on life behind Serb lines and he said I was pushing too hard and getting kicked in the head too often.

That morning I had heard on the BBC that a "renegade" Serb tank unit was attacking the UN enclave at Bihac and decided to run up there. As we came flying over a hill near the smoldering town we ran into General Ratko Maladic standing in the middle of the road running the attack. He was not happy to be caught. I figured, what the hell, and walked up to him had got a rare but short interview.

"Get the fuck out of my country," he spat.

"You can't do anything with these assholes," Haley advised as we got out of there and got back to Doboj, where we thought we were safe;.

I called a Serb officer I knew to come and join us to try and explain what had happened that day. Like most of what occurred in that war, there was no rational explanation.

The officer was local hero for his exploits, slithering across Bosnian lines with knife in his teeth and slitting the throats of sentries, but for the most part he semed rational. Though I had my doubts when, after a few brandies, he confided that he didn't hate Muslims. In fact, he whispered, he had one of the most wanted Muslims in his home where he was protecting him.

Before I could delve deeper, the hotel manager came over and whispered in his ear. His mood quickly changed.

He looked at us with pity and explained: "The Serbska army is surrounding the building and that have orders to execute you."

There was no time to lament our demise. We hastily got the name and number of the unit, the officers names and rushed to the front desk of the hotel, grabbed the phone and started dialing. The hotel manager stood by, quietly listening. It was to late to call anyone—no cell phones in those days—but the news agencies.

Reuters picked up and we began dictating our own obits.

"Zoran this is Tom and Ed and we are about to be executed. Do not believe we were killed by Bosnians. The killers are . . ." We named the unit and officers. "If you don't hear from us come to Doboj our bodies should be . . ."

We never got to finish.

The doors swung open and soldiers, guns drawn and faces taut, rushed through the door. We were grabbed and about to be hustled out the door when the hotel manager walked over to the officer in charge. Everything stopped as they walked away and huddled in a corner.

As we stood there the officer came back and talked to the officer we were eating with and a few others. We couldn't tell what was going on but we could see the anger in his face turn to concern. We were taken to a local prison and ignored as we heard the officers argue heatedly.

A few hours later we were taken out and put into a car, convinced that we were headed to some empty field with an open ditch. Instead, we were taken to another unit and sat again while another argument ensued.

And it was that way for the rest of the night.

A ride, an argument and another transfer. After dawn, an officer who spoke English came over, confused, and asked what the hell we wanted.

"We have to get to Belgrade," I said, "It is important."

Another argument and another car.

But this one, a grey staff car, sped away, without escort and to our surprise, drove through the border crossing into Serbia proper. We were safe.

Stunned, it took us an hour to figure out what happened: It was the phone call that saved our lives. When the hotel manager had told the officer that his name and unit had been given to Reuters he knew that if he executed us he was in trouble. So he tried to pass the job off and, each time, the new unit decided that "if they won't do it why should we?" They then passed us off to the next unit. As we moved down the line the story got muddled and provided us with an escape.

Ed Barnes

Tales from the Chief

1999: The eve of the 50th anniversary of the People's Republic of China. The entire contingent of the China newstour has been invited to attend the gala banquet in the Great Hall of the People. It is pouring rain. Sheets of it. Word is that clouds have been seeded so that October 1st is clear and all the parades and fireworks can go off perfectly. As we leave the Hall, the rain keeps us under the portico as we wait for a brief break to make it to the buses. Before us is Tiananmen Square. To our left, the Tiananmen Gate to the Forbidden City, with Mao's iconic and strangely expressionless portrait. Ted Turner and Steve Case are engaged in a not so friendly discussion about who is the wealthiest. Case has just been ranked ahead of Ted and is teasing him about it. Ted is not amused. Neither is Jane. So Case decides to cajole and tells Ted that the ranking does not take landholdings into account. On that front, Ted leads the pack. The rain breaks a bit. We head to the buses. And Mao stares ahead.

-0-

1993: We've flown into Tripoli for the last interview of The Peacemakers, TIME's 1993 MOY. Mandela, DeKlerk, Rabin and now Arafat. The call comes in early morning and we are taken to one of Arafat's residences. The security is the tightest of all, even more thorough than the Israelis. They even open my compact, to make sure the spring mechanism isn't rigged. As I am introduced to Arafat, he greets me in French and proceeds to say that Charles De Gaulle is one of his heroes. De Gaulle, he adds, gesturing to the Huguenot cross I wear on a neck chain, gave him the same. He then asks me about my student days in Paris. They have dug into a lot more than my compact.

-0-

1991: Jonathan Beaty and Sam Gwynne do BCCI. With a hefty assist from John Dickerson. Beaty and Gwynne are in New Mexico, finishing their work on the outlaw bank and its particularly dubious management and clients. At the suggestion of John Moscow, Robert Morgenthau's deputy, they agree to call in daily so we know they're okay. Works fine, until they don't. Ann King checks in with family and friends. No one knows where they are. We call Moscow to let him know 'the boys", as Ann calls them, are nowhere to be found. Hours later, they call in. They'd taken Jonathan's boat out on the lake and couldn't understand why law enforcement had turned out in force to meet them upon their return to the dock. Boys.

Joelle Attinger

A Strategic Leak

It was sometime in the mid '80s when the Reagan administration (probably not consciously) seemed bent on breaking the Soviet Union by spending it into the ground, particularly on weapon systems (remember John Lehman's 600-ship navy?). It was touch and go whose economy would crack first given the amount of money being flung at the military. Waste, fraud and abuse at the Pentagon were hot topics and the Washington bureau had been working on a cover about the military spending tsunami that was about to engulf the budget. We were all set to go, but then those familiar messages from New York started arriving: were we getting ahead of ourselves? Were we sure of the numbers?

It seemed likely that New York was about to whimp out. There was only one thing to do and (now that I can't be fired) I admit responsibility. On the Friday the cover was due to close there were hearings on the Hill involving some of the key figures warning of the military overspend. The network correspondents were already planning their weekends, so it seemed unlikely that the hearings would get any coverage. So we leaked the information that Time's cover the following week would be on Pentagon spending. The networks, being just as insecure as our masters in New York, took the bait and dispatched vast teams to cover what proved to be a fairly low key event. But it was enough. The hearings made the nightly news, New York was reassured, and the cover was put to bed that weekend. A small victory for the News Service. It was an important story.

Years later I confessed this ruse to Ray Cave over drinks at the Dorchester in London. Ray sipped his martini and confirmed that I would have been fired on the spot had he known.

Chris Redman

From Hollywood to Baghdad

Looking back at my 30-odd years reporting for Time, I'm still amazed by the wonderful breadth of that experience: I started in Boston, then Washington, the White House, the State Department, Jerusalem bureau chief, New York editing, chief foreign correspondent covering the world. I wrote about a million different things from thermonuclear fusion and fashion models, to arms control, politics and diplomacy. I spent a fair share of my career in places where danger was the norm and those memories are colored in the grim shades of terror, horror, anguish, misery. While you're doing it, it's bearable, but it doesn't make for moments to recall. So I'd rather tell a few other tales from the Time trenches, like:

I was still a stringer in the Boston bureau when I was sent on my first big cover story to interview a little-known guy from the south who was defending the America's Cup in Newport, R.I. I met him one morning on the dock and he started talking, and was still mouthing on four hours later, moving from the art of sailing to his big dreams for expanding his billboard business into never before imagined regions. Having run out of notebook space, I wrote my summation of the guy on my wrist: "Napoleon complex." The guy, of course, was Ted Turner and he was explaining to me his wild idea of broadcasting news 24 hours a day. I know I called him extraordinarily ambitious in my files, but can't remember if I even reported the nature of his dream.

When I got to Washington, I thought, ah, now I'll be doing the big, serious stuff. So when then Bureau Chief Bob Ajemian called me into his office not long after my arrival, to undertake a cover assignment, I thought, wow this is it. Then he told me I would be the correspondent assigned to hang out with supermodel Cheryl Tiegs for a couple of weeks. I said something like: but I didn't come here to do THAT stuff! Bob just looked at me with his eyes closed and murmured: "Johanna, you don't understand. The ME wants YOU to do this." For years, that was one of the biggest selling covers I worked on.

I laugh when I remember the vagaries of pre-computer reporting. I was once sending a medium-size file from Marrakech while covering a Secretary of State, and handed it over to the telex (remember them?) man laid on for reporters. I blithely went out to a lavish dinner, returning late in the evening to gather up my sent file—only to discover my English prose had been dispatched by an arabic teletype operator as one incredibly long word.

For years, our wonderful colleagues on the Newsdesk in Washington and New York used to have to phone us correspondents up in the middle of the night Fridays to read us our playbacks and type up our checkpoints. (I'm sure Jonathan answered more than a few of mine.) I think it was on the same trip to North Africa that Waits May, then a stalwart news clerk in the DC bureau, called me in Tunisia in the wee hours to read what must have been a pretty boring playback. As he tells it, at some point, he thought he'd lost the connection and kept calling my name. There was no answer from my end, and Waits began to worry something bad had happened. Then, he heard my heart beating with perfect regularity: I had fallen asleep with the phone resting on my chest. And then there was dictation, a long lost art form of my generation, constructing an entire file verbally on the fly—but then you could also go reporting with no more equipment than a pen, a notebook and a quarter for the phone. It could get hairy though. When Reagan went to Reykjavik for a seminal summit meeting with Soviet Premier Mikhail Gorbachev, the final session was set to conclude Saturday night, Iceland time, maximum deadline for Time. So the three of us covering the story set up open phone lines to New York, one to the ME, one to the World editor and one to the writer, all hanging on as we waited to discover what had transpired between these two practitioners of the unexpected. I can still see our first fleeting glimpse of Reagan's bitterly disappointed face as he exited the meeting, knowing something dramatic had happened, and having to dictate to the writer, who I believe was Walter Isaacson, virtually in sync with the briefing, as the collapse of Reagan's astonishing bid to forego all nuclear weapons was revealed.

Luck played a role in my career, as it must in journalism, but I sometimes felt like the bad penny turning up at tragedies. I happened to be lunching with photog Diana Walker a block away from the

Washington Hilton when Reagan was shot: we heard the sirens and raced up the street, among the very first reporters to arrive. I also happened to be friendly with a presidential security agent from my days covering Jimmy Carter—Jerry Parr, the one who shoved Reagan into his limo—who took my calls right away. I happened to be sitting in as Jerusalem bureau chief, where I was having dinner with a photographer friend whose husband snapped for Reuters and who had dutifully gone to shoot a boring rally for the Prime Minister in Tel Aviv. He phoned home the minute Rabin was shot and Time was able to get a great start on a deadline cover. I dictated much of that story too, in the wee hours of a Sunday to ME Jim Gaines in New York. Time won a lot of prizes for its coverage of that assassination. And I happened to be on my way back to NYC from a vacation in Australia, stopping for a break overnight with family in Los Angeles, when our sleep was rudely interrupted by the Northridge earthquake: I spent the rest of the week out there reporting, aided hugely by a young nephew who knew all the back roads in the area and a brother-in-law's functioning landline phone.

In all the years I spent covering the stiff and formal George Shultz, I only saw him disconcerted once: when I asked him if he really had a tatoo of a Princeton tiger on his derriere. He wasn't a lying man and he had no repartee, so he admitted he did, then changed the subject. As we reporters trooped back to our seats in the rear of the plane, I passed Mrs. Shultz, who patted my arm and said: "Good girl! You're the only one among those old sticks who had the balls to ask him." And then she leaned over and guffawed: "And he used to roar like a tiger when his kids would push on it." My opinion of the important man was never quite the same.

In fact, it's hard for any experienced reporter to feel much sympathy for the pols and presidents they cover: my years in

Washington taught me the closer you get, the less you like or admire or respect most of them. But I remember a truly poignant moment aboard the plane carrying outgoing president Jimmy Carter back to Plains after his single term, watching him watch the American hostages in Iran being freed immediately on the accession of his successor. The anguished look of pain and sadness and failure mixed with relief that his countrymen were finally free was an unforgettable image of his presidency and gave him a stature in defeat that he never achieved in victory.

And I will share two moments when war was strange rather than terrifying. After a lot of smarmy sucking-up to Iraqi officials who later appeared high up on the infamous Deck of Cards, to get an interview with Saddam, I was invited to Baghdad in Dec. 1998. Few other reporters were on the ground and there wasn't much news in the offing so we were hopeful Saddam had decided to liven things up by talking to Time. After a few days, it looked promising enough to send for the chief of correspondents of the day, John Stacks to join me, and he set out from New York. As he was winging east, so were a fleet of U.S. ships and warplanes loaded with Cruise missiles and other heavy stuff sent by Bill Clinton to punish Saddam for alleged violations of UN sanctions. The night the bombs started dropping I was in my room at the Al Rashid, talking on my forbidden satphone to Jonathan at home in New York. The phone only worked if the window was open. I watched a Cruise missile fly by remarkably slowly parallel to my window at just about my 8th floor level, while Jonathan in NYC watched it simultaneously, in glowing green film broadcast from the CNN window downstairs from mine. Suddenly, the missile turned and hit its target a couple of kilometers away with a tremendous blinding concussion that knocked me flat on my butt. Jonathan says the last thing he heard was me saying "Oh, shit . . ." (I was able to reassure him in short order that nothing more damaging than a big bruise had resulted.) John, who spent as I recall a grim night crossing the desert amidst the bombs, arrived next day in Baghdad. Our interview, needless to say, was off the agenda. But John and I spent the next several nights standing on the top of the government press center in downtown Baghdad, convinced the missiles would never hit us journalists, while the most dramatic sort of fireworks display flashed and flared around us. Thank god both of us had smuggled in whiskey . . . (Editor's note: I believe I arrived, after the all night drive across the desert with bombs illuminating the sky, the morning of the day the bombing started. Johanna and I deployed to the roof of the Interior Ministry to watch the action, but noticed that all the other pressies were wearing flak jackets and helmets. We repaired to the alRashid, opened the windows, and watched the cruise missile get the Bath party headquarters. JFS

And my skin still crawls when I remember the terrifying incongruity of sitting with Bobby Ghosh in the living room of one of the baddest of bad guys in insurrection-era Baghdad, while he called me his "little flower" and whispered poetic compliments, wondering all the while if he meant to kidnap us . . .

I could never have done my job without the help, support and camaraderie of the many researchers and stringers and other correspondents I worked with—I was lucky to work with so many and they were always one of the best parts of Time. But I especially want to mention two late colleagues who made Time's foreign coverage the stuff of legend it was and whom I was so proud to call friends: Jamil Hamad and Yuri Zarakovich.

Johanna McGeary

Back to the Convent

Getting the story is journalism's mantra. Getting *TO* the story is the trick in Africa. So far I'd been grazed by a bullet in one of Somalia's countless street battles and spent three mainly boring days as a prisoner in Liberia's war for control of the diamond and timber trade. The smell of unburied body parts in Rwanda I'll never forget.

May 1991, after decades of fighting, the Eritreans and Ethiopians drove Mengistu's tanks into Addis Ababa. Mengistu himself fled to Zimbabwe. Isaias Afwerki closed the borders of Eritrea. Was this Cambodia's killing fields all over again? I had interviewed him and spent time with his army. With the borders closed, the only way to get to him was by water.

Off to a sitdown with the U.S. ambassador in Djibouti. Of course you can do what you want, he said. But we've heard that they're taking people to the middle of the Red Sea and then throwing them overboard. He gave me the names of three men he trusted. That evening, which could have been my last, I went drinking with the U.S. press officer. "Gotta see this," he said," before you die."

It was a bar . . . of course. But not just any bar. A bit of Waugh in Abyssinia. T'was boys from the French Foreign Legion. In a huge room of mirrors one legionnaire danced with himself. Moving his hands all over his body, looking at his image in the mirrors.

Turned out the "boat" I hired was a small dhow. It had two motors that never broke down. It had a sun roof that blew off on the second day. It had a place to cook on the forward deck. Hah!! "Forward deck . . ." Fish for breakfast. Fish for lunch. Fish for dinner. All freshly caught and cooked in a barrel on the forward deck.

Amidships is me. The sun roof was for the crazy lady. Me. They loaded bottled water for the crazy lady. For themselves, they drank Nestles milk out of a can. Not for the crazy lady. Smiles of introductions all round. Crazy Lady is making nice with her three crew members. One Afar is at the engine. The second is the cook. The Captain comes from a higher caste tribe and speaks French, as in "Ca Va!"

First day sun. More sun. As the pain in the butt sun gets the hell off the water my crew starts to chew a godawfully bitter green plant. I watch the khat melt their faces.

Day two. I can now see the Eritrean coast on our left side. The morning went by fast. Water, water everywhere . . . one of the Afars carried me to the beach so my shoes stayed dry.

OH MY GOD!!!!!

My period!!!!!! What if they notice!! Are they like most tribes? Women menstruating are "unclean!" Will I be thrown off? I spent two days holding my stomach, playing the wretching role. Changing the tampons were tense moments. Me, huddled in my "bathroom"—a sheet artfully hung—watching in horror the tapon's paper cover bounce around in the whirling air on the right side of the boat. "Ca Va" "Ca Va" smiles the African Frenchman who doesn't speak French. I think I prayed. Told God I would go back to the nunnery.

Marguerite Michaels

Scooping the Supreme Court

During the '70s and '80s, Time employed many of the world's most talented photojournalists. They were a swashbuckling crew. One day in the Washington Bureau dart throwing area, AKA the photographer's lounge, Stan (Stormy) Cloud saw one prominent photographer, probably Steve Northrup, returning from one boondoggle or another.

To his fellow dart-throwers, Cloud declared: "You know, photography is what we have in the 20th Century instead of stagecoach robbery. The same type of people go into it." From then, we correspondents universally referred to photographers as The Stagecoach Robbers.

I worked with a number of great ones—David Burnett, Dick Swanson, Alan Nogues, Dennis Brack, among others—but I had a special bond with David Hume Kennerly. As a bachelor living the bachelor life style in Washington, Kennerly was a constant inspiration and role model. He also did unbelieveable professional work.

Kennerly and I were working the Watergate trials at the U.S. Courthouse in early 1974 when the word came down—"New York" wanted a fresh picture of burglar Bernard Barker. No cameras inside the courthouse at that time, so the shot would have to be made outside. But there were four entrances, one on each side, and only two of us. And, of course, I couldn't be trusted with a camera. Kennerly and I gambled Barker wouldn't be coming into the garage on the north side. So I took the southwest corner, where I could cover the west and south entrances, and Kennerly stood at the southeast corner, about 200 yards away.

About 8:50 a.m. that morning, I spotted Barker and his lawyer arriving by cab at the west entrance. I yelled "He's down here" to Kennerly, who immediately began sprinting on the lawn from one end of the courthouse to the other. I moved towards the cab, asking Barker an innocuous question in hopes of slowing him down, but he kept walking. As Barker approached the courthouse door, Kennerly came roaring full tilt around the corner, took a few more steps and launched himself into the air in front of Barker, his motorized camera clacking away. The following week, the picture of a somewhat startled-looking Barker appeared in Time, looking perfectly composed, almost as if it had been set up and posed.

When the Nixon tapes case hit the U.S. Supreme Court, anticipating the verdict, New York ordered up fresh candid photos of each Justice. Kennerly did most of the assignment. The idea, as I remember, was that they were human beings, not minor deities, and should be seen out of their robes, in a human setting. Most of the justices, after it was explained, played along, except for two: Warren Burger, still holding a grudge against Time, and William Brennan, an ardent defender of First Amendment rights who prided himself on 100 percent non-cooperation with the press. We heard Burger was attending a judicial conference at the Greenbrier, so Kennerly and I went down in hopes of catching him offguard, but Burger was alerted, and demurred. I kept harassing his aide. Finally, I got a call. "Chief Justice Burger intends to visit the Rose Garden at 2 p.m. today." Of course, the stiff Chief Justice was wearing a sport coat and tie, but Kennerly managed to get about three dozen pictures of Burger carefully inspecting the flowers, while Burger studiously pretended he didn't even know either one of us were there.

Brennan was a tougher nut. The deadline was approaching, and we had nothing. I'd heard Brennan went walking every morning, so in desperation Anne Callahan placed two photographers outside his Georgetown townhouse one morning at 5 a.m., at the front and back doors. Precisely at 5:30, an unshaven, dumpy man in a dirty T-shirt and soiled trousers came out the back door. Both Brennan and the (second-string) photographer were startled to see each other. The photographer, thinking a homeless man had somehow found his way into Brennan's house, said, "Are you Justice Brennan?" The unkempt figure assured him he was not, that a mistake had been made, and disappeared back into the house before the photographer could even get off a frame.

With disaster looming, providence intervened. Former Chief Justice Earl Warren died. All current Court members would attend the funeral at Arlington, out in the open. By this time, our determined pursuit of Brennan—and Brennan's success in one-upping us—was common knowledge within the Supreme Court building, a matter of great amusement. As the Justices, in a loose pack, started walking down the hill and back to their cars after Warren was interred, there in front of them was Kennerly, standing and waiting. The other Justices started laughing at Brennan as he realized he'd been had. In desperation, Brennan tried to duck behind the rather ample torso of his friend, Justice Thurgood Marshall, but Marshall nimbly dodged out of the way. We could hear Marshall calling out, "Smile, Billy. He's got you, Billy. Smile!"

Kennerly danced around, happily getting the final image. The assignment was completed, in time for the Court's announcement of Nixon v. U.S. Can anyone imagine any publication taking that kind of professional care today?

-0-

After reporting the Supreme Court's 8-0 decision in Nixon v. U.S. in late July, 1974, I was feeling pretty satisfied with myself. My preview of the decision—keyed directly off a subtle but strong hint from an unimpeachable source—virtually stated the verdict would be unanimous against Nixon, and would put tremendous pressure on him. By contrast, Newsweek had floundered about attempting to cover their keisters by alternatively predicting every possible combination of eight votes known to mathematics. 6-2 this way, or 4-4 in a deadlock, or 6-2 the other way . . . you name any vote combination, and that's what Newsweek claimed the Justices were allegedly considering. In other words, I'd reported there was no real debate—it would be unanimous—while Newsweek alleged there was all this back-and-forth in judicial chambers that later turned out to have been pure fiction. When the Court very quickly released its unanimous decision against Nixon, I took a bow and prepared to take a break.

I was really looking forward to "covering" the American Bar Association meeting in Honolulu a week later . . . had never been to Hawaii, was planning on taking a surfing lesson, perhaps attending a seminar or two. Watergate had already lasted close to three years, and we all expected more months of delay in handing over the tapes, and the prosecutor listening to them, and whatever charges were made, etc.

On Thursday, just days before my flight to Hawaii, I was visiting my parents in Bryan, TX. That evening, a phone call from Washington desk officer Ed Jackson. Nixon had just announced he was resigning the next day. It's all hands on deck, and you've got to come back to D.C., Jackson told me.

My mind went into overdrive. It would take me most of Friday to fly back, putting me out of action on the key reporting day. And there would likely be no trip to Hawaii. I started telling Jackson why I should stick with current plans. It's not really my story any more . . . Dean Fischer and our crack White House team would handle it . . . legal sources are really irrelevent at this point. An inspiration struck me. Besides, I said, there would be various insiders at the ABA convention—I remember mentioning Justice Lewis Powell, and former deputy attorney general William Ruckelshaus—who might unload some real information for the next week's inevitable follow up.

A half-hour later, Jackson called with a new play call. Henry Grunwald, basking in Time's success on Watergate, had devised a new feature called "Letters to Time." He envisioned a national dialogue among intellectuals, celebrities, glitterati, politicos—all of whom would share their absolute best pithy thoughts for the week in a special Time letters column. Your mission, Jackson told me, was to proceed to Honolulu, track down Ruckelshaus, and get a solid, meaty paragraph from him on how Nixon's resignation showed that the rule of law was still working in the U.S.A. This will be a beautiful way to kick off the "Letters to Time" feature, he said, with commentary from a prominent victim of the Saturday night massacre. Of course, that sounded good to me.

After arriving in Honolulu, I learned Ruckelshaus was in my hotel, the Sheraton Waikiki. I telephoned his room the next morning.; his wife said he was down on the beach. I headed down to the sand, feeling somewhat Nixonian in a blazer and tie, and cordovans. I quickly found Ruckelshaus, taking the sun in a chaise lounge, reading a book, a fruity drink at his side. Within seconds, I had given him the full Grunwald concept, assuring him what an honor it would be to start this national dialogue. It wouldn't have to be more than a few sentences, I noted, even verbally outlining what he might consider saying.

When I finished my sales pitch, there was silence. Ruckelshaus quietly looked away, out over the ocean, to the horizon. Then he looked back at me. "I don't have the time," he said. I staggered backward, reeling, aghast that anyone would take a pass on being part of Time magazine history. "What if I do a draft for you . . . you can change it around," I suggested. He replied: "That might work."

I rushed back up to the ABA press room. A row of typewriters had been set up. I put a sheet of paper in one, and typed out a rough version of the proper message on the rule of law. I made a couple of mistakes, but instead of erasing them, I just put XXXXs over the offending words. Then back down to the beach I went, paper in hand. Ruckelshaus was where I had left him, perhaps one shade darker. He took the paper, read what I'd written—and handed it back. "Fine," he said. "Do I have to sign it?"

The next week, Ruckelshaus's "Letter to Time" was printed, inaugurating the promising start of a national dialogue on public affairs. Alas, while Henry Grunwald had countless good ideas during his tenure at Time ME, this was not one of them. "Letters to Time" collapsed of its own weight within weeks due to lack of interest, the project quietly abandoned.

But for 30 years afterwards, whenever I ran into Ruckelshaus around Washington, his eyes would light up and he would greet me: "Ah, my writer!"

-0

On Monday, Jan. 22, 1973, perhaps the most eventful day of his career, Justice Harry Blackmun returned home in mid-afternoon to his Washington condo. That morning, he had announced the landmark majority opinion in Roe v. Wade, declaring that abortion was now a constitutional right. Protestors were already gathering at the Supreme Court. Blackmun, seeking some diversion, decided to relax at home with his copy of Time Magazine delivered that morning.

To Blackman's chagrin, an account of the Roe v. Wade decision—obviously written the previous week—was already in the magazine. The story included some behind-the-scenes details on internal court maneuvering in the case, including a mention that Chief Justice Warren E. (Big Juicy) Burger had delayed announcement of the decision by withholding his final vote, apparently so he wouldn't have to face President Nixon at his second inauguration with the decidedly non-conservative opinion in the news. An angry Blackmun telephoned Burger, who promised to investigate the leak.

The Time scoop had received relatively little attention in the media. It was long, with an extensive discussion of the abortion question and its ramifications, but was couched in terms of what was likely to happen. It was published amidst the hullaballoo of an inauguration weekend, when attention was elsewhere. And sensing the firestorm to come, I had pleaded with New York to soft-peddle our press release, knowing there would be hell to pay from a historically-rare leak of inner court deliberations.

Two weeks later, Washington Bureau Chief Hugh Sidey received a call from Burger's office. He wanted a meeting with Time executives to discuss our reporting. At the time, I'd been in the Washington bureau as the junior correspondent for only a year, a reportial sapling among giants in the bureau. Until this episode, I wasn't sure the top editors in New York even knew who I was.

Within days, the top brass—Hedley Donovan, Henry Grunwald, Murray Gart and others—flew down to Washington on a Time Inc. plane for dinner with Burger. To avoid publicity, the dinner was catered in the bureau conference room. I was sent in a limo to the general aviation terminal at National to meet the plane and brief on what Burger was up to. I sat in the front seat, next to the driver. As we drove to the bureau, I outlined how I'd reported the story. Donovan, whom I'd never previously met, asked me, "What will Burger's position be?" I said he'd claim the court must operate in complete confidentiality, since leaking of pending decisions could move markets and erode respect for the law.

I wasn't invited to the dinner. Copy assistant Kim Eisler and I briefly entertained the idea of rigging the conference room telephone—this was prior to widespread availability of tiny recording devices—but we feared somebody might try to use the phone and catch on. So I spent the evening lurking in my windowless office in the back hall of the bureau.

Burger showed up with an aide, toting a large looseleaf binder, "Time Magazine matter" on the cover, containing fruits of his exhaustive leak investigation. As the dinner proceeded, he read liberally from his findings, in the manner of a prosecutor laying out damning facts. "On December 3, 1972, at approximately 3:30 p.m., Beckwith telephoned Justice Marshall's clerk, Joe Jones, and attempted to arrange a lunch appointment. He was turned down." He had even documented my failed attempt to get a dinner date with one of Justice Powell's attractive secretaries, an effort that was doubtless more social than journalistic. Of course, these points were all music to Murray's ears, because they merely showed enterprise. A participant later related that Burger used the men's room at one point, and when he returned to dinner, he had somehow failed to zip his fly . . . an apt metaphor for the entire evening.

After Burger left, I walked into the mail room, next to the conference room exit, and pretended to read "the board," copies of files teletyped to New York. I could hear laughter from the brass still in the room as they rehashed Burger's complaints. After a few minutes, Donovan came out, his face all ruddy, en route to the men's room. We were now clearly fast friends. When he spotted me, he slapped me on the shoulder and said, "You know, Dave, haw, haw, you explained Burger's position better than he did! Haw, haw!"

Needless to say, Burger's inquisition dried up most Supreme Court sources over the short term, and his fears of regular "eavesdropping" by the press on Supreme Court deliberations proved unfounded. A few years later, Bob Woodward trained his considerable talents on reporting inside the high court in "The Brethren," methodically interviewing former high court clerks for stories about past cases—and only past cases. As a rule, the secrecy of Supreme Court proceedings remains secure.

I got the leak by bluffing out clerks. I figured out what was likely to happen, and talked to them as if I already knew. They then inadvertantly confirmed it. I also used another reinforcing technique—namely telling the argument that I suspected would be used to justify the decision, the expanded right to privacy, and asking them to supply the best lower court decisions advancing that argument. Instead of steering me away from that argument, they readily complied, effectively re-confirming what they had indicated in other conversations.

David Beckwith

TIME Bomb

Reporters working for Time Magazine championed "Breaking News" long before TV channels "patented" it! Still, it really was another world.

I recall in 1995, Beant Singh, the Chief Minister of India's terrorism-wracked Punjab province was assassinated in a bomb explosion on a Thursday. That was deadline day for us in the Delhi Bureau. I was told the edition could be kept open till Thursday late night for my report. I had only a few hours to put together this dramatic story, but fortunately, I had the best contacts in Punjab, thanks to my years of extensive reporting from the region. Just as I was wrapping up my report to New York, sixth sense made me call Punjab's top police official, K.P.S Gill, one last time, for a final update. Gill was notoriously inaccessible, infuriating, difficult and taciturn. The interview went something like this:

Q: Are you sure it's a car bomb?

A: No

Q: Then why is everyone saying it's a car bomb?

A: Ask them.

Q: I am asking you.

A: I replied.

Q: What is your reply?

A: Your memory is poor.

Q: You said you are not sure it's a car bomb.

A: Hmm.

Q: You are saying you are not sure it's a car bomb.

A: Is this an interview or a stuck record?

Q: If it's not a car bomb, then what could it possibly be?

A: Possibilities—there always are many.

Q: Ok, let me ask you upfront. Do you know what killed Mr. Beant Singh?

A: Hmm.

Q: So what killed Mr. Beant Singh?

A: Wrong Question.

Q: What do you mean wrong question?

A: Like me, you are a student of English literature. Your question is grammatically wrong.

Q: (Exasperated as I am past my deadline) Mr. Gill, happy to discuss Literature with you any other time, but not now. What killed Mr. Singh?

A: Isn't Journalism about the 5 W's. Your question is wrong for that reason too.

Q: Where, why, when, all that I know about this bomb explosion. We know it's a bomb, but we don't know what type of bomb

A: Think again. That's not the only thing you journalists don't know.

Q: Who, who?

A: Yes.

Q: I don't understand.

A: You Journalists never do.

Q: We would if you guys did a better job of explaining.

A: We owe you nothing.

Q: Then don't expect anything. Don't expect accurate reporting. Don't complain later about how journalists always get things wrong.

A: I expect only the worst from journalists.

Q: Why are you being difficult?

A: It's not my job to make your life easier.

Q: My question is simple—what killed Beant Singh?

A: Bomb.

Q: I know that! What type of bomb?

A: That's a better question. A human bomb.

Q: Whaaat! A suicide bomber?

A: Yes.

Q: Are you sure?

A: Yes.

Q: Thanks Mr. Gill. I have to rush to print or I will miss this edition and then it's too late. I asked you this question and you kept deflecting saying I am asking the wrong question.

A: You asked "What killed Beant Singh?"

Q: Who killed Beant Singh?

A: Dilawar Singh.

Q: A suicide bomber named Dilawar Singh killed Beant Singh?

A: Yes.

Q: Thank you so much Mr. Gill.

A: Next time, please remember, I am a cop, not a professor of Literature or Journalism.

I had an exclusive on a breaking story, but Time would hit the stands only next Monday. Surely, some other journalist would scoop my scoop. Never were five days so excruciating.

Monday morning, Indian newspapers were still reporting about the time-bomb that killed the Chief Minister, when TIME came out with its explosive exclusive! When angry journalists demanded to know why he had not told them the truth for the past several days, Gill replied "You asked the wrong question!" And then adding salt to their wounds in his inimical style, he said: "But you are right—there is a TIME-bomb."

A major development in a breaking news story remaining an exclusive five days after the event! That world is extinct. Now we cannot even imagine it existed a mere 17 years ago! But then again, in today's Instant Era, 17 years is perhaps ancient history.

Anita Pretap

The Jones Project

By July 1970 Strobe Talbott, working covertly on the code-named Jones Project, had secretly translated a full draft of the first volume of Nikita Khrushchev's memoirs from a Russian language transcript of tape recordings Khrushchev had made for his family while under house arrest in a dacha outside Moscow. However, there were still translation knots to be untied and ground rules to be finalized before publication. Strobe had requested access to the tape recordings in order to compare them to the transcriptions and clarify his translations, especially in controversial sections. Time Inc had still not voice printed the tapes to confirm that the speech patterns were all in Khrushchev's voice. Victor Louis, the intermediary and manager of the project on the Soviet side, was anxious to see samples of the manuscript to confirm that nothing damaging to Khrushchev had been inserted.

In August Strobe flew to Copenhagen and joined Murray Gart and me. Gart had called a meeting of *Time's* European Bureau Chiefs in Copenhagen as a cover for his rendezvous with Victor. He planned to meet with Victor after the bureau chiefs left town. Gart was not anxious for Strobe to be distracted by a meeting with Victor and did not want him to come to Copenhagen. When I argued that Strobe had to listen to the tapes to preserve the authenticity of the project and obtain some sample tapes to be tested for voice printing, Gart relented. However, he insisted that Strobe not stay in the five star Hotel d' Angleterre with us, but at the modest Hotel Royal so not to attract attention from any of the European *Time* Bureau chiefs attending the meeting.

The three of us and Victor sat around a tape recorder in Murray's suite, carefully listening to sections of the tape I had asked Victor to bring to Copenhagen. We compared the transcript to the translation and discussed the nuances of word meanings. Strobe then urged Victor to lend us the sections of tape long enough for them to be voice-printed. Murray and I left Strobe with Victor and agreed to meet for dinner.

In his personal journal Strobe wrote that when he asked Victor to borrow the tape samples, "He became testy and accused me of trying to take advantage of him. Didn't I realize how vulnerable he was? How vulnerable 'the family' was? Didn't I realize that the tapes were their only 'insurance policy'? The logic of his position escaped me, but the logic was clear: to make him appear to be farther out on a limb than he had ever intended to go—lured there by the wealthy, powerful manipulators with whom he was dealing."

"From this first taste of an adversary proceeding with Victor Louis," Strobe continued," I began to appreciate that for him a business negotiation was an exercise in histrionics. He would cast himself in the role of the naïve but proud amateur entrepreneur who is only just learning how unfair and exploitative the big time can be. His petulance was fine tuned to transmit just a hint of threat that he might walk out at any moment, shocked and disgusted at the bullying greed he had encountered. He bluffed not from a position of faked strength, but from one of faked weakness; he played the game as though he was down to his last chip, mostly because the rest of the table cheated, and besides, he had never meant to get into a game of such high stakes and low sportsmanship anyway. For me—a genuine novice—it was all fascinating and disorienting. I did not know it at the time, but it was a fleeting preview of similar, though more elaborate drama in the years to come."

Victor was still grumpy at dinner that night with the three of us in the Tivoli Gardens until I suggested we also pursue a *Time-Life* film based on the book, using the tapes as the basis for the script. Until that moment Victor had still not agreed to Khrushchev telling his story in the first person and wanted the book to be a biography in the third person with extensive quotes from the transcripts. Now, with the promise of a film, Victor seemed convinced of *Time Inc's* commitment to the project and readily agreed to the plan for the book to be written in Khrushchev's voice from the tapes.

Then came Victor's conditions. The cover and title page should not list Nikita Khrushchev as the author and the book could not be described or advertised by *Time Inc*. as a memoir. After a torturous negotiation we agreed the book would be billed as K's "reminiscences."

The next morning Victor's phone rang in his room. A man identifying himself as a Danish reporter asked him what he was doing in Copenhagen and what he was discussing with representatives of *Time-Life*. Victor hung up the phone without replying and marched furiously down the hall to my room. accusing me of "stupidity" and a "double cross." We had blown his cover and jeopardized the project, he charged angrily. Grabbing a pair of scissors, he began to cut up the tape and throw the pieces into the toilet, muttering "Nobody will get these tapes." I tried to calm him and warned that we had no knowledge of how he had been discovered, but we had to limit the damage and end the meetings immediately. I insisted that we needed the sample tapes and that to destroy them could force the project to be terminated. We had all gone too far toward publication planned for the end of the year to halt it now. Victor, still angry, handed over the rest of the sample tapes and left Copenhagen, as did Murray, Strobe and I, to avoid running into any journalists.

The next day's edition of the Copenhagen's *Berlingske Aftenavis* carried a five-column headline: "Mysterious Russian Journalist Meets American Colleagues." The story, written by Mogens Auning, a former Danish military intelligence officer, reported that "news of international interest is being made in Copenhagen, and important international newsmen are in Denmark." It noted that Victor Louis, Gart and Schecter were occupying rooms on the same floor at the Angleterre. There was no mention of Strobe or Khrushchev in the story, which speculated that the outcome of the meetings might "affect Sino-Soviet relations." The memoirs remained on track and we had agreed on how we would try to prevent reprisals against Khrushchev once they appeared.

On the flight home Gart surmised that Time's Copenhagen stringer Knud Meister, a respected Danish journalist, angered at being cut of the secret meetings, might have been the leak to show his own skills as an investigative reporter. After the first volume appeared in December, 1970 the Copenhagen meeting was cited as the connecting link between Time and Victor Louis, but was never confirmed by those of us who took part.

Before Victor Louis died in 1992 he dictated his own memoirs to former KGB General Vyacheslav Kevorkov, with whom he had worked closely in his role as a KGB asset. The book was published in 2010 in Moscow in Russian.

In discussing the Khrushchev memoirs and their authenticity Victor said: "After a while I've managed to get in touch with most of the authors who wrote on that subject. To my question of why they never thought of the most correct version, that at the end of his life the ex-ruler decided to rehabilitate himself before history and his people, they had replied as one:

'Dear Victor, don't you know that nobody needs the boring truth. No paper will take it. You yourself had benefited from sensations.'

"By that time I gave up trying to persuade people that I was not working for any agency beside my newspaper. But I also learned that it was much more beneficial to belong to a mysterious department than to be just a journalist. I was treated with respect and sometimes even with servility in most countries. I was received by ministers, heads of state, assistants to presidents and vice-presidents. The aura of a man belonging to a mysterious government body, even if it is the secret police, would open many doors for me which would be slammed in front of an ordinary journalist. I have learned to puff my cheeks, spread a tail like a peacock and prophesy as if I really were 'the hand of Moscow'. I had been doing that for so long that I came to believe myself in the high purpose of my missions and finally they have stopped asking me salacious questions."

-0-

At the head of the receiving line in the hushed Great Hall of the People stood Mao Zedong's wife. Jiang Qing, and her three anti-American cohorts, together, the Gang of Four, were responsible for the excesses of the Cultural Revolution of 1966-67. It was now coming to its end. James Schlesinger, hurriedly designated America's ambassador to Mao's funeral, and our party of six was carefully inserted into the receiving line by a protocol officer. I carefully studied Madame Mao's thin face and those of her collaborators before shaking their hands and offering condolences. I had first seen Madame Mao up close during President Nixon's epoch-changing visit in February 1972. She had hosted a performance of the revolutionary opera, *Red Detachment of Women*, which offended Mrs. Nixon with its anti-American slurs.

On the receiving line she was cold and restless, but still sure of herself. Her three Shanghai stooges stood grim and stolid. Clearly, they were a power to be dealt with. In my file I wrote: "The Gang of Four, headed by Jiang Qing, appeared as if they could hardly wait to seize power." During Mao's illness it had become apparent that a power struggle for succession was underway. I wrote about this in my file which was sent through the Chinese cable office.

Schlesinger had been invited to tour China after he was fired by President Gerald Ford on December 2, 1975 after Ford's visit to China earlier in the year.

After Ford's return to Washington, Secretary of State Henry Kissinger had indicated that normalization with the People's Republic of China could not be accomplished until after the 1976 Presidential elections. Chairman Mao had been furious. He had hoped for complete diplomatic normalization with the US and was angry that Ford would not give in to Mao's demand. The Chinese Communists were insisting on a complete US break in relations with Taiwan and the end to US arms sales to Taiwan. Strong pressure from the right wing of the Republican Party forced Ford to delay normalization. Schlesinger, a hardliner on improved nuclear armament to counter the Soviet Union was an ideal choice for an invitation to China.

Ironically, Schlesinger, who was fired by Ford because he pressed Congress for a bigger defense budget for improving nuclear weapons, had become a Chinese favorite. He was seen by Mao as a player against the Soviet Union, whose intercontinental ballistic missiles threatened China. A Schlesinger visit could be interpreted as a warning to the Soviet Union.

Schlesinger was given unofficial state visitor status, short only of an honor guard arrival ceremony. The Chinese provided an airplane to fly our party across China from as far as Sinkiang and Inner Mongolia to Tibet. We were in Lhasa visiting a Chinese-built propaganda museum. She committed suicide, by hanging in her jail cell in 1991 after being stricken with cancer. None of the Shanghai Communist Party leaders, her co-conspirators, survived.

Zhang Chungqiao's death, sentence was, commuted to life imprisonment. He died in 2006

Yao Wen Yuan, sentenced to 20 years in prison, was released and died in 2006, as was Yao Wenyuan, who died in 2006 and dedicated to the horrors of Tibetan feudalism when Chairman Mao died on September 7, 1976. We were quickly flown back to Beijing in time to see people wailing in the streets, distraught at the Great Helmsman's passing. Schlesinger and the members of our party were invited to attend the funeral and file past Chairman Mao's open ceremonial coffin to pay last respects.

The morning after the funeral I was summoned to Jim Schlesinger's suite. Our Chinese hosts were up in arms over what I had filed to Time. Schlesinger appeared unperturbed. "I want to let you know that the Chinese head of protocol angrily protested against what you wrote about the Gang of Four. He said it is an unwarranted interference in their internal affairs. I told them I do not control what American journalists write even if they are guests in China." Jim and I discussed how the Chinese had gotten hold of my copy and what the repercussions might be. Schlesinger showed no serious concern and made no effort to influence what I had written or would write.

I believed my message to the editors, warning of the Gang of Four's intentions, tipped them off that the internal power struggle against Jiang's extremists had come to swords point with their appearance at the funeral. Since there was no other foreign correspondent in the receiving line shaking hands with the Gang of Four, I thought I had a colossal scoop. I was wrong. Time's lead story on the funeral that week eliminated any mention of the Gang of Four in the receiving line and the internal power struggle cracking open. Thirty days later, on October 6, 1976 the Gang of Four were arrested, charged with treason and jailed until their show trial in 1981. At that time all of the Four were air brushed from official pictures of the funeral; Time's prescient editors had already edited them out.

Jerrold Schecter

"Rescuing" Patty Hearst

In the early stages of the Patty Hearst kidnapping in 1974, confusion reigned. I was the San Francisco bureau chief and my bureau was responsible for all of the coverage, with assistance from Los Angeles from time to time. The young heiress' whereabouts were of course a mystery, but from tape recordings left in phone booths and other locations in the city, it was learned that she was being held by the Symbionese Liberation Army. The SLA, as they called themselves, were domestic terrorists who already had taken credit for the assassination of an Oakland schools official and the wounding of another. They were a motley crew of self-stylled anarchists, most of them college dropouts with middle class roots, who had turned violent.

At first, no one knew who exactly made up the SLA and the mood in San Francisco was fear bordering on paranoia. The person seated next to you on the streetcar or in a restaurant might be part of this frightening, unpredictable organization. The atmosphere made the media, the Hearst family and law enforcement a potential target for con artists and crazies.

However, like firefighters who must answer every alarm even if false, those of us covering the story couldn't ignore any tip that came our way, even if it bordered on the outlandish.

Consequently, I took with utmost seriousness a call to the bureau one afternoon asking for me by name, from a fellow who would only describe himself to Pat Newman, the bureau's administrative assistant, as "Hollywood." when I got on the line, Hollywood, in a voice between a rasp and a whisper, identified himself has a member of the SLA.

"We have Patty," he said. "We're holding her in a safe house. The other members of the group are out and left me and my girlfriend to watch her," he continued. "Man, this chick ain't no revolutionary. We should release her. I heard you're an ok guy and I would be willing to release her to you personally. I wouldn't be asking you for anything, but all me and my girl need is money to get out of here before the others find out what we did." That amount would be $250, he said.

I would be directed to an address in Oakland and was to go on the porch and knock and an exchange would be made in which Patty would be turned over to me and I would hand over the money.

I decided to take the chance, mainly to rescue Patty but perhaps get an exclusive. It didn't occur to me until a little later that paying felons to get out of Dodge might be illegal.

I did have enough presence of mind to be skeptical and cautious enough not to go alone. I asked one of the bureau's best stringers, Paul Ciotti, a former naval officer, if he'd like to go along, making it clear he was under no obligation to do so. Paul accepted without hesitation.

So, minutes later, we were crossing the Bay bridge to Oakland, with $250 from petty cash in a brown paper bag and the address of the "safe house."

It was an afternoon in spring, with the sun shining in the quiet Oakland neighborhood of decaying bungalows with a brilliance that seems to be found only in California. The street was deserted and the house we were directed to stood silent and foreboding, curtains drawn, no evidence of any activity. I had Paul stay in the van with the keys in the ignition and instructions that if anything went down wrong, to get out as fast as he could and notify the police.

I stood on the porch and knocked. And knocked. No answer, I went to a pay phone and dialed the number Hollywood had given me. "We saw you pull up in your orange van," he said. "The first time was a test. But you had that white boy with you and that spooked the deal."

It took me a bit, but I convinced him Paul was not a cop. Then I got new instructions. I was to go to a vacant lot several blocks away and place the money behind a certain bush. Then I was to call for the pick-up spot for Patty. "She really wants to go home-and with you," Hollywood insisted, repeating, "This chick ain't cut out to be a revolutionary."

Paul and I found the vacant lot and, again, he stayed in the car with orders to flee if anything went wrong. I found the special bush and placed the bag of money beneath it.

By this time our nerves were nearly at the breaking point. Twice now, we had exposed ourselves to alleged members of a group that had already committed murder and bragged about it.

So this time, when I called Hollywood, I wanted some proof that indeed, he was who he said he was and was holding Patty Hearst.

"I'll prove it to you," he said, somewhat indignantly. "I'll put her on the phone."

After about a half-minute a female voice came on the phone. Her words were slurred and she didn't sound anywhere nearly as refined as I thought young Hearst would.

"Patty," I said, after introducing myself, "I want to take you home. Are you ok?" "Yeah," she responded.

After a couple of innocuous remarks about her coming home, I said, "Patty, I need to make sure you are who you say you are. I need to ask you some personal questions, ok?"

Yeah," she said.

Steven Weed had been Patty's fiance and they had been living in a condo together and attending UC Berkeley when the SLA broke in, beat Weed and abducted the heiress. I had interviewed him and he had stopped by the bureau a couple of times.

"Patty," I said, "I want you to tell me something about you that only your parents would know, that not even Steven might know."

There was a hesitation on the other end of the line. "Well," she whispered finally, "there's this tattoo . . ." Silence.

"Where is the tattoo,?" I asked softly.

"Whaa . . . ?"

"Where is the tattoo," I asked again, trying not to sound too pressing.

A moment of silence and then, "Shit, if I wouldn't tell Steven, why the hell you think I'd tell you?" blurted the alleged kidnap victim.

Hollywood got back on the phone and tried to explain that his hostage was strung out on drugs, but it was too late. The game was up.

Paul and I hurried back to the vacant lot. Fortunately, the bag containing $250 was still there.

We learned later that Hollywood had successfully taken a local TV station for $2,500 using the same scam.

Joe Boyce

Dateline: Timbukto

I was based in the Paris bureau of TIME for six years, from 1988 to 1994, but I often yearned for exotic assignments further afield. Once I persuaded the editors to let me go to Vietnam with Pierre Cardin, when it was still a Communist country: he was the first Western designer to stage fashion shows in Hanoi and Hong Kong.

Years earlier, the Maghreb had been covered out of Paris, which made sense to us in the bureau since Morocco, Tunisia and Algeria, as former French colonies, were largely Francophile. But the Cairo bureau had managed to wrest it away. Still, we in Paris frequently argued, it was logistically impractical to cover those countries from Cairo when the airplane traffic to the Maghreb was largely routed through Paris. There were no direct flights from Cairo to Casablanca for example. And while we were on the subject of jurisdiction, why cover French-speaking West Africa out of Nairobi, when their main flights were routed through Paris, and Nairobi correspondents for the most part didn't speak French?

I would use any excuse to get to the Maghreb to show editors in New York that it really should be covered from Paris. There were trips to Tunisia and Algeria with President Francois Mitterrand. And, for an Olympics issue, I wrote a story out of Constantine on a female Algerian runner criticized by Islamists for showing leg. When a tanker spilled a huge quantity of oil off Morocco, I jumped on it before the Cairo bureau had a chance to flag New York.

Once the oil spill story was filed, I wrote the editors that a great feature I'd wanted to do was ripe for the picking in nearby Niger and Mali. It was the annual Paris-Dakar road rally with thousands of trucks and motorcycles roaring across the desert. I could file a great story, I suggested, on the lone motorcyclists who competed and often floundered in the sand. The French called them "poireaux"—exact translation: leeks. Because they were sunk into the dirt.

So the editors said, fine, since you are down there, you can go do that story—even if it is in the Nairobi bureau's territory.

What I didn't tell them is that there was no air service between Morocco and Niger or Mali. I had to fly back to Paris and catch a plane back to Africa. It was worth risking their ire, if they found out.

After all, how often does one get to file a story with the dateline Timbuktu?

Margot Roosevelt

The Scoop on Bert Lance

As a rookie Washington correspondent in 1976, I stumbled onto a great story about Bert Lance, Jimmy Carter's budget director and fellow Georgian. Lance's financial disclosure forms showed that he was deeply in debt, so much so that he would have trouble paying the interest on all his loans. This fact had somehow escaped the attention of the Senate committee that had confirmed him, not to mention the Washington press corps.

Coming off a year-three run as Time's sports editor, I was not exactly an expert on financial matters. To fill the expertise gap, I sought help from the best person I could think of, someone I had come to know during my first months in the Washington bureau—Stanley Sporkin, head of the SEC enforcement division. To my amazement, Sporkin agreed to go over Lance's financial statements with me, explaining the intricacies and confirming my suspicion that Lance could not afford his debt payments.

After several weeks of reporting in Washington and Georgia, including some teamwork from Ru Rauch, the Atlanta bureau chief, I was ready to interview Lance. We met in his huge office at the Old Executive Office Building, adjacent to the White House. He seemed stunned to find himself being questioned by a twentysomething reporter. I was as astonished at the tableau as he. The interview was bracing but productive and a few days later I filed my dispatch.

I think it fair to say that top editors in New York were not thrilled to have a hot story about one of the new president's top aides and best friends land on their desks. Marshall Loeb, editor of the Nation section, was anything but enthusiastic. By the time the story was published, the edge had been sanded down. What should have been displayed as a big scoop ended up as a single page story under the bland headline, "Budget Chief's Balance Sheet," or something close to that.

When I tried to follow up with additional reporting, Marshall and his colleagues were uninterested. I was left to watch enviously as Bill Safire at The Times picked up the story and ran with it all the way to a Pulitzer Prize.

A year or so later, I discovered what had given Time pause. Time Inc., heavily dependent on the U.S. Postal Service to deliver millions of copies of its magazines every week, had decided to lobby Bert Lance to hold down postal rates. Barry Zorthian, a Time Inc. executive based in Washington, had been handed this assignment by his bosses in New York just as my story was being edited. I learned all this from Barry a year later, who graciously filled me in. "We figure you cost us millions of dollars," he told me. Nice.

-0-

Fresh out of college, I arrived at Time in 1970 as a correspondent in the Boston Bureau. After getting settled, I realized that Edwin Land was working on a new instant photo camera at Polaroid, which was based in Cambridge. I pitched Land and the new camera as a possible cover story, and to my amazement, the idea was accepted and I was given the assignment.

Land, a brilliant inventor and businessman, was the Steve Jobs of his day, turning out sleek, consumer-friendly products and dazzling shareholders and reporters with his masterful performances at Polaroid's annual meetings.

When the time came to shoot the cover photo, John Durniak, the Time photo editor, came up with the brilliant idea of assigning Alfred Eisenstadt. The setting was the front steps of Polaroid headquarters. "Eisie," as Eisenstadt was known, showed up with a single Leica camera and one roll of film. This astounded Land and me. Every photographer I had worked with at Time up to this point had burned through dozens of rolls of film—just for routine stories.

But Land was flattered that the great Eisenstadt was going to take the cover photograph. And Eisie was thrilled to meet the inventor of instant photography. So Land stood on the steps, holding up one of the new SX-70 cameras as though taking a photograph. Eisie snapped a dozen frames. "That's it," he announced. "You're done?" Land asked. "I am done," Eisie said. A few weeks later one of the photos was on the cover.

-0-

As Time sports editor, I had the chance to report and write a number of cover stories. It always surprised me when Henry Grunwald, hardly a sports fan, put a sport figure on he cover, but he seemed to like the change of pace and I ended up producing half a dozen cover stories over the course of a few years. (Reggie Jackson, Jimmy Connors, Dorothy Hamill, Bernie Parent, Charles Finley, among others.)

Grunwald was absent when the time came to do a cover on the "Steel Curtain" defensive line of the Pittsburgh Steelers—"Mean Joe" Greene, L.C. Greenwood, Dwight White and Ernie Holmes. Jay

Rosenstein handled the reporting and I wrote the cover story. As it happened, the Steelers were playing the Jets in New York as he story was in the works, and Ernie Holmes agreed to come by Time to meet with Hedley Donovan, who was sitting in as managing editor.

Jay and I had warned Hedley that Ernie was a robust cognac consumer, and Hedley had a bottle of Courvoisier VSOP on hand as the meeting began. As Jay and I took a small sip from our snifters every few minutes, Hedley and Ernie started draining their glasses. It wasn't long before the bottle was empty. As the meeting ended, Hedley somehow managed to get up from the sofa without falling over and said something vaguely coherent. Ernie popped up as if he had just sacked Joe Namath and seemed stone sober.

Phil Taubman

Playing a Journalist

The best part of the business is the weird juxtapositions we always encountered.

In 2009, at the American Colony Hotel, just after Obama gave his Cairo speech. I was writing about West Bank settlers, spending the days running around hilltop settlements where young men with prayer shawls and beards and guns and wives with a half dozen babies under five lived in trailers within sight of Nablus.

Returning from one of those forays, in the hotel lobby, I encountered, successively, Jimmy Carter (nabbed a quote), Fiat heir Laapo Elkan in an eye-catching powder blue suit, and Julian Schnabel in a dirty white gelabiya. Schnabel was there filming the "Oslo scene" for the movie he was making of his Palestinian girlfriend's book, Miral. He had a cast of extras posing as journalists waiting in the courtyard for the movie version of Oslo accords announcements, and he asked if I wanted to play a journalist. They started filming at midnight and I spent that night sitting next to Frieda Pinto, doing take after take of a scene in which I had to say one line: "Yes, please sit down." When the sun rose on that scene, Time's then-Jerusalem driver, an Israeli archaeologist and I set off on a wild goose chase all over an Israeli army proving ground in the wilderness outside Jerusalem, searching for an archaeological site to which the Mormons in Utah had dispatched a team of young people to excavate, which supposedly held proof of their holy book. Our hunt led deeper and deeper into no man's land, and was fruitless, mainly because our driver got spooked when we got into the artillery ranges. My archaeologist sources assure me the American kids have been digging for Levi back there. Oh and I have an IMDB "actress" entry now.

Nina Burleigh

James Willde and the Naked German

I have heard many versions but this is the one Karsten told about the Saigon bureau: One morning, when Jim Wilde did not appear for a meeting, Frank Mc Cullough sent Karsten to speed Jim's progress. They all stayed in the same old hotel and I believe the office was also located there.

Karsten entered Jim's second floor room and was astonished to see Jim on top of his bed, fully clothed and covered with broken glass and odd splinters of wood. "My God, Jim, what the hell happened?" Karsten asked. Jim looked dazed but finally responded. "Well," he said, "I was quietly lying in my bed, listening to my Foreign Legion dirges when this little drunk German man came in. He was quite naked. He screamed that he hated my music and demanded that I turn it off. When I refused, he ripped the window out of the frame and broke it over me. Then he grabbed my jacket, put it on, and jumped out of the window".

Jim had not moved since.

Since Jim was reported to frequently indulge in the pipe, Karsten thought this might not be an accurate description of what went on. After ascertaining that Jim was not injured, K returned to the office to tell Frank. A group of correspondents went to the Jim's room and he repeated the story, adamant that it was a true recounting of fact.

They then trooped down to the lobby and noticing shards of glass and a few spots of blood, they asked the Sikh doorman if anything unusual had occurred the previous evening. He allowed as how, yes, something very unusual had happened. Around 4 am, he had heard a crashing and tinkling that seemed to come from one of the rooms above. Before he could get outside to look up, one of the guests came tumbling down, his fall arrested by the awning. He was naked except for a sports jacket. "I rushed over to help him", he said, "but he jumped up, brushed himself off and marched back into the hotel. He checked out later this morning". The office never really learned who the German was or why he was running around the hotel naked. They paid for the replacement of the window, Jim's jacket was delivered to him by the dry cleaners, I think with a brief message of apology, and that was the end of that (except for the many times it has been recounted).

Laverne Prager

Colonel Pham Xuan An

The greatest irony, and the greatest surprise, of my years at Time was the discovery, after the fact, that Pham Xuan An was a spy. Mr. An-who was the bureau's esteemed local correspondent in the Saigon Bureau-was a spy for the other side, a spy with the world's greatest cover, a spy on us. I didn't suspect a thing—except once.

I'd landed in Saigon late in 1974 equipped with all the usual advice about how to deal with the quirks of the bureau. One of the caveats was that you couldn't expect ever to quite understand An and how he worked. He just did things, and he came up with the goods. He was considered the best Vietnamese reporter in the game. He would sometimes disappear for a while and then come back to talk.

And that's exactly what happened. Of course, there wasn't much war going on when I first arrived-we were more concerned with street protests by Father Thanh and the Third Way, with deterioration in Cambodia, even with politics in Thailand than with the low-level bang-bang between the ARVN and the VC (we thought) out in the provinces. Still, An briefed me from time to time and it all seemed right. The only hitch came when I left for a Christmas break and, for the first time, An was asked to be the sole correspondent in the bureau and to file copy. He was not used to that and was a bit freaked out.

Only later, shortly before the fall of Saigon, did a single incident give me pause. I was in Bangkok when a good friend, the French AFP correspondent, Paul Leandri, was killed by the South Vietnamese immigration police when he was called in for a tense meeting (they wanted his sources for a story about Montagnards going over to the other side). I rushed back from Bangkok to join the uproar in the western press corps over Paul's murder. But when I ran into An in the bureau at the Continental Palace Hotel, he shared none of my indignation. To the contrary, all he could do was rail against Leandri, complaining that the wire reporter was a haughty Frenchman who had once shown a superior attitude during a confrontation with a South Vietnamese government spokesman.

It was an outburst of outrage that I had never before seen in An-utterly out of keeping with An's normal posture as a western-oriented reporter. How could bad manners justify murder? Where was the dudgeon?

I got my answer only months after the fall of South Vietnam—when it was announced that An was a colonel in the National People's Army and was being decorated for his work as a spy. The pieces fell into place. An had always told me that, politically, he was simply a nationalist. But that, combined with all the pieces others were able to put together later, especially about his early decision to join the Viet Minh and go to college in California, made it clear that his passion for the national cause was much greater and more deeply rooted than most of us had imagined. It was visceral, it was pure, it was sometimes bitterly angry. An's hatred for the colonial masters, the same impulse that recruited him originally to Ho Chi Minh's cause, had burst forth in the moment of Leandri's demise—the tiniest window of insight, at least for me, into An's true political position.

Figuring it all out ex post facto didn't make his antipathy for my murdered friend any more palatable, nor did it assuage my now very mixed feelings about the guy we all seemed to love so much—RIP. But it gave me the smallest retrospective look at a moment that should perhaps have told me more than it did.

Peter Ross Range

Stalking Sosa

New York editors could be shameless about expecting—okay, demanding—miracles from their news service colleagues. Days before Christmas in 1998, editor Dan Goodgame called me and said, in his trademark baritone: "We need you to get some time with Sammy Sosa."

At some point, in the frenzy of pulling together our annual Person of the Year issue, New York (that's what we affectionately called our HQ bosses) decided that I needed to commission and ghost-write an account by Chicago Cub slugger Sammy Sosa of his historic home run race with Mark McGwire, his big swinging rival from the St. Louis Cardinals.

It was a good idea, weighted by bad timing. As Chicago bureau chief, I asked my ace reporter Julie Grace to look into it. If anyone could snag Sosa in the pre-holiday rush, it was Jules. Funny, charming, and disarmingly clever in getting to sources, Julie was my go-to in the clutch.

Julie made a few calls, and returned looking grim: as it happened, Sammy had just hopped on a flight to D.C., where he was scheduled to join President Clinton and Hillary in lighting the White House Christmas tree. Next, Julie said, Sammy was off to his home in Santa Domingo to relax for the holidays. In other words: not a chance.

I called Dan and delivered the bad news. He was silent. Hours later, I arrived in the sun-drenched Dominican Republic and was checking into a hotel, with my dogged news assistant Andrew Keith, fluent in several languages, including Spanish.

Over the next three days, we went after Sosa—who, at some point during his hitting streak had come to loathe media-types. No matter, we sought out Sosa—by car, by email, by phone. At one point, Andrew and I drove two hours along the dark coastline and showed up at a Gloria Estefan concert where we managed to get a few feet away from Sosa backstage—at least until his entourage spirited us offstage and back into the crowd. At the concert, one of Sosa's handlers did slip us a business card with the address of one of Sosa's daytime haunts—a travel agency owned by a longtime friend—and the next day, we hung out there for hours. Sosa arrived at dusk

"What you want?" he said, striding past us. We followed Sosa into the office. I took out my notepad and recorder.

"So tell me," I began, and then the lights suddenly went out. I would later learn, electrical outages were commonplace there. In the dark of the office, I pulled away the curtain and scribbled into the sliver of light on my notepad. After twenty minutes or so, Andrew and I headed back to the hotel, banged out Sosa's first-person essay, emailed it to his agent, got the fixes, reworked it and sent the piece to Goodgame.

"Good work," Dan said, and headed off to a meeting.

That night, Andrew and I ordered a good dinner at the hotel and flew back to Chicago to following morning.

On December 28, 1998, Time published Sammy Sosa's essay under the headline "Mi Amigo Mark", at 665 words.

Ron Stodghill

Getting Bono

For me, Joey Ramone's death on April 15, 2001, had two meanings. On the one hand, as an avid Ramones fan since the 6th Grade, I was crushed to learn that one of my heroes had fallen. On the other, Joey's passing coincided with me finally convincing the higher-ups at TIME Magazine—where I'd been working since mid-90's—to let me do some more hands-on reporting (up until that point, I'd been simply a news desk editor with precious little creative input). The sorry event of Joey's death provided a fitting opportunity for me to contribute.

As it happened, at that morning's story meeting, the editorial staff sat around discussing how to handle the passing of Joey Ramone. Traditionally, when a public figure died, the magazine sought out a fitting contemporary to compose a eulogy. Several editors jumped right in suggesting "Johnny Rotten," largely oblivious to the fact that John Lydon has rarely-if-ever expressed a kind word about the Ramones. Moreover, roping the notoriously thorny Lydon into penning a eulogy for a mainstream American news weekly seemed like an unlikely task at best. Buoyed by my boss' recent show of support for my abilities, I spoke up. "We should get Bono." For the first time at a story meeting, I suddenly had the floor.

I reasoned that since Bono had been floridly outspoken in the past about the Ramones' influence on the nascent U2 (however remote their respective sounds might seem), he'd be a great fit, further citing Bono's tireless penchant for pithy, printable soundbytes and the simple star-power of his name. "Alright, Alex," the deputy managing editor said, "Make it happen."

Within seconds, I was back at my desk making phone calls. After slogging it out as an ersatz "freelance music journalist" since 1989, I knew the procedure for petitioning publicists and record labels, but never before had I been calling under the mighty auspices of TIME Magazine. Where before I'd have been put on hold interminably or simply told to call back some other time, I was now plugged right into the matrix. I only had a few days to make this happen before the magazine went to print, and U2 were on tour in Europe in support of their then-new album *All That You Can't Leave Behind*. It was going to be a difficult game of tag, but I was determined to make it work.

With my news desk buddies gamely picking up the slack of my normal gig, I spent the next two days attempting to pin down a time with U2's people for Bono to call me. It was going to be down to the wire. Friday was the only conceivable time. I confirmed with the U2 camp, stalled with my editors and feverishly made sure my tape recorder worked, hoping to God that I didn't blow this.

After a tense Friday morning, Bono finally called. He rang from a tour bus somewhere in Germany. His voice was hoarse and raspy and he sounded exhausted, but very generous and professional. I politely told him about the space limitations and word counts we were working under and suddenly we were off and running. Bono waxed rhapsodic about the profound effect of the Ramones on his life and his music, barely pausing for a moment's breath. When the connection was momentarily lost, Bono promptly called me back, needlessly apologizing like a mad man. In the end, he gave me a dizzying amount of information (I still have the tape), and kept apologizing and offered to call me back to work on revisions the next day. I thanked him profusely, but told him that the deadline was looming. "Well, I have your number," he laughed and that was that.

I spent the rest of the day transcribing and managed to submit the piece on time. It hit the stands the following Monday and became my first reporting credit for TIME (though you'd never know it *from the online version*). I only wish we'd have had more space.

Alex Smith

Taking KP to the Bang Bang

In 1991, I was the Time bureau chief in New Delhi, and the then editor of Time International was the legendary Karsten Prager, a former foreign correspondent himself who had seen plenty of wartime reporting, especially in Vietnam. He never lost his taste for that excitement, and when he came to visit, which he did on occasion, I knew he'd want to get up close to the main activity of the bureau at that time, which as covering the many wars in the region—Afghanistan, Kashmir, Sri Lanka, to name a few. In fact, he specifically asked what "bang bang" I was planning to take in while he was in town, and that caused me some worry.

Karsten was a heart transplant survivor; in fact for some time he was one of the most successful cases in his generation. I knew he wanted to go to Afghanistan, but I had fresh memories of a trip to Khost that almost ended very badly. A Soviet-made Scud rocket had landed not very far away from me and photographer Bob Nickelsberg when we were literally running from the city as it came under aerial bombardment. I could still feel the concussion that passed through my body. I remember wondering whether, quite literally, my organs might have become detached. Weird, I know, and I was ok, but I wondered if someone whose ticker was literally stitched into place could withstand that. I didn't think we needed to find out.

I sold Karsten on a trip to a new and less concussive battlefield—the city of Srinagar in India's Kashmir, where the Indian army was engaged in a panicked counter-insurgency against Kashmiri guerillas. Karsten was intrigued but there was only one problem: Foreign journalists were banned from Kashmir. In the past I had snuck in anyway by driving overland and posing as a dim-witted lost flyfisherman. But we did not have time for those hijinks. I consulted friends in Srinagar who said they would help. They were not specific. They just said to fly to Srinagar.

As soon as we stepped off the plane, two border guards closed in on me and Kartsen and brusquely ushered us to a desk where a police intelligence official was sitting at a pile of papers. He barely looked at us and asked what we were doing there, "didn't we know all foreigners were banned from Kashmir?" I hesitated, not sure whether to get assertive, beg forgiveness or what. But then out of the corner of my eye I saw, outside the window of the small airport, a friend, who was gesticulating to me in a way that suggested I should stay cool. I got the idea. Just play along. I looked at the intel guy again, and he was busy writing something, based on our passports, which we had handed him. We stood there for a few minutes, and Karsten, who no doubt had been in similar jams many times, just followed my lead. I said nothing. After what seemed like an eternity, he shoved the passports across the table toward us and, without really looking up, tossed his head off to the right, toward the door. I wasn't sure what he meant, but I guessed we should just move. We started walking to the door, and no one stopped us, and then out the door, where the friend and car were waiting. We got in and drove in silence for several minutes. Then I asked what happened.

Our Kashmiri friend said, "You will be reported to the police." I was puzzled, and asked, "Does that mean they'll be looking for us? I don't especially want to get arrested in the middle of the night." Yes," he replied, "but it will take time to file the report, and time for someone to issue an order to find you. By then you will be back in Delhi." Karsten laughed. He knew this was going to be a great trip, and it was.

Ned Desmond

I am often asked if I have a favorite story from my years as a newsmagazine correspondent. My usual answer is that with a combined 27 years at Newsweek and Time, there are way too many to pick just one. In addition to "Brothers", the 1987 Newsweek cover story of 11 black men I grew up with on the South Side of Chicago which led to a best-selling book by the same title and covering Jesse Jackson's 1984 presidential campaign, two stories stand out. Both were done during my years as a correspondent for the Time Life News Service.

The first was getting to meet Nelson Mandela in Cape Town a few hours after he was released from prison. I was sent there to accompany Rev. Jesse Jackson who traveled to South Africa because of unconfirmed rumors that Mandela might be released. At the time, I was a correspondent in the Los Angeles bureau. Rev. Jackson was just being "Jetstream Jesse", injecting himself into yet another high profile news event with or without a formal invitation. Neither Rev. Jackson nor I was particularly welcome in South Africa at the time. When we arrived in Johannesburg, we both received rather chilly receptions. Jackson's came from South African government officials and others including some black leaders and others who met with him more as a matter of international courtesy than anything else. Mine came from the Time Johannesburg bureau chief who was not happy to see an uninvited Los Angeles correspondent encroaching on his turf in the middle of a big story.

Ironically, given Jackson's gift for finding his way onto center stage in the middle of some of the biggest stories in the world, he got to meet with Mandela before many of those who snubbed him, and I got to speak with Mandela and his wife Winnie days before the Joburg bureau chief did his formal interview with Mandela for that week's magazine. Though I filed extensively about Jackson's trip, not a word I sent made the magazine. Instead I ended up writing a freelance story for Emerge Magazine, a black monthly, about an encounter with a White Afrikaner member of the South African Parliament who told he how disappointed he was with Mandela's first speech upon his release from prison.

"I am so disappointed," the man said. "After 27 years, Nelson is still saying the same things he was saying when he went to prison."

"What did you expect him to say?" I replied. "Things are pretty much the same as they were when he went to prison."

Apartheid was still very much alive in South Africa. After an awkward silence, the man changed the subject by noticing a twin-faced Time Magazine watch I was wearing. It was a Time promotion given to me by a Time ad salesman.

"That's a nice watch," he said. "Where did you get it?" When I told him, he said, "It's very difficult for us to get such nice things like that here." What I wanted to say to him, but did not, was that the reason he could not was because the international economic sanctions against his country for continuing apartheid were working. Instead, I told him that when apartheid ended in South Africa, I would send him the watch. Three years later in 1994, the oppressive system was officially ended, and I sent him the watch.

Though no story of mine ever appeared in Time magazine about this trip, it still ranks among the most unforgettable experiences of my professional career, and it was all made possible because I was a member of the Time Life News Service.

Another story that stands out was being the lead reporter on a Time cover story about the Nation of Islam leader Louis Farrakhan. This time, my work, including an exclusive interview with Farrakhan at his palatial Chicago home, was not only published but won the National Association of Black Journalists magazine writing award for 1994. What makes this experience so memorable was not just the cover package, which I believe remains one of the most fair and balanced stories ever published in the mainstream media about this most controversial of African American leaders.

From inception to final edit, tensions flared over the decision to do the story sending shockwaves from the Time Life Building in New York to the Nation of Islam headquarters in Chicago and beyond. Throughout the process, Time editors, reporters and others, particularly Jewish members of the staff, loudly disagreed not only about how we should do the story but whether we should do it at all. One New York-based reporter-researcher burst into tears arguing that it was a disgraceful affront to Jews for the magazine to put such an "anti-Semitic hater" on the cover. If we published such a cover story, she said, she would feel like she had betrayed her race.

I tried to remind her that our job was not to report on people we like, but people who made news. And Farrakhan was big news. There were heated debates about whether the cover image should be a photograph or a classic Time portrait and over the cover language, especially about the use and treatment of the word "hate."

Ultimately, we did what great journalists do and set aside our personal biases and produced a fair, balanced and accurate piece of work that most of us at Time were proud of. I was particularly proud of it because producing that February 28, 1994 cover package entitled "Ministry of Rage" pushed each of us involved to a place we rarely go in order to produce great journalism. Personally, throughout the entire process, I felt like I was walking a tightrope above a pit of hungry sharks. Assigned to get the interview with Farrakhan who was speaking to almost no one in the mainstream media, I had to convince the man—despised and fear by many of the people I worked with; loved and revered by many of my own friends and family—that he could have a voice in the pages of Time without having his words distorted.

On the other side of the tightrope, were white colleagues and editors I had to convince that I would, indeed could, put my journalistic integrity above my blackness. I was well aware that there were many people at Time and other news organizations who believed that black reporters could not be objective covering black civil rights leaders. I had been told as much by an editor at Newsweek while covering the Jackson presidential campaign in 1984. When the top editors at Time, including Managing Editor Jim Gaines, wanted to fly to Chicago and sit in on the interview with Farrakhan, I suspected it wasn't just because they wanted to meet the man up close and personal.

After days of waiting in Chicago for an answer, Farrakhan's people finally called and told me "The Minister" would meet me at his home. My relief was almost indescribable. It wasn't just that I'd landed the interview. But because it had come so close to deadline, there was no time for the editors to fly from New York to sit in on it. I don't know if Farrakhan would have allowed them to sit in. What I do know is that he had given the interview to me, not me and my white bosses. If they had come, I would have lost the respect and trust that got us the interview in the first place and been forever viewed as a black lackey bringing white men where they could otherwise not get by themselves.

The interview, conducted largely at the dining room table in the ornate mansion that had once belonged to Nation of Islam founder Elijah Muhammad, was supposed to last about 20 minutes. It went for nearly two hours and included a personal tour. During the tour Farrakhan took me to a room where he said he liked to relax and play the violin. I have done countless interviews with people of great stature, but this one stands out as one of the most challenging and rewarding of my career.

The interview, however, did not get me completely across the tightrope and away from the perils of the pit below. The last hurdle was the language in the publisher's letter at the front of the magazine where the managing editor generally highlighted the top stories of the week. My heart dropped when I read Jim Gaines' first draft, which said in effect that the reason Time was putting Louis Farrakhan on the cover was to reveal the truth about the racist, anti-Semitic hater who was spreading fear across the country. Such language would have destroyed every other effort we'd made to be fair and balanced in our treatment.

Thankfully, my good friends and colleagues Jack White and Jan Simpson and several other African American members of the staff had the same reaction and together we went to see Jim. To his credit, he told us that if we did not like the language in the letter, then we should rewrite it. We did, telling readers that the reason Louis Farrakhan was on the cover of Time was so that they could read the facts for themselves and hear his voice unfiltered through the usual mainstream media prism and decide for themselves what to think of him.

I never heard directly from Minister Farrakhan what he thought of the cover story. Some of his top aides told me they did not like the painted cover portrait. But one of them did say to me after reading the package, "Nice try, Brother Monroe." That was enough for me.

The stories got both widespread acclaim and criticism, which is as it should be. But the recognition that meant the most to me was winning the National Association of Black Journalists magazine writing award. More than any other accolade that told me that in the highest tradition of newsmagazine journalism, my Time colleagues and I had successfully crossed the tightrope. When I walked off the stage after accepting the award at the NABJ national convention in

Philadelphia and handed it to Jim Gaines, I had never been more proud to be a Time correspondent.

Sylvester Monroe

Veterans' Advice

I don't recall stories so much as I remember the lessons. Johanna McGeary pulled me aside in my first week and said of the mysterious editors in New York, "Tell 'em what you know but, more importantly, tell 'em what you think. They want to know what you think." Bruce van Voorst pushed me to ignore the office politics and just do my job. Chris Redman warned me one day when I was seeking guidance, "Never ask permission. Just do what you think is right and if it turns our to be bad, they will probably give you points for initiative." Those three can take you pretty far no matter what you do in life, and I pass those along now to all the youngsters, including the latest, a 24 year old whizbang out of University of Missouri whose papers, when they finally arrived from Payroll a few weeks ago for me to sign, read simply: "Reporter/Washington/TIME Domestic News Service."

Michael Duffy

Slaughter in Liberia

It was April, 1980 and I had been chief of the Nairobi Bureau for less than four months. I had just arrived in Kinshasa, Zaire for some story or other when I received a message from someone at the

American Embassy. They thought I'd like to know that there had been a bloody coup in the west African republic of Liberia and that President William Tolbert had been slaughtered.

I immediately went to the airport, fought my way through the mob of local thugs, tipsters and hangers-on, and got on a flight to Abidjan, Ivory Coast, where my good friend Leon Dash of the Washington Post was stationed. I wasn't by any stretch of the imagination an old Africa hand, but I knew it was always better to travel with at least one other correspondent in unstable situations. You always wanted to have someone around to watch your back.

By the time I got to Abidjan, other journalists were already swarming, trying to figure out how to get into Liberia. Pranay Gupte of the New York Times, a guy named Tony from the Voice of America, Nick Profitt from Newsweek and David Lamb of the LA Times were already there. I had one complication to deal with: I didn't have a visa for the Ivory Coast and the immigration officer didn't want to admit me. I solved the problem the old fashioned way, with a bribe.

A day or two later, we got word that the airport in Monrovia might be open and the six of us boarded a small chartered plane and flew out. When we landed a couple hours later in piercing sunshine and the kind of humidity that turns strong men into pulp, a band of nervous looking soldiers armed with a motley assortment of weapons rushed out and surrounded the plane, demanding to know who were were and why we had come. They seemed to think that we might be the first wave of an armed force invading Liberia to reverse the coup and put the old regime back in power.

I don't recall exactly how we got out of that mess, but I remember that they confiscated all of our weapons, which means that one of them pocketed the VOA guy's little Swiss pen knife before sending us on our way.

We set up in the Ducor Hotel, a nice place that like much else in Liberia reminded me of home back in America. Founded by freed slaves during the 19th century, Liberia was a lot like rural Alabama or Mississippi as seen in a funhouse mirror. There were real hamburgers, and peanut butter and Breyers ice cream just like back home. The cops wore uniforms modeled on those of the NYPD, and the currency was used American dollars. It was really eerie.

We soon learned that the coup had been mounted by a small band of noncommissioned Army officers who called themselves the Peoples Redemption Council. Their leader was a sergeant named Samuel K. Doe—who the VOA guy immediately started calling Earnie Kaydo, after the soul singer whose most popular hit was "Mother-in-law" ("the worst person I know is my mother-in law, mother-in-law").

But I digress. Word soon came that Doe was going to have a press conference the next day to explain why he and his fellow PRC members had risen up against the Liberia's ruling elite, descendents of the freed slaves who founded the country and known as Amerigo-Liberians, on behalf of the indigenous folk known as the Country People.

The presser turned out to be quite a show. By then camera crews from the BBC and other networks had arrived, along with dozens of print reporters. At the appointed time, Doe strutted up to the podium, dressed in a U.S. style special forces uniform with a swagger stick under his arm and an enormous nickleplated pistol dangling from a shoulder hoster. He read a short statement, very haltingly, then said he would answer two questions.

The first one came from the BBC correspondent, who asked Doe in impeccable British tones whether, considering that he was a drop-out from a Liberian (heavy stress on Liberian) high school, he really felt qualified to be a head of state.

Doe fixed him with a glare and responded, "Yes."

That was all he said.

I can't remember if there was a second question.

In any case, Doe marched out and his newly appointed minister of information, Gabriel Nimely, took his place at the podium. "Ladies and gentlemen of the press," he declared, "there are are going to be some executions tomorrow and you're all invited."

The next day was a classic mix of absurdity and horror. As a group of us sat down for breakfast in the Ducor restaurant, we were approached by a couple of tired looking men who looked a bit like Mutt and Jeff. One was short and chubby and dressed in a cowboy hat. The other was tall, lean, and wearing a battered safari jacket.

"Say, are you fellows foreign correspondents?" asked short and chubby in a Texas drawl. "We're from the Fort Worth Star Telegram. We would have got here yesterday, but we took the wrong plane and flew into Lagos, Nigeria. We just got here a little while ago."

It turned out that Fort Worth is the home of a large seminary from which the slain President Tolbert had graduated. So for the Star Telegram this faraway coup had a local angle. The short chubby guy was a reporter whose name I've forgotten. The tall, laconic guy was a photographer named Larry Price, and I'll never forget him.

After we had exhausted all the jokes we could wring from the ineptitude of our newly arrived colleagues, we all headed down to the Barclay Training Center, an army installation on the shore of the Atlantic where the executions were going to take place. A huge crowd had already gathered and there was a group of soldiers drawn up in sloppy ranks on the beach. Some of them had obviously been drinking heavily. Between them and the waves, workmen were planting nine telephone polls in the sand.

They hadn't finished the work when a yellow bus drove up, filled with soldiers and what turned out to be thirteen frightened officials from the fallen regime who had been condemned to death by a military tribunal after hearings that might have lasted 15 minutes or so. As we watched, soldiers yanked nine of the men out of the bus, and marched them to the telephone polls, dragging them if necessary.

Leon, who had been to Liberia several times, recognized some of the hapless men, including Charles Cecil Dennis, a distinguished diplomat who had been Minister of Affairs.

The next few minutes were unbearable to watch. As the crowd cheered, the drunken soldiers fired volley after volley of shots at the men lashed to the telephone polls. I watched as bullet after bullet whizzed past Cecil Dennis who, unlike most of the victims, stood as erect as a soldier at attention, defying his fate. I could see the misfired shots kicking up little wavelets in the ocean behind him. At last an officer came out and cut Cecil Dennis down with a burst of fire.

All the while, the four condemned men still in the bus had been watching this gut-wrenching spectacle. The bodies of the dead men lashed to the telephone polls hadn't even been removed when soldiers stormed unto the bus and dragged the remaining victims out to the beach. They were tied to the polls and slaughtered in a barrage that probably lasted a few minutes but seemed to go on much, much longer. Then the soldiers in the disorderly firing squad romped out of their ranks, climbing unto the bodies and striking heroic poses like hunters showing off their trophies.

One of the photographers taking pictures was the tall laconic Texan, Larry Price, whom we had met only a few hours before. His stunning depictions ran with my first hand account of the grizzly event and were later awarded the 1981 Pulitzer Prize for spot photography.

As we left the scene, a tractor trailer pulled up. It was loaded with more telephone polls.

-0-

In November 1983, the day after the Rev. Jesse Jackson formally announced his candidacy for the Democratic presidential nomination, another black journalist from a major newspaper and I flew with him and one of his top aides from Washington to Tuskegee, Alabama.

On arrival, we were met by a local activist who drove the four of us in his white van to the campus of Tuskegee University, the famous school founded by Booker T. Washington. Jackson and his aide, Lamont Godwin, began discussing campaign business. Godwin, an economist with a Ph.D from I think the University of Texas, started talking about various persons being "Jew boys." Jackson mentioned that he would soon be in "Hymietown," by which he meant New York City. He also used the name, "Hymie," in a collective reference to Jews as a group, who might be opposed to his campaign because of his prior embrace of the Palestinians

Both the other black journalist and I were stunned by Jackson's casual use of such inflammatory language and flummoxed about how we should respond to it. There had been no explicit agreement on the "ground rules" governing the ride in the van—whether it was on or off the record. Yet it seemed pretty obvious that Jackson and his aide believed that they could speak freely in front of us and that we would not report what we had heard. They would never have lapsed into that kind of talk if they believed it would wind up on the pages of a news magazine or one of the most widely circulated newspapers in the U.S.

Later that day, the other journalist, who was a good bit closer personally to Jackson than I was, and I talked about how to handle what we had heard. He told me that he had heard Jackson use the same ugly words in several telephone conversations. Though this was the first time I had ever heard Jackson use anti-Semitic epithets, he had used similarly loaded language about other racial groups with me while I was reporting a cover story on his potential run for the White House a few months earlier.

He had, for example, referred to blacks by what is now known as the N-word, to homosexuals as "faggots," and to Hispanics as "Spics." But he had only uttered those words after I had agreed to, in his phrase, "take your reporter's cap off and put on your black hat"—which I translated as his way of saying, "this is off the record." That meant that I had agreed that I could not report on it.

As uncomfortable as I was with the arrangement, I felt honor bound to uphold it, as I had upheld similar deals with other politicians, mostly white. In those instances, there was a clear demarcation between what was on and off the record—what could be reported and what couldn't be. Usually, this allowed the source to more openly discuss a controversial issue. Occasionally, it allowed the source to tell a ribald joke, as when a congressman from a Midwestern state recounted salacious stories about the supposedly loose sexual behavior of women from a bordering state, without fear that it would wind up in print.

But the conversation in the bus was different, and the ground rules, if any, were ambivalent. Like most black reporters of my generation, I had been drawn into journalism by the civil rights movement of the 1960s and I identified completely with the black struggle of which Jackson had emerged as, perhaps, the most prominent leader. Since childhood, I had heard fellow blacks, when talking amongst themselves, refer to each other by the N-word, whose usages were remarkably flexible. I had often done it myself. Depending on context and intonation, it could be used to express everything from affection and solidarity toward other blacks to disgust and contempt for them in those private conversations. But I would have bristled if anyone outside the group—i.e. any white person—had used the term. Indeed, on one occasion, I had upbraided and threatened to punch out a colleague at TIME for crossing that line.

Beyond that, I didn't believe that Jackson, who grew up in segregated South Carolina with little or no exposure to Jews, was really an anti-Semite. Though he had outraged some prominent Jews by hugging Yassir Arafat on a highly-publicized tour of the Middle East during the 1970s, he had maintained close personal and working relationships with others. But I also knew that Jackson was a manipulator who had absolutely no qualms about co-opting black journalists by appealing to their sense of racial solidarity. Using ugly racial language in seemingly candid conversations was one of his ways of trying to draw us in, compromising us by making us feel that he trusted us with his little secret. Taking off our reporters caps and putting on our black caps was tantamount to joining his team. I felt insulted by his seeming belief that we could be so easily swayed.

What to do? Over the next few weeks I gingerly discussed the matter with a few of the other veteran black reporters on the campaign. Some said they had heard similar language, but others denied it. Those who had heard it seemed to agree that the remarks had been off the record and that we could not write about them. But I still felt uneasy. I filed a long item to TIME's National Memo, a weekly in-house confidential newsletter in which correspondents shared off-the-record and unconfirmed stories that they were working on with the editors back in New York. In it, I drew several contrasts between Jackson's public and private conduct, including his use of the words "Hymie" and "Hymietown." Though items in the National Memo often provoked exploratory queries from editors seeking to find ways to turn them into stories, in this case there was silence. I never heard a peep.

That's where things stood until early January 1984, after Jackson returned from a triumphant journey to Syria, where he had arranged for the release of Lt. Robert Goodman, a U.S. Navy flyer who had been in captivity there since his plane was shot down in a bombing run over Lebanon. Ronald Reagan had sent Air Force One to bring home Jackson and his party, which included Rev. Louis Farrakhan of the Nation of Islam. (Among the traveling press was AP bureau chief Terry Anderson, who was later taken captive by Hezbollah militants in Lebanon and held hostage for eight years.) The mission concluded with a joyous celebration at the White House.

Jackson's stock had never been higher. He started going up in the polls for the upcoming New Hampshire primary. His press entourage expanded dramatically as other news organizations leaped to cover a candidacy that many had written off.

And then the boom fell. Near the bottom of a long story by Washington Post reporter Rich Atkinson came this brief passage: "In private conversations with reporters, Jackson has referred to Jews as `Hymie' and to New York as `Hymietown.' And all hell broke loose.

It turned out that Atkinson had learned about Jackson's ugly words from Milton Coleman, a veteran black reporter who had briefly joined the Jackson press corps. Coleman later wrote that in a conversation at the private aviation terminal in Washington, Jackson "talked about the preoccupation of some with Israel. He said something to the effect of the following: 'That's all Hymie wants to talk about, is Israel; every time you go to Hymietown, that's all they want to talk about.'" He also wrote that since other journalists covering Jackson's campaign had heard similar remarks, he considered them to be "sorta semi-public."

As I said, all hell broke loose. Nasty stories charging that black journalists had covered up what they knew about Jackson's secret anti-Semitism started coming out. In one instance, a black correspondent for one of the nation's leading newspapers was replaced by another black correspondent whom editors believed would "get the goods" on Jackson. Jackson began to drop in the polls under a non-stop barrage of questions.

It got really ugly in Chicago where Jackson was scheduled to address Savior's Day, an annual observation in honor of the late founder of the Nation of Islam founder Elijah Muhammed. He invited a handful of black journalists who had been on the campaign trail to his home where his wife Jacqueline was preparing a dinner of pork chops. There was a lot of joking about whether Farrakhan, who like Jews and mainstream Muslims, kept strick Kosher would put us through a "pork detector" when we arrived at the rally.

It turned out to be a raucous and nasty spectacle. While Jackson sat on the stage, Farrakhan whipped his followers into a frenzy with an angry speech warning Jews that "If you harm this brother (Jackson), it will be the last one you harm."

And I had a conversation that I've rarely talked about since, with one of Jackson's ministerial advisers, a well-known black clergyman whose name I don't feel comfortable revealing. I asked him what advice he was giving Jackson about handling the persistent questioning he was facing about the issue, and he gave me a reply I'll never forget: "I'm going to tell him to lie about it. He has to preserve his political viability. He can't admit this."

I was appalled. I had not expected to hear such a cynical response from a man of the cloth, nor to get what amounted to a confirmation of what I already knew about Jackson's loose talk. I was also in a pickle because I had told TIME's editors about Jackson's language in that National Memo item. That night, over drinks with other journalists at Chicago's Hyde Park Hilton, I reached a decision. The next day, as we flew off in Jackson's campaign plane, I had a brief conversation with another of Jackson's ministerial advisors. I told him that I had months ago reported what I knew about Jackson's bigoted phraseology to my editors and that if he kept denying using the language, I would have no choice but to do a story that said he was simply lying. The minister said he would convey the message.

Not long after that, Jackson delivered an emotional speech at a synagogue in New Hampshire, admitting that he had said those hurtful word and asking for forgiveness. I think he used the phrase, "God is not finished with me yet," which he later repeated in a deeply moving address at the Democratic convention in San Francisco. TIME did a straightforward, and I thought superficial, story on Jackson's confession.

I don't know if the conversation I had with his ministerial adviser on the campaign plane had any part in persuading Jackson to come clean. I've never discussed it with Jackson himself. I've always had ambivalent feelings about these events and the way I covered them,. My second thoughts have to do with the ambiguous circumstances under which I had first learned about Jackson's behind the scenes rhetoric, and my unsureness about what ground rules applied. Nearly 30 years later, I'm still trying to figure it out.

Jack E. White

Thankless Assignments

Sarajevo February 1984. Witnessing a rising war at Pension Bob. With a few exceptions, like Sports writer Tom Callahan, correspondent, BJ Phillips and her translator Jane, who were staying in the Olympic village, the Time team (Edit and Pix) was packed together at the "Pension Bob" up the hill from Sarajevo. Rooms were the size of closets and the thin wooden partitions could not dampen the heavy snoring of neighbors. After a few days tensions started rising, between Edit and Pix—no wonder with such a group of strong personalities: Editor Karsten Prager (and his wife Laverne), Bureau Chief John Moody, Correspondents Bill Rademaekers and Jack Skow, Vienna stringer Traudl Lessing, photographers Neil Leifer and Rudi Frey (who brought along his female Italian cook), and Gérard Bouland, one of the Paris bureau's telex operators. Bill, Gérard—with his precious telex machine—and I had flown from Paris to Dubrovnik and then driven through Mostar before arriving in Sarajevo.

Both Edit and Pix had drivers and a fleet of Mercedes. Invariably every morning one of the photo team's cars had punctured tires—Frey, who is Austrian, had rubbed the Bosnians the wrong way, stirring up past historical memories and that was their way of vengeance.

One morning we were woken up by a horrible shriek: a piglet had been slaughtered in the nearby farm house and that same evening had landed on the table where Rudi was playing host to his photographer pals. Bill Rademaekers who was having an early dinner that night was asked by Rudy to get out of the dining room. A nasty shouting match followed. And soon after a blanket was hung, separating the Edit space from the Pix one. Paris Bureau Photo Editor Barbara Nagelsmith who joined our group later on in the game could not believe her eyes. "It was like a war zone", she recalls. This was like a premonition of what was to come, but that's another story

-0-

Barcelona: Summer 1992 Paul Witteman defending his troops:

Late one Friday night, acting bureau chief Paul Witteman and the Edit group arrived on the TIME cruise ship, anchored in the Barcelona harbor, where the business side had been lavishly entertaining their Olympic celebrity guests. But the Edit team, exhausted and starving after closing the magazine, was told that the kitchen was closed and no more food would be served. Witteman went ballistic. Soon after some leftovers appeared, and we were basking in bubbles.

-0-

Lillehammer: Winter 1994

Worst memory: covering the bobsleigh events and having to answer a checkpoint from Howard Chua: what is the speed of an eye blink? Driving every morning on icy roads to the bobsleigh venue at minus 25 degree Celsius temperature to watch the trial runs and track down Prince Albert of Monaco whom I had to address as "Monseigneur."

Best memory: Meeting Paul Witteman at our favorite local delicatessen to share hot camembert with gooey strawberry sauce.

-0-

Lech Walesa at Maxim's:

I seem to remember that the News Tour group was supposed to meet Lech Walesa in Warsaw but on that date Walesa was in Paris, having been invited by the French Trade Unions. So the bureau had to arrange a last-minute secret meeting with him and the group. The TIME plane made an unscheduled stopover at Charles de Gaulle airport, for only of a few hours, so that this group of high-powered capitalists could meet with Walesa, for a 6 am breakfast at the Maxim's airport restaurant. Sandy Burton and I had to scramble to find Polish-English interpreters. On the day before the meeting we rehearsed the bus route to the airport with one of Walesa's advisors and found a way for Walesa to enter the airport building incognito: the Maxim's kitchen back door. Unfortunately the restaurant's walls were not sound proof and anyone passing by could hear the whole debate. So much for secrecy.

A few days later martial law was imposed in Poland and both Walesa and his advisor were arrested.

-0-

On my way to Hanoi, I had to stop at the Bangkok airport, where a member of the bureau handed me a box full of soap bars, because there would be no soap at the Hanoi Government House, the official government residence for foreign dignitaries, where half the News Tour group was staying. On departure day, around 6 am, there was no staff in the kitchen to serve breakfast, so I had to rope in guests to set the table, and to convince Hank Luce to monitor the only toaster available.

-0-

In and out of the airport to meet Jerusalem Bureau Chief David Halevy in the transit section of the Zurich airport. We had never met before, but he had to entrust me with a bunch of highly sensitive documents about Menahem Begin's health, that had to be pouched from Paris to New York.

-0-

Manilla, Mindanao, the Philippines: Fall 1983

Visiting Hong Kong Bureau chief Sandy Burton, along with Judy Fayard, Life's Paris bureau chief, who was on her way back to Paris from China, where she had been covering Chinese athletes preparing for the 1984 Olympics. On our first night in Manila, we ended up at the home of Joyce, a friend of Sandy's where a lively party was going on. Very late that night, Judy ended up on top of the piano, dancing and singing with Senator Homobono Adasa from Cagayan de Oro.

A few days later Sandy, photographer Sandro Tucci and I took off to Mindano with Adasa. Sandy, busy with interviews with Filipino army generals, suggested I go off to tour the island on a jeepney with a total stranger that Sandy had judged (from a one minute encounter in the hotel lobby) trustworthy. For security reasons he insisted we share the same room during the trip. We later discovered that he was the local CIA agent . . . but he had indeed been very proper.

On another night, I returned to our hotel late, but Sandy was still out. Then suddenly I heard the noise of a chaotic scene in the corridor, and Sandy burst into my room, very distraught, running from the grasp of a Filipino general she had dined with after interviewing.

-0-

I was assigned to take the Concorde to New York to courier pictures of Ivan Lendl, winner of the French Open, and discovered that Lendl was sitting two rows in front of me.

-0-

The Paris Office: Fending off a mentally disturbed and drunken English mercenary who had just gone awol from the French Foreign Legion, and had burst in the office on Avenue Matignon to tell his story to Time. Going awol from the Foreign Legion was then liable to long-term imprisonment

Trying to convince the bureau's accountant James de Bovet, the epitome of an English gentleman that there were mice in my office at Matignon (I get hysterical at the sight of one). For the next ten days, upon his arrival in the morning he would find a dead mouse on his desk, deposited by Marc Bénard, a dedicated telex operator.

Turning a blind eye when a correspondent who was supposed to be at his post in a far away country appeared in the office accompanied by a gorgeous blond woman in a voluminous fur coat, who said to me: Claire, you have never seen me, right?

Shipping back ONE shoe to a correspondent who had inadvertently left it behind at some Parisian lady's flat.

Best memory of all: Paris, Nov 2007

My farewell dinner to Time (after 32 years) with almost all my bureau chiefs: Greg Wierzynski, Henry Muller, Jordan Bonfante, Chris Redman, Jamie Graff, Paul Witteman (Tom Sancton could not make it and Friedel Ungeheur was no longer among us).

Claire Senard

A Logistical Miracle Saves A Manchurian Scoop

"This is a ghost city," I cabled *Life*'s editors in New York on October 29, 1948. "Most of the government's troops are camped near the rail sidings waiting evacuation. In the heart of the metropolis freezing blasts whistle down the broad empty thoroughfares. Shop fronts, and even army pillboxes at the main intersections are boarded up. Jagged walls in factory areas, built by Japanese invaders, blasted by American bombers during World War II, and later pillaged by the Russian occupation forces, stand silhouetted against the steel-gray sky. Mukden, the capital of China's richest industrial area, looks as ragged as the half-frozen refugees picking their way through the debris on the few streets where people can still be found."

Just a few days earlier, in a rare interview with Generalissimo Chiang Kai-shek in Beijing, he had told *Life* photographer Jack Birns and me that the strategic city would be defended to the last man. Now, it was obvious that it and the rest of Manchuria, a chunk of China bigger than California, Oregon, and Washington state combined, had just been wrested from his control. Remarkably no other reporters or photographers were there, a situation hard to imagine with today's media saturation of even the smallest most remote war.

At the U.S. consulate we found everything moving in reverse. Instead of preparing to evacuate, the 56-year-old Consul General Angus Ward and his staff were busy digging in for the long winter, barricading themselves behind a year's supply of canned food and flour. Out in the courtyard an Army major was chopping up a shortwave radio transmitter with an ax. All the files had been flown down to Qingdao for safekeeping. But the State Department had ordered the consular personnel to stay put. The hope was that they might start a dialogue with Mao's hardliners that had been broken off two years ago when an exasperated General George Marshall finally gave up trying to mediate a peace agreement between Mao and Chiang.

Out at South Field thousands of civilians were waiting their turn to board one of the C-46 and C-47 cargo planes shuttling back and forth to Tianjin. As soon as an arriving crew finished tossing out it's cargo of rice, a wild human phalanx would surge towards the plane's open hatch. Kicking, punching, and clawing, men, women, and children would then try to fight their way aboard. The pilots had to stomp their cowboy boots on the outstretched fingers of those still trying pull themselves up into the already overloaded planes.

Twenty-four hours later photographer Birns and I were back in Shanghai. The Central News Agency still hadn't announced the fall of Mukden. Even more surprising none of our reporter friends at the Foreign Correspondents' Club had caught wind of the disaster.

The challenge now was to get the pictures and exclusive eyewitness account into the issues of *Life* scheduled to be put to bed that night in New York. My eyewitness account that went by cable posed no problem. But Birns's dozen rolls of undeveloped film had to go by plane. And the transpacific flight on Pan-Am's propeller-driven DC-4s took 40 hours, minus the 13 hours of clock time gained by crossing the International Date Line.

Fortunately our editors in New York refused to let the almost impossible logistics deny us a scoop, even if it meant the expense of holding the presses for 24 hours. They ordered a portable photo lab set up in the San Francisco airport. Processed between planes, the wet negatives were then couriered in jars of water to Chicago, where *Life*'s printing plant was located. But Chicago was socked in and the plane landed in Cleveland. A charter pilot was persuaded to fly the courier to fogbound Chicago. Holding the now-dried negatives against the window of a taxi, the managing editor, who had flown out from New York, was able to select five pages of pictures on the way to the printing plant.

People looking at *Life* the next day had no idea of the extraordinary effort that it took to get those pages into their copy of the magazine—and probably couldn't have cared less. But knowing that millions of Americans were seeing those pictures and reading that story made Birns and me feel pretty good. The thought, too, that Chiang Kai-shek could no longer hide the truth that a vast industrial province had just slipped from his grasp, made us feel that we were helping to set the record straight on China.

-0-

Slithering through the jungle of Malaya was an army of 5,000 Communist insurgents. Divided into regiments they had been quietly gaining strength since the Japanese occupation. Suddenly in 1948 they went on a rampage, Killing and burning, they launched an all-out war aimed at driving out the British.

The military leader of the insurgents, *Life* photographer Jack Birns and I soon learned, was Lau Yew, a 34-year-old Malay Chinese who ironically had been feted in London as a World War II guerilla hero.

Whole companies of Gurkha troops had been combing the jungles unsuccessfully for Lau Yew. Captain Bill Stafford, the police superintendant in Kuala Lumpu finally decided the only way to fight Lau Yew's kind of terror was by employing similar terror tactics himself. The stocky, barrel-chested Stafford, nicknamed the Iron Broom, had the reputation of always spoiling for a fight. He carried a pair of submachine guns slung over each shoulder and a revolver tucked in his belt. He even slept with a pistol under his pillow in a bedroom lined with mirrors to spot any intruder.

Jack and I were told the only way to appreciate the Iron Broom's raw courage was to follow him into the jungle. Not all of his sweeps bagged terrorists. In fact we spent several nights tagging along on raids that got us nothing more than barked shins and a rash of insect bites. Then one morning a frightened Communist informer was led into Stafford's headquarters. The informer claimed he knew where Lau Yew was hiding.

"I don't trust the bastard," Stafford whispered to me. He had good reason to be suspicious. There was a $400 bounty on any terrorist killed or captured. But several hours of interrogation finally convinced Stafford to risk it. "Probably a wild-goose chase," he warned. "But if you want to, come along."

We left Kuala Lumpur at 2 A.M. the next day with the nervous informer hidden in the back of Stafford's weapons carrier. About a mile out of town the red taillights of our convoy of jeeps and several more weapons carriers blinked off. Tires crunched the gravel as the vehicles pulled off the onto road's shoulder. Stafford first recommended that Birns and I stay with the vehicles, but then relented and let us go along.

The squad moved down the road. Occasional flashes of heat lightning caught the black-suited men and held them silhouetted against the sky for an instant, and then let them slip back into the night.

Stafford motioned to the informer up ahead and whispered to his Chinese sergeant, "If you think he's pulling a fast one, shoot him."

The squad stopped. Coconut torches carried by a group of tappers on their way to work in the rubber plantation where the informer claimed Lau Yew was hiding, flickered dimly in the road ahead. Stafford signaled for the squad to move off the road and into the jungle.

For an hour we trudged through dense thicket. Moist ferns brushed our faces. I could hear feet tripping over roots and carbines catching in vines. "You've got to be crazy to do this," muttered Stafford. "I think the bloody bloke's lost."

When the stars faded and pink streaks lit the sky I could see we were huddled on a ridge. A thick mist rose from the hollow below. We followed Stafford and the informer down the steep slope into the mist. A narrow path opened into rows of freshly tapped rubber trees with white driblets of latex coming from the spiral cuts in their bark.

The rows of rubber trees ended abruptly on the rim of a deep basin blanketed with yellow kunai grass. At the bottom were three flimsy shacks beside a little brook. The informer pointed to the center shack where a woman puttered with her morning chores. It was a peaceful scene.

The squad fanned out as Stafford led them cautiously down into the basin. Creeping through the deep kunai grass, they moved toward the shacks.

As they approached, the woman glanced up and shrieked. Three men burst from the house brandishing revolvers. The crack of carbines firing in rapid succession rang through the ravine. There was another scream followed by more shots. Then it was quiet. Two terrorists were dead. Six women and two other men were in custody.

Stafford hurried up the hill where one body lay in the grass. It looked like Lau Yew. Blood trickled from his neck. A Lugar lay on the ground beside him. Two of Stafford's men came up and dragged the body down toward the now handcuffed prisoners while other members of the squad hauled maps, rifles, uniforms, and a burlap sack of ammunition from the shack.

One of the squad members recognized Lau Yew's wife among the prisoners. "See if it's her old man," Stafford said. They forced the woman close to the corpse. She stared blankly at it and nodded.

"All right," Stafford yelled. "Let's burn this place and get out. There may be more of them around." A squad member lit a torch and touched it to the thatched roof. In a moment the shack was in flames. Jack snapped my picture standing in front of the clouds of thick yellow smoke.

I was about to zip up my shoulder bag containing the exposed rolls of film Jack had shot when the whole hollow exploded in a blast of Bren guns and rifles firing in rapid bursts. A band of some 30 guerillas had been hiding in the jungle and were counterattacking. Bullets spat in the dirt. Two hand grenades exploded. A third bounced harmlessly on the ground.

Stafford and his men sprawled on the ground with their faces pressed hard against the turf, crawling toward a brook, and then burrowed into the kunai grass on the other side.

I clutched the shoulder bag and and then dove headlong over the embankment, shattering my glasses on the ground and rolling into the brook. A few feet away two squad members poked their Tommy guns through the deep kunai grass and fired ear-splitting bursts directly over my head. I crawled from the creek into the grass behind them.

In the grass I noticed that my film bag was open—and empty. In my wild dive for cover I had dropped the whole photographic record of the raid. I shouted for Birns, but there was no answer. For ten minutes I groped around, calling his name, expecting any moment to stumble on his body. When I finally found him he was crawling around, waving one of the cop's revolvers looking for me. "I thought you were dead," he said.

The house still burned fiercely and more guerillas were slipping down the hill into position behind it. Birns and I lay flat, afraid to raise our heads to take pictures. One of Stafford's weapons carriers suddenly appeared in the narrow cart tracks near our position.

"Here come the Gurkhas! Here comes the army!" shouted Stafford, hoping the sight of the weapons carrier would fool the guerillas. His men took up the cry and moved forward in a fake charge. The firing finally subsided until only the sharp report of single shots echoed in the hollow. Then it was quiet. The guerillas had gone as suddenly as they had come. "That was bloody promiscuous shooting," Stafford growled.

One of the men raced back to the smoking house and found our film lying in the mud. Nearby were the crumpled bodies of the eight prisoners with their arms still handcuffed behind them. Stafford claimed they had been killed in the crossfire. But I believe his men had intentionally sprayed them with bullets during the counterattack. His killer squad, after all, was not trained to show mercy.

Roy Rowan

The Death Beat

During the mid-90s, I wrote stories on death row claims of innocence and helped save four men. Bobby Shaw, a retarded share-cropper's son with paranoid schizophrenia, was the first. His voices ordered him to kill twice, and with a half-formed IQ he obeyed despite liking his victims.

A Missouri judge rejected an insanity plea. Bobby was assigned an inexperienced lawyer, and one of the state's staff psychiatrists testified that he was maybe "a little depressed." Instead of a hospital for the criminally insane, Bobby went to The Row.

I visited him at Potosi State Prison with an appeals lawyer named Sean O'Brien and a muscular guard introduced as Tom. Death row was in the prison's sub-basement. I remember thinking about lost souls crossing over, probably because I was nervous interviewing a psychotic killer. It got worse when I realized O'Brien and Tom hadn't followed me into the interviewing room. "I've got other clients to see," O'Brien said, "and Tom has to take me. The door locks from the outside, so everything is secure."

Something in my cognitive apparatus passed a message to my brain's emergency room. I was about to be locked in with an unstable killer and no guard in sight. "You'll be fine," O'Brien added. "Bobby's door is also locked." I whispered a feeble joke to myself. "I hope his voices like me."

A tall black scarecrow with angular movements, bony arms and saucer-eyes entered. I shook off my fear and got focused. Bobby had lost his legal right to be judged insane, and perhaps a Time article, heavy on evidence, could untangle this gloomy mess. "Hello," he said, shaking hands with a goofy bar-buddy smile. "My name is Bobby Shaw." His divorce from reality was obvious. Curious if he had religious beliefs, I asked what he thought would happen after his execution. "Breakfast, I guess," he said." Maybe grits." O'Brien told me that the governor's staff read the Time article just before halting his execution. They sent him to a prison wing with medical facilities where he eventually died.

-0-

I pulled out a handkerchief to wipe my wet forehead as we parked in a dusty farmer's field. I heard the American ambassador, ringed by bodyguards, muttering about "getting it right" this time. It was too late.

This was my first day in El Salvador as a new bureau chief. My Spanish lessons had ended when word came that three American nuns and a lay missionary were missing in a country where death squads owned the night.

Campesinos wearing bandanas like an old cowboy movie waited with shovels by the half-dug grave. I looked down and saw a woman's leg sticking out of the dirt. She and the others were kidnapped at a roadblock, raped, shot and dumped in this field. Peasants were ordered to bury them. The smell was so strong that tears came to my eyes. The diggers tied ropes to the women's arms. Slowly Maryknoll sisters Maura Clark and Ida Ford, Cleveland sister Dorothy Kazel and Jean Donovan, a Cleveland accountant, came out. What remained of them was a mocking caricature of humanity: a body whose face was missing, a woman with her panties around her ankles. Another's sweet face even in death made me impulsively wish I'd known her. A living nun appeared and covered them with tree branches.

I counted about forty journalists, maybe a dozen nuns and priests plus local farmers with their families. We were halfway through this obscene mess when two squads of Salvadoran national guardsmen arrived in trucks and started pushing people around. The danger was obvious.

Then something made them stop. Weeks later, I ran into an embassy security man I'd seen that day cradling an M-16 and asked him about gossip that the guardsmen came to kill us. Did he agree?

"Affirmative," he said. I was stunned. "Why didn't they?" I asked. "We had more firepower," he smiled.

-0-

There are special moments when journalism tests you. Here are a few favorites:

. . . Guatemala's president in 1982 was Romeo Lucas-Garcia, a general who governed through death squads. One rainy afternoon angry crowds gathered outside the Presidential palace, and gunfire filled the air as I joined a few reporters walking toward the action. Suddenly a Guatemalan army captain drew his gun and forced us to walk backwards.

He was pushing us into a firefight a block behind us. A tear-gas canister exploded, blinding everyone. Now we were stumbling backwards into a crossfire in the rain, sightless and terrified. We passed a blurry side street and knew that fleeing was our only hope—if the captain was too blind to shoot. He apparently was.

-0-

I was fairly new to Time in 1972 when mobster Joey Gallo died after a gunfight in Manhattan's Little Italy in the restaurant, Umberto's Clam House. I went down to talk to cops and bystanders and noticed a burly guy behind the bar. After I asked a few questions, he said, "if you quote me, I'll come after you." I belatedly realized I was talking to a mob button man. After some thought, I included his quotes in my reporting. The editors didn't use them. For once, I didn't mind.

-0-

I flew to Boston with Robert Redford when he screened All The President's Men for a mix of local politicians and reporters. I was sitting between Boston's mayor and Redford when his honor leaned across to Redford as if I wasn't there and said something unflattering about politics. Then he remembered I was a reporter. "This is off the record," he growled. "You understand?" I became unprofessionally annoyed. "If you want to go off the record, Mr. Mayor," I growled back, "you have to say so first." His jaw dropped. The editors used the quote after I mentioned special circumstances in the file. To my amazement, I got a congratulatory note from the legendary Dick Clurman. No longer chief of the TLNS, he was still reading files.

-0-

I was doing a story on the late Crips founder, Tookie Williams, sentenced to death for multiple murders. He'd started writing children's books warning against gang life, an ironic turnaround. Problem was, San Quentin barred reporters from death row. His editor, Barbara Becnel, suggested I sign in as a "friend," and it worked. The condemned men and their families were gathered unrestrained in a bigroom as if on a picnic. Just before Tookie came out, a man with demonic eyes walked up and stood beside me. "Barbara," I said innocently, "he could double for the Night Stalker." I meant a serial killer so vicious I assumed he'd be locked up today. "That is the Night Stalker," she answered. I didn't attempt to interview him.

Tookie came out, and we got along just like "friends."

-0-

I've never liked flying, particularly on the day Dick Duncan and I boarded an ancient Royal Air Laos turboprop to fly from Vientiane to Bangkok. We were airborne only a few minutes when dark smoke began to fill the cabin. Duncan advised relaxing and started telling me stories of his near-crashes, which of course helped. Finally, in a panic, I asked a steward about the smoke. Don't worry, he said, that happens every time we fly.

James K. Willwerth

—

Shortly after Saddam invaded Kuwait on August 2, 1990, Prince Bandar embarked on a whirlwind tour of America's media outlets to make the case for U.S. intervention. As usual with Bandar, it was all fighter-jock bombast—I don't recall him leaving much time to indulge questions—and he was gone almost as quickly as he had arrived. The Kuwaitis soon realized they needed a similar presence and a soft-spoken genius named Ali Khalifa al-Sabah arrived on the 24th floor. As Kuwait's oil and finance minister, Khalifa had been the guiding force behind the phenomenally successful Kuwait Investment Authority and his calm presentation was far more persuasive than the Saudi's.

After checking with Muller and Stacks, I asked Sheik Ali if I could accompany him as he went around the world drumming up support to repel the Iraqis. And thus began a fascinating—and very expensive—five month journey during which I spent a fair amount of time in Taif, the mountain town about two hours from Jeddah that King Fahd had turned over to the Kuwaiti government-in-exile. To the discomfort of the American ambassador and CIA station chief, I developed a close relationship with the Kuwaiti high command and learned a great deal about the plans for the coming war, all of which I dutifully reported back to New York. I left Taif on January 23, 1991 to attend my son's fifth birthday party back home. No sooner had I arrived at JFK on the morning of the 24th, I learned that the ground war had just begun. (All the intel I accumulated in Taif did *not* include that all-important date.) Naturally, I turned to TIME's secret weapon for help, and within an hour, Richard Nigosian had arranged for me to get back to Saudi Arabia as fast as humanly possible—which was no mean feat since air space in the Middle East had been severely restricted.

(Like many of us, I had long been a beneficiary of Nigosian's magic. Once, when I was in Moscow as part of the team producing our "Greatest Person of All Time" issue on Mikhail Gorbachev—all I can recall about my own contribution to that effort is Stacks lying on a sofa drinking vodka at a Soviet government dacha as he methodically drew careful Xs though page after page of my copy—Nigosian managed to hold the Concorde at Heathrow so I could get back to New York to make a Friday deadline.)

Thanks to the relationships I'd developed, I was the first American journalist inside Kuwait, accompanying a group of Kuwaiti commandos who made it home several hours before Norm Schwazkopf's coalition forces crossed the border. Once inside Kuwait City, I came across the December 25, 1990 edition of the occupation paper the Iraqis published daily for those who hadn't had the good fortune to escape their country in August. And there, on the front page, was a piece about my TIME cover story titled "What is Kuwait, and is it Worth Dying For?" Needless to say, the Iraqis had completely distorted our effort, summarizing our take as concluding that no one should give a rat's ass about Kuwait.

All I can say at this remove is what I suppose everyone can honestly say: my time at TIME was the highlight of my journalistic career. I will forever be grateful for having had the opportunity to serve with all of you. I wish we could get together and do it all again.
Michael Kramer

Prior Restraint

They must have thought it was important because they sent the number two and number three men from FBI headquarters in Washington to the Time &Life building to confront the Magazine. Crowded into a cubicle office with John Stacks, Time attorney Bob Marshal, and me, the Feds, stiff and adamant, said they were cooperating with the CIA and that we could not publish a story I had just finished, Terrorism: Fat Man, Tailor, Soldier, Spy, because of national security considerations. It was the first whiff of prior restraint anyone could remember since the Vietnam war, and we were surprised. There wasn't any question of fact, because the Mafia had handed us the story on a platter.

Three weeks earlier, an old source, a catholic priest of blemished reputation, had invited me to a party in upper Manhattan to meet 'some interesting people'. Father Lawrence Zorza was a young Vatican comer until he was jailed in New York for smuggling stolen 16th century Italian paintings. Temporarily banished by the Church to the New World, he provided spiritual counsel and international courier service to a mob connected family in New York.

The adjoining suites in the prestigious residential hotel were crowded when I arrived and was introduced to the Fat Man, a Brooklyn consigliere who provided such valuable service moving Italians with legal difficulties between the U.S. and Italy that his travel agency was used by all but one of the five New York Families. He was the ostensible host of this champagne, caviar and cognac affair celebrating, it turned out, the first anniversary of the liberation, after 42-days of captivity, of a top NATO General, American Brigadier General James Dozier. He had been kidnapped from his home in Verona by Red Brigade terrorists the evening of Dec. 17, 1981, setting off the biggest manhunt in Italian history. Why would they be celebrating that?

After a few drinks, I realized the party had been orchestrated for my benefit, so that certain people could tell me how American and Italian Mafiosi had cooperated with the CIA and found the general, not the Italian police who had been given public credit. And now the CIA had double-crossed their man who made the rescue possible. Instead of giving him a green card so he could safely stay in America as they had promised, they were trying to have him extradited to Italy where he would be jailed for life for Mafia activities there.

Their story of the mob's role was labyrinthine. Within days of Dozier's abduction, officers in SESMI, Italy's super-secretive military intelligence apparat, realized the Mafia, which knew everything, should be able to find the general. They couldn't be seen cooperating with the mob in Italy, so they tasked Marcello Campione, military attache to the Italian mission at the United Nations, to search in New York Mafia circles for someone with the right connections in Italy. He was steered to the Fat Man, who in turn produced a fugitive from Italy who was hiding out in New York. He was Dominic Lombino, 40, a lawyer from Milan. Lombino's sole client was Franchino Restelli, the top boss in northern Italy. Campione offered Lombino a half-million dollars and protection from the law if he would ask Restelli, then incarcerated in Milan's notorious San Vittore prison for mafia activities, for help. At the party, Campione told me how the FBI discovered he was moving Lombino about, captured them, then turned the operation over to the CIA, who gave the lawyer false id and then spirited them off to Italy.

Lombino arrived at the party and provided details of what Time would later call "a remarkable tale of triumphs and bungles, of Brooklyn consiglieri and Milan Mafiosi, of chases along New York city's Fifth Avenue and gun-toting criminals trailing intelligence agents along the Italian autostrada." He assured me he was a man of good will. "It is true I sat on the Council, but never once did I vote for death; I always said if a lesson was needed, break the man's legs or take away his business. Death isn't necessary." He smiled sincerely.

The Machiavelli of this party, the real host, to whom all paid deference despite his relative youth, was an elegant Italian introduced as Dr. Francesco Pazienza, Knight of Malta. I had no clue who I was dealing with and was charmed by his polished manner. Father Zorza stood by and translated when Pazienza had trouble with an English phrase. I assumed, correctly, that *il doctore* was a high level international mafia executive, but he turned out to be quite a bit more than that.

It would take months to learn that the charming Pazienza was also recently a high level SESMI officer, heading a special espionage unit, the Information and Military Security Service, suspected of bombings they blamed on local communists. When Mehmet Ali Agca tried to assassinate Pope John Paul II, two years before, Pazienza took part in his interrogations. When I met him he was also the the number two man to Licio Gelli, head of Propaganda Due, Italy's notorious and then-recently outlawed secret masonic lodge, "a state within the state", whose members included right wing politicians, members of every Italian intelligence agency, military leaders and Vatican-backed bankers.

The next day it took John Stacks about 30 seconds after listening to the story to send me to Rome to see what this was all about. It turned out to be surreal. Met at DaVinci airport that night by Pazienza's aide in a grey armored Mercedes, I was taken to his house, a mausoleum like mansion stripped of furniture, to await his arrival. In near dark, the aide built a fire in the fireplace and began feeding it papers. "His P-Due cards", he said at one point and I nodded as if I understood. When Pazienza arrived we packed into another Mercedes sedan with driver and bodyguard, and sped off into the night and a demonstration of power and influence such as I had rarely seen. First stop was the home of a Roman senator, the head of what we would call the Judiciary Committee, who answered the door in pajamas and a silk robe. At Pazienza's request he offered coffee and described visiting a hotel room in Rome, where Dominic Lombino, surrounded by CIA and SESMI agents, was waiting while arrangements were being made to spring Restelli from San Vittore prison near Milan. As we raced north, one of the bodyguards recalled the original Lombino caravan a year ago. Lombino was in an Alfa Romeo with four policemen, followed by Campione and other SESMI officers, followed by two Mercedes sedans filled with Mafia soldiers and machine guns. Belatedly notified CIA officers joined the parade to the prison near Milian.

When Pazienza and I arrived at 4 a.m. at Milan's Palace of Justice, where the interviews with Restelli had transpired, the two magistrates in charge of that meeting were waiting for us in the darkened empty offices. At a gesture from *il doctore* the magistrates described what had happened: Restelli, who had already shut down heroin deliveries in much of northern Italy to drive out informants had already narrowed Dozier's location to Padua. Now, expecting he would be assigned to a better prison, and that Lombino would be provided sanctuary, he handed over the address of an apartment above a bakery shop. Within hours Lombino, in a car with CIA agents, watched as the building was stormed by commandos and the general freed. Because of political considerations, the U.S. gave the Italians total credit for the police work that led to the General's release.

The FBI men, trying to face down Stacks in the Time office, insisted our facts were wrong, and the CIA didn't work with the Mafia, and that if they did the Mafia wasn't any help. We told him how the American Ambassador in Rome, who had sworn to God nothing like this had happened, had became so rattled when he was shown evidence he said the hunt for Dozier had become so frantic that Nancy Reagan had sent her personal psychic to Rome, and he had led the Italian police and army on a merry chase for weeks. Well, if it wasn't a national security issue, the feds said, we were still endangering the life of their confidential informant. We told them their CI was our main story source, and he wanted his green card and we could add the fact that they welshed on their promise to the story. They folded and we published.

In the end, Lombinio got his green card, but his $500,000 vanished within SESMI and was never found. Campigone was banished to Khartoum. Pazienza survived long enough to head up damage control after the Vatican bank scandal. Later he and P-2's Geli were convicted as a conspirators in the bombing of the Bologna train station in 1980, which killed 87. Red Brigade terrorists had been first blamed. In a splendid example of Italian Justice, after five years, Pazienza was exonerated and freed.

Father Zorza called me at my ranch just a few weeks ago, to ask if I was interested in doing a story about the Pope's mistress.

Jonathan Beaty

"We Gotta Bomb"

The first important news source I acquired after joining the Washington bureau in the fall of 1963 as backup man on the diplomatic beat was, shall we say, a meaty one.

On arrival, I had almost no contacts in the Capitol of any kind and even less awareness of Time's power and access. But having misspent the previous two years as a graduate student at Harvard, I did have some academic names to drop. So I made a cold call to MIT economist Walt Rostow, then head of the State Department Policy Planning Council, and invited him to lunch. To my surprise, he accepted.

We met the next day at the Madison Hotel. Walt ordered steak tartare, and after we exchanged the names of some mutual friends in Cambridge, he began filling me in about the Vietnam policy debates raging among administration insiders. The immediate issue, he explained, was whether and when to start bombing the Ho Chi Minh trail in Laos and key targets in North Vietnam.

The food arrived. A lusty, messy eater, Walt made his own superhawk position vividly clear.

"We've got to start bombing," he said. Gobs of the raw steak trickled down his chin. "We gotta bomb, we gotta bomb."

The bombing of North Vietnam began the following June in the wake of the Tonkin Gulf incident.

To this day, I've never ordered steak tartare.

-0-

Shortly after succeeding Bill Radaemakers as diplomatic correspondant I had my first encounter with Henry Luce at a small dinner hosted by bureau chief John Steele. I think it was John, bless him, who warned me beforehand that the key to surviving Luce's typical fusillade of questions was to come up with quick answers. Content was secondary.

After a popgun series of queries about European and Vietnam policy, he asked what I thought of Secretary of State Dean Rusk. I gave a long, highly critical response. He listened attentively for awhile, then barked: "OK, who would do better?"

I had no idea and started to clutch. In the nick, I remembered an interview earlier that day with a friend on the National Security Council staff and his reference to the U.S. Ambassador to Japan.

"Ed Reischauer," I blurted. Luce grunted approval and not only moved on but warmed up. I later learned that he knew Reischauer well and admired him greatly. Close call.

-0-

Although I disagreed with Rusk about many a policy issue, I liked him personally and enjoyed most of our contacts. One of those occasions, however, was uncomfortable in the extreme.

In 1967, his daughter Peggy became engaged to a black college classmate. Raised in rural Georgia and always reticent about his private life, the Secretary was as dismayed by the publicity as by her decision.

Managing editor Otto Feuerbringer immediately laid on a cover story about intermarriage, pegged to the nuptials, and I had to call Rusk with both that news and a request for interviews with the family. Deeply distraught, he called me at home, again and again, literally begging me to talk Otto into canceling the cover. It wasn't a legitimate social trends story, he argued, just a private family matter.

Fat chance. Otto was unmoved. He was right in news terms, but he reacted so coldly that I concluded he must have had a thing about miscegenation. The Rusk family refused all interviews. The cover appeared.

Rusk, a gentleman albeit a southern gentleman, maintained our cordial relationship as before.

-0-

Let us now praise the old-time expense accounts, no pun intended. Having broken into journalism at the Chicago Sun-Times, where every bus fare required the services of a defense lawyer, it was culture shock on steroids.

We all have our favorite stories. Mine involves an assignment in Paris—covering a NATO conference or maybe the Paris peace talks—during which Dick Clurman arrived in state. He invited two colleagues to dinner, myself and the Newsweek bureau chief of the day. Arriving at his suite in the Ritz, we found Dick standing beside a telephone and an ice bucket stocked with Dom Perignon.

He greeted us with one hand, picked up the phone with the other, and ordered the concierge to send up a butler to pour the champagne. For three.

-0-

In June, 1969, worried that the lessons of the 1968 riots were already being forgotten, civil rights leader Whitney Young organized a cross-country "ghetto-a-day" tour for a dozen or two top editors and columnists, including Henry Grunwald. Whitney was a persuasive, highly respected guy and almost all accepted. Boeing contributed an executive jet. Almost every leading print outlet was aboard.

Now Henry loved to travel, but a ghetto-a-day as part of a pack was not his style. He called and assigned me. He doubted there would be a story for us but he did want Time represented.

In the event, I got a press piece out of it. More important, I got one of my more indelible memories.

The scene: a hotsheet motel room in the San Francisco ghetto. The cast: half a dozen whores and pimps in sporting life regalia. The journalists: William F. Buckley Jr., and your correspondant. While I sat there, a fascinated fly on the wall, Bill quizzed them at length about their trade, ghetto life, national policies, the works. They peppered him with scornful comments about conservative credos. He deployed his customary vocabulary. They taught him a few new words. He flashed his eyebrows. They ogled him back. The banter got hotter, the laughter louder. Better than Firing Line by far.

Why did they like Bill so much, I kept wondering. The fly finally figured it out;. They had style. So did he.

-0-

They don't party like they used to.

In 1975, shortly after I became Los Angeles bureau chief, someone back in New York decided I should have a proper bar mitzvah party. Meaning that Hedley and Henry wanted to mingle with the Hollywood glitterati.

Leo Janos, our entertainment correspondant, suggested that we talk with producer Bob Evans (The Godfather, Chinatown, Love Story) and see if he would throw the bash at his Beverly Hills estate. Bob, whose movies regularly made Time's cover, was eager to cooperate. He offered to assemble the A list if Time would split the cost. New York agreed.

The party took glitz to a new level. Every star of note was there. Evans glowed with triumph. Henry circled delightedly among the stars (mostly among Raquel Welch, if memory serves). I recall Hedley, gazing contentedly into the distance, with a nubile Goldie Hawn on his lap. Wine flowed. The food was scrumptious.

Bob telephoned us with the tab a week or two later. I think our share came to $20-25,000, no small sum in 1975. New York declined to pay. Someone evidently decided that he had already gotten that much free publicity out of Time and more.

Maybe someone was right. Bob was amazingly gracious when we gave him the bad news. Leo and I took him out for a good dinner and all was forgiven.

-0-

Pat Brown, the two-term California governor, had a difficult relationship with his son.

I knew, from covering Jerry during his own first term as governor, that he didn't like talking about his dad. But I didn't realize just how prickly it all was until the day, in March 1976, that Jerry announced his first presidential candidacy.

Pat and I had lunch fairly often during that period and we had one scheduled that day. When he arrived at the table, I let him know I was irritated.

"Pat, I thought we were friends. Why didn't you give me a heads up that Jerry was going to announce today."

"Give YOU a heads up," he exploded. "I heard the goddamn news on my car radio driving in to work."

-0-

Remember that hair pulling contest between Nancy Reagan and Betty Ford as their husbands fought for the 1976 GOP presidential nomination? Here's a related story I never used.

Mrs. Ford, asked on 60 Minutes what she would do if daughter Susan told her she was having an affair, responded that she would "counsel her." Mrs. Reagan then slammed her for not condemning such behavior. Shortly afterward, someone in our LA bureau—Roland Flamini I think—discovered that the Reagan's daughter, Patti, was living near Malibu with a member of the Eagles band.

I was covering Reagan in the New Hampshire primary. Finding a moment alone with Nancy aboard the campaign plane, I asked her the obvious question: how could you?

Her eyes grew wide with surprise that the word was out, but I had to admire her instant comeback. "The difference," she snapped, "is that I don't condone it."

-0-

When it comes to the conundrum of dealing with nuclear waste, plus ca change is alive and well.

Back in 1973, Jerry Hannifin and I had a Washington bureau lunch with Dixie Lee Ray, the biologist and onetime Washington state governor who was then chairing the Atomic Energy Commission. Ray was pushing hard for more nuclear power plants.

What about the radioactive wastes, we asked.

"Oh, we'll have that problem licked in the next year or two," she shrugged.

Jess Cook

Free Spenders

One reporter who nailed the Bay of Pigs story in such authoritative detail that it caused an uproar in the Kennedy White House was my bureau colleague Charles J.V. Murphy, the Washington editor of Fortune.

Charlie Murphy was a silver-haired veteran of Time Inc.'s earlier days and latterly one of the reigning savants on national security affairs. One of Luce's favorites, Murphy boasted a Richard Harding Davis-like career full of scoops and colorful capers. His creative expense accounts (he once charged the company for a $700 fur coat he'd bought for an assignment to the Antarctic) were the despair of Time Inc. accountants.

Murphy had a roguish charm, complete with theatrically raised eyebrow, that fit well with his patent Anglophilia. He was an expert on the Royal Family, the author of a biography on Edward VIII whom he'd come to know. His sources were legend, impeccable as his bespoke double-breasted suits. A White House aide confided that Murphy had so many highly placed sources "we treat him as a separate State Department."

When you ate with Charlie it was always four-star. Late in the week when our heaviest filing was done, if fortune smiled, my phone would ring and Murphy's melodious voice would issue a luncheon summons. We would decamp to a favorite hangout of his off Connecticut Avenue. There Murphy would ensconce himself on a banquette, light up a filtered Parliament, and order a dry martini straight up. When the entrée arrived, Murphy would seamlessly switch gears from dishing out the latest Capital gossip to dispensing his wisdom on weightier matters. I'd ask a leading question. Murphy would blow a lazy smoke ring, lean back expansively, and begin the tutorial. For the next hour I'd be instructed on everything from the intricacies of breaching the Berlin Wall to the inanities of television reporting. All on the company's chit.

If I had doubts about Murphy's sumptuous expense accounting, I was soon set right on such matters by my boss, the chief of corespondents, Richard Clurman. Clurman called me in one day to complain that my expense accounts were subpar for a TIME correspondent. I obviously wasn't taking enough outside sources to lunch. Henceforth, I began taking my sources' culinary needs more seriously.

Lans Lamont

If It's Not in the Times

I filed my first copy as a correspondent during my second week when Ed Goodpaster, the Washington news editor, dropped a query on my desk concerning a coup in Mali reported in that morning's New York Times. "Call the State Department Africa desk and ask them what they have on the coup."

The Africa desk said that the situation was extremely murky. I decided to call a friend who worked Africa on the National Security Council staff, a lunchmate at the White House mess, and told him the truth—I was filing to New York for the first time and wanted to look good. As he filled me in, on background, I had the feeling he was reading almost verbatim from the overnight CIA report to the President. He gave me the names of the young Mali lieutenants who were involved and said they had just been in Paris meeting with military and civilian officials. Clearly the French were deeply involved. I filed to the World section.

Next morning, Goodpaster came into my office with a troubled look and closed the door. "Leo, we have a problem here. Your advisory is being challenged in New York because none of this stuff was in the New York Times. They want to know your sources."

I told him. Nevertheless, Time's account of the coup in the next issue was basically a rewrite of the newspaper story. That slavish following of the New York Times would hold the whole ten years I was at the magazine.

-0-

One of my early assignments was to join the White House press corp' "death watch" in Austin Texas while LBJ spent a long weekend at his nearby Hill Country ranch. As luck would have it, the Time Inc. magazines had just reversed years of strong support for the Vietnam effort and begun to criticize the President's war policies.

My former colleague, Press Secretary George Christian, called me at seven in the morning, said it was time I started acting like a reporter, and put me in the press pool for a Johnson appearance in Austin to inspect some low-cost government housing development. When Christian led me into a crappy little apartment, crammed with city officials, Johnson eyed me as if I were a six-inch tarantula.

George wore his most evil smirk. "Mr. President,' he chirped, "'you remember friend Janos, now the property of Time Inc."

Those Johnsonian eyes narrowed. "How do you like working the other side of the street?" he asked.

"'Mr. President," I said, "I'm doing my best to keep them honest."

Johnson shook his head mournfully. "Well, you're sure fucking up."

-0-

During the first months of the next administration I enjoyed a couple of memorable moments covering Nixon.

Going to sea with him for naval maneuvers off the Virginia coast, we choppered onto the deck of the carrier USS Enterprise, then watched missile-firing frigates unleash their hardware in roars of smoke and flame. A jet zipped by at eye level and unleashed a sonic boom that caused Nixon to jump three feet off his chair.

Finally, at the end of the day, I trailed behind the President as he moved among the sailors, overhearing his small talk—always awkward and stilted.

"You boys do any fishing off this deck?"

-0-

In November, 1969 Time decided to put Spiro Agnew on the cover. I suggested interviewing my old boss Hubert Humphrey for a sidebar about the torments of the vice presidency as he had suffered them under LBJ. Hugh Sidey thought it was a terrific idea and so did the editors. I called Humphrey in Minneapolis and he quickly agreed to see me.

When I began quizzing Humphrey, all the accumulated frustration and anger of those unhappy years spilled out. I used most of it in the sidebar but not all of it because Humphrey, trusting me as a former staff member, said some intensely personal things.

"You know what it was like being Johnson's vice president? You're up to your balls freezing naked in a snow drift and nobody even offers you a match."

By sunrise in my hotel room I had almost finished filing when the phone rang. It was Norm Sherman, an old friend and Humphrey's former press secretary. "Humphrey asked me to ask you—are you going to use what he said last night?"

I was furious. "Goddam it, Norm, is he still so scared of Johnson? Where's his balls?" Norm laughed. "Johnson still has them in his freezer."

-0-

Time was in Houston primarily to cover the nine historic Apollo space missions to the moon. John Wilhelm did most of the heavy-lifting science reporting. I focused on the activities of the astronauts themselves and interviewed most of them for a piece on how going to the moon affected their lives. In some cases, I learned, the answer was profoundly.

Charles Duke said it was the most deeply moving experience of his life seeing his own footprints in the lunar dust. Jim Erwin saw the mystery and majesty of God and left the program to become a minister. Ed Mitchell left the program and devoted himself to the study of ESP. Rusty Schweikart left the program to work with drug addicts. "I am not the same man," he said. "None of us are." Even Al Shephard noticed a difference. "I was a mean SOB before the launch. Now I'm just an SOB."

-0-

In retrospect, the Hollywood years were my most enjoyable at Time and I did some of my best reporting and writing. The beat was fun but also pressure packed because Henry Grunwald demanded that we beat Newsweek to the punch on all the best stories. Still, not all planned covers made it. I remember warning Mel Brooks not to spread the word that Time was planning a cover to coincide with his latest movie, "Young Frankenstein," because show business covers were notoriously vulnerable to last minute, hard news events around the world.

Mel ignored my advice and spread the good news all over the Twentieth-Century Fox lot. Fox trumpeted his expected triumph with a full page ad in Variety congratulating him on the upcoming Time cover.

Later that day, I had to call and tell him the bad news. "Mel, our cover has been bounced." "Bounced for what," he demanded to know. The answer was Legionnaires' disease; a mysterious bacteria that was making scores of American Legion conventioneers dangerously ill.

"You're telling me that Mel Brooks was bounced for a fucking germ," he raged.

Leo Janos

Leo Janos joined the News Service in 1968, following a two-year speechwriting stint in the LBJ White House (he had earlier worked for Hubert Humphrey). He subsequently reported out of the Washington bureau, as Houston bureau chief, and as Time's Los Angeles-based entertainment correspondent. A superb storyteller and writer—he hit the bestseller list with his Chuck Yeager book—Leo was working on his memoirs at the time of his death in 2008. These anecdotes are distilled from that draft by Jess Cook.

With His Spats On

On a luminous late October day in 1979 I ran into Jay McMullen on the Michigan Avenue Bridge. We had been pals back in the city hall newsroom, the city hall of the old Mayor Daley, the real one. With more than twenty years in the hall for the Chicago Daily News, Jay was the senior dog in the room and I was a puppy, cranking out bulletins for the City News Bureau. As such, one of my informal duties was to answer McMullen's phone when he stepped over to the Blackstone Hotel for a nooner with Jane Byrne, who was then Daley's head of consumer affairs.

The city desk understood well enough when I said he was getting a shoe shine and would not be back for a couple of hours. His wife was less understanding, but that was okay. She was the last person to know she was getting dumped. Jay and Jane got hitched and by the time I saw him on the bridge she was mayor and he was her press secretary.

"Fucking Suro," he says to me, I figured you were dead. As I laughed and tried to protest, Jay added, "You haven't had a byline in a fucking blue moon. You are dead." And, indeed after prolific years of newspapering in Chicago, I had descended into the splendid anonymity of the Time-Life News Service about 14 months earlier. But I had a reply. "I am working for a national rag, and I am getting the fuck out of Chicago before you and Jane wreck the place."

That day on the bridge, 27 years old and tanned, I was feeling extremely full of myself. Duncan had pretty well promised me a billet in Washington, and nobody had said no when I talked about eventually getting to a foreign bureau. Better yet I had just come back from what remains one of the best boondoggles of my career.

The Soviets supposedly had put a combat brigade in Cuba. Hysteria in Washington generated hysteria in the News Service.

Bernie Diederich was smart enough not to be bothered, and so I went off to cover the impact of the crisis in the Caribbean. It was a fool's errand, but under princely circumstances--like many, many other assignments to come. I was then still enjoying the life and not yet missing the work, and so I kept busy. At the bar of the Pegasus in Kingston, I noticed a fetching young woman reading our then glam mag while eating Shepherd's Pie and drinking Scotch.

I identified myself as her dinner company and sat down. A bawdy British ad exec, she was intent on salt and pepper but relented later than night after some reflection and study. We decamped to the north coast the next day to sit on a beach near Ian Fleming's house, and for several days we searched the horizon for mushroom clouds while washing the ganja down with Myers's. Then the telex came from New York. Strobe had decided against starting World War III, and so it was time for me to go home.

"You don't look like a fucking Time correspondent dressed that way." The day I met McMullen on the Michigan Avenue Bridge I had no plans to go into the bureau. It must have been the beginning of the week, or the end of the week or maybe the middle of the week. In any case I was wearing jeans and sweater. Jay undoubtedly was wearing a turtleneck, it was his signature, probably baby blue or cherry red with a broad lapelled plaid sports coat. It was the 70's, and I was grossly underdressed for the decade. "Holy mother of God," McMullen says, "I can remember when Time correspondents used to fuck with their spats on." And indeed we did.

Roberto Suro

The Doubtful & Uninformed
Peacemakers of the Year

In the fall of 1993, TIME named four Persons of the Year for their efforts at peacemaking: Palestinian and Israeli leaders Yasser Arafat and Yitzhak Rabin, and black and white South African leaders Nelson Mandela and F.W. de Klerk. Arafat's Palestine Liberation Organization had just completed the Oslo peace accords with Yitzhak Rabin's government, providing for limited self-rule for the Palestinians in parts of the Gaza Strip and West Bank, and for negotiations on a final settlement, which everyone understood would one day be a Palestinian state.

I was then the Jerusalem bureau chief. Gaines sent me a letter, officially informing Rabin he would be named POY. I arranged with the Prime Minister's office to bring it to Rabin personally at his apartment in Tel Aviv one evening. Possessing almost no social graces, Rabin was difficult to talk to, but we managed a short conversation about the peace agreement. I took it as a sign that he was pleased by the POY announcement that he saw me to the door when I left. As I was walking out, he expressed a sentiment I've never seen attributed to him. "It might not work, you know?" he said to me. I questioned him with my eyebrows. "The peace. It might not work," he said with a little shudder, and stepped back inside his apartment.

Those were still flush days at TIME, so Managing Editor Jim Gaines rented a private plane so a team could jet around the globe to interview the four Persons of the Year.

The interview with Arafat took place at the PLO chief's headquarters in Tunis. He was still living in exile then. As was always the case with Arafat, we were merely told we'd get to see him sometime that night, which meant a call to head over in the wee hours of the next morning. The team was Gaines, Chief of Correspondents Joelle Attinger, Cairo bureau chief Dean Fischer and me.

Only Fischer had met Arafat before. He had plainly been briefed on who we were individually. Each time he mentioned Jerusalem he looked at me, as if he knew I was based there. There was something about Arafat that was buffoonish but cute. He was so eager to be liked. I was not at all expecting it, but I was charmed by him, as were the others.

It was not what one would call a hard-hitting interview. Arafat spent a disproportionate amount of time showing us a medal he kept around his ghostly white neck and explaining its origins, each of us leaning in to look at it closely. Ah, fascinating.

But it wasn't fascinating, and it wasn't useable. When we broke after two hours of talking to him, we somehow managed to sober up and realize, we didn't have an interview. We had almost nothing we could use, just a bunch of conversation.

We had to ask Arafat's spokesman if we could have more time with him. It was granted, but before we were allowed back in, the spokesman pulled me aside. He wanted to rule out a question I'd asked Arafat earlier: whether he would have been a Zionist had he been born a Jew instead of an Arab. Arafat had deflected the question. Now the spokesman told me, hotly, that this was the wrong question because the PLO could never recognize that the Jewish religion made Jews a separate people from the Arabs. "For us, if we accept that . . ." he said, and flung his hand out in a gesture that meant "it's over."

When the interview resumed, the TIME team took a more sober approach. Feeling empowered to pursue the tougher questions I'd mapped out in advance, I asked Arafat what I'd thought was a basic question. I noted that under the Oslo agreement, he would be the governor of Gaza, however thousands of Israeli settlers, over whom he'd have no control, would remain. I asked how he thought that would work. Arafat looked at me like I was stupid. He said, "I will have sovereignty," and added that he'd be in charge of the settlers.

I thought maybe there was a language issue. I started quoting the agreement, saying sovereignty would remain with Israel while the Palestinian Authority would have autonomy, or self-rule, limited to governance over specified functions in specified districts that wouldn't include the Israeli settlements.

Arafat interrupted. He pointed his bony finger in my face, leaned in and said again, loudly, "I will have sovereignty." His eyes bulging, he said, "Do you think I have not read what I have signed?"

I tried again. "But the agreements say . . ."

Now he was truly angry, close to shouting. "Do you think I have not read what I have signed?" He was accusing me. I felt the room grow close. I looked at Arafat's belt and wondered if he carried a gun in his office. I noticed that my colleagues were staring at me and that the half dozen or so aides who'd been milling around the huge office, some armed with rifles, had gone quiet and still. I dropped the matter and waited for a colleague to ask a different question.

But I always wondered, what the heck happened in that exchange? Did Arafat really think the Oslo agreement gave him sovereignty over the Jewish settlers in Gaza, or over anything? Did he think he was going to move to the Palestinian territories and have real power? If he did, he learned very soon after his arrival half a year later that his authority was very constrained by Israel's superior authority. Over the years, as Arafat turned on the peace process, I asked myself, did he misunderstand what he was getting into?

But no, it turns out, he didn't misunderstand anything. After he died in 2004, his aides confirmed that Arafat hadn't read the Oslo agreement before he signed it, if at all. That day he waved his finger in my face, his accusation was as empty as his holster famously was when he first addressed the UN General Assembly, having been forced to leave his pistol at the door.

Secrets of the Druze

During my time as the Jerusalem bureau chief, I read a story in a local paper about a Druze author who'd been banished from his community for exposing the secrets of his religion, which is notoriously secretive about its practices and beliefs. I suggested the story to the editors in New York. They bought it. I got a message back saying something like, "Very much looking forward to reading your expose on the secrets of the Druze."

My Palestinian colleague Jamil Hamad and I did some preliminary reporting and discovered that the author was not ex-communicated for writing about the secrets of the Druze but rather for including sex scenes in his latest novel. I wrote the editors, informing them of this and asking whether they still wanted the story. They wrote back, "Story is still of interest. But please see if the author also unveiled some secrets of the Druze for inclusion in your story."

Jamil and I traveled to Druze country, interviewed the author and other members of the community. I informed New York that the author did not reveal any secrets of the Druze but, as I'd noted before, was banished for writing about sex and that I thought the story was still worthwhile. I got a message back: "Please come ahead, but also pursue reporting to see if you can independently uncover any secrets of the Druze."

Jamil and I did our best to uncover the secrets that the Druze sect has kept from the rest of humanity for ten centuries. We talked to

Druze friends and religion scholars and together ended up with what we started with: rumors that the Druze believe the messiah will be born from between the legs of a man, which is why the men wear loose, billowy trousers.

I delivered the story about the ex-communicated author with a note to the editors that I was sorry, I did not possess the secrets of the Druze. I was relieved to receive no further instructions from New York.

The next week, the magazine came. The story was headlined: The Secrets of the Druze.

Lisa Beyer

A Glass of Something

Billy Martin was drunk. Billy Martin was often drunk during his difficult, self-inflicted life. But on this sparkling sunny afternoon in May of 1980 on the beautifully groomed grass of the Oakland Coliseum, he was well oiled. His team had just won another game in a remarkable start that propelled the Oakland Athletics and Alfred Pesaro Martin, his very own self, to the top of the baseball heap It was what baseball lifers called getaway day when teams going on the road play in the afternoon before getting on the plane. Martin had a glass of vodka, no ice, no chaser in his hand. Maybe it was his second.

Photographer Annie Liebowitz was setting up for a potential cover shoot, and I was there as the go-between and to take any quotes that tripped from the lips of the man genius. Annie was nervous because this was an alien shoot to her. I was nervous because Billy in the Bag was unpredictable. To ease the tension I proposed a happy snap of Billy appearing to threaten me as if I were an umpire who had displeased him. Annie snapped away.

The more serious part of the shoot was problematic. Annie was kneeling on the grass, setting up a bottom to top shot as Billy chugged away. Did I say it was a water tumbler? Martin, ever Mr. Smooth, proposed something else entirely, something raunchily sexual, and it had nothing to do with cover shoots. Annie was aghast. I was speechless. Martin smirked. The shoot went forward but was unsuccessful. Not Annie's fault.

Off to the plane with the team I went for the two hour flight to Seattle. We bussed to the hotel where Martin was met by someone I presumed was his daughter. One of the beat writers informed me that, no, it was his paramour, all of 16. Shock number two. What to do with this material, since we were not yet in the People Magazine era, I did not know.

In the cover story we settled on a reference to Martin and his glass of post-game vodka, relatively innocuous, I thought. The day the cover appeared, I showed up at the Coliseum and at Martin's post game press conference. He railed at me, holding up a water tumbler. He was a wine drinker, he said. I had gotten it wrong, he claimed. I didn't think so. I was banned from his press rants for the remainder of the season, during which his team won the American League pennant going away and the World Series as well.

Postscript. Billy Martin died in a pickup truck accident near Buffalo, N.Y. where he lived with his girlfriend who was then his spouse, perhaps common law The road was icy and the pickup went off the road. Happens all the time. His partner survived. There was no mention of alcoholic intake in the postmortem. I have always wondered about that.

Paul Witteman

-0-

In March of 1979 there was a whiff of Persian Spring abroad in Iran. To wit, the men in power, who were not yet the mullahs, but secular politicians, who had been educated in Paris and other Western venues, decided that an election was in order. There was but one question posed to voters: are you in favor of an Islamic Republic or against it?

I was agnostic but the citizenry seemed enthused by the opportunity to express their opinion on this weighty matter. There were wooden ballot boxes and flimsy paper ballots. The ones marked in red said "No" in Farsi. The ones marked in green said "Yes" Voters told the monitors which ballot they wanted, then slipped said ballot into the ballot box. No one was asked for identification and voters did not have to sign the ballots to identify themselves. There was a festive mood around most of the polling places. Two attractive young women in semi-chador were in charge of the polling station I found near the American Embassy.

They were students at the university and bored because business was slow. I asked for a yes ballot and a no ballot because I wanted mementos of the historic occasion. They obliged. Then I was struck with the sudden impulse to vote and help determine the political future of Iran. I was inclined to vote "no" but the coeds were having no part of that. They covered the slot in the box with their hands. I switched ballots and went with green. Down the slot it went. A photographer captured the moment. Maybe it was the late Kaveh Golestan, a talented shooter and wonderful companion with whom I often paired. Maybe it was even his idea, although he took the transformation his country was experiencing very seriously. More than likely it was one of my harebrained impulses. I have looked everywhere for the print, to no avail.

So if you are looking for an inflection point when the Iranian revolution tipped from secular to ecclesiastical, look no farther. It happened that morning when my ballot disappeared down the slot. It was the vote that no doubt gave the good Ayatollah the momentum he was seeking and sent the country in a direction from which it's never returned. My bad, folks, my bad.

Night Flight with Howard Hughes

It had been a long, hard day at Bevedit—12 or 15 story suggestions from our end, almost that many queries from New York—and I was grateful when I got to bed that night. At 10:30, the phone rang and before I could figure out what the noise was, my wife had answered it. "No", she told the caller, "he's not home. You can reach him in the morning at his office", and she recited the Bevedit phone number. Then, a little nervously she turned to me and said "that was Howard Hughes."

Because Hughes was virtually untouchable and had multiple interests in stories at the time, I had a cup of coffee and called him back. With the usual result that he wasn't there and insofar as the phone answerer indicated, might never be again.

Okay, I said, then let him know that I am just as tired as he is but returned his call.

Lights out again. Sleep rolled in and took over so completely that I didn't even hear the next ring of the phone, but the conditioned response of a Time correspondent took over and I managed to ask my wife croakily if that had been another call.

There was a long hesitation before she answered, then: "yes, it was Hughes again. I told him how exhausted you are and he apologized for bothering you this late at night", she said.

By this time sleep had moved to another planet, so the next call—in about fifteen minutes—shook the foundations of the house. It was, of course, Hughes.

"Mrs. McCulloch" he said hesitantly, "is Mr. McCulloch any better rested?"

So I took the phone and Howard's unmistakable nasal voice asked me to meet him at the far, then unfinished side of the Los Angeles International Airport.

"At one o'clock in the morning?" I asked.

"Of course," said the voice, "and if you don't want to drive yourself, you'll find a two-tone Dodge parked on the street outside your house, and the driver will bring you here."

It was pitch black on the far side of the airport and I stood miserably outside the high fence until a figure shambled up from out of the dark.

It was Hughes himself, and a few minutes later we were aboard the original Boeing prototype of the 707 transport.

We—Howard, his wife, Jean Peters and a Boeing co-pilot—took off without a word to the tower and flew aimlessly over most of the Southwest United States until daybreak.

We got back to the L.A. airport at dawn, and Hughes, who had piloted the craft himself most of the time, brought it in for a perfect landing—again with no communication with the tower.

At the far, deserted side of the airport, we rolled to a stop, Hughes shut the engine down, went to the door with his wife, and vanished into the dark.

And that was how I became Hughes' sole media contact for much of the rest of his life. It was an intensely valuable meeting for me, and I had pretty much an inside track with the man all the way down through the fantastic story about Clifford Irving's phony Hughes biography. As for that, the outstanding memory for me is of a lie detector test conducted at McGraw-Hill headquarters by a New York detector operator by the name of Rudy Caputo. Irving had started the meeting by announcing he had a flight to Spain to catch, and then he and Caputo vanished in to another room. After about an hour, the two of them emerged and Irving fled out the door.

"Mr. Caputo" said Harold McGraw, president of the company, "please tell us how this test came out."

Caputo finished buttoning his three piece suit coat and then said "the best I can say, Mr. McGraw, it was highly equivocal."

"Thank God" said McGraw.

From there on—until the end—the story went steadily downhill.

-0-

In the spring of 1965 Henry Grunwald, then Assistant Managing Editor of Time, visited Viet Nam. Like most visitors from New York he wanted to see action, so I included his wish in ordering transportation for his first field visit. Our destination was a special forces camp near the Cambodian border, and it was our understanding that while fire was being exchanged, the camp was in no danger of falling.

Our escort officer on the 30 minute flight from Saigon to the camp was an aged Army captain obviously counting the seconds until his pending retirement. Midway to the camp our helicopter pilot received a radio message to the effect that the camp was now under heavy fire and, without replacements, was in some danger of being lost. he turned nervously to me and asked "Who is this guy?"—pointing to Grunwald—"what does he do?" "He is the assistant managing editor of Time" I said. "Time Magazine?" the captain gasped. Yes, I said, that's right.

His retirement plan obviously in danger, the captain blanched, shuffled his feet, and then moaned, "Ohhhhhhh, shit."

Frank McCulloch

"Katie, Rip Up That Letter!"

I'm not sure how many of those huge and expensive news tours we undertook when I worked for Murray Gart and Dick Duncan and Henry Muller, but it seems like there were a lot and they were definitely a huge pain for those of us who had to organize them and then become nannies to the rich and important corporate types we showed around the world.

One of the weirdest experiences came on the news tour that began in Cuba, went on to Russia and ended in China—a kind of grand tour of the Communist world. We were in Havana waiting to see Castro when one of the businessmen called me in the hotel to say that one of his shoes was falling apart and that he couldn't go see El Jefe with a damaged shoe. I naturally asked if he hadn't brought another pair with him, since I, as always, had packed at least a dozen pairs (you never know when a girl will need lavendar stilletoes in Hanoi). No, he replied, this was his only pair. The man was worth millions but came with only a single pair of shoes for an around the world trip.

It being a weekend and it being Cuba, no shoemakers were available. So with some spit and tape we fixed him up well enough for him to hobble off to the Castro dinner at the Revolutionary Hall. He was a little glum with this outcome fearing, I guess, that Fidel might take this opportunity to wear his Gucci loafers. I prayed that this was the end of the story—or at least until we got to Hong Kong. But as Sunday dawned and we made our way from Cuba to Moscow he made his way from the front of the plane to me in the back wondering if I could get the shoe repaired once we landed. I wasn't too confident but when we arrived and were greeted by our long time local correspent, Felix Rosenthal, I whined pitifully to him and miraculously, he called a friend who owned a toy factory and lo and behold he was able to take the shoe, sew it up and return it before this CEO dinner. I have never been more grateful to anyone than I was to Felix that Sunday morning in Moscow.

-0-

I also remember receiving urgent Saturday morning calls at home from several correspondents over the years (they shall remain nameless) who having had a rough time closing their stories the night before had fired off a letter to Dick resigning after their story suffered some indignity at the hands of an editor. "Please, Kate, you've got to go in early on Monday and track down the packet, find the letter, rip it up—and above all don't read it!" This ensured lots of lovely trinkets and a fair amount of drinks at the Dorset.

Katie McNevin

Bios from the 2011 Reunion

JOELLE ATTINGER

Back in Washington since 2007, working at The European Institute, a small public policy organization that focuses on European-American Relations. Done wonders for the Euro and world peace so far. Celia and Abigail are happily settled here as well, and my 89 year-old Dad is just down the road in Charlottesville.
jattinger@aol.com

KEN BANTA

I'm currently the head of strategic affairs at the global eye health company, Bausch + Lomb, as part of the management team working to turn the company around. I also work with Warburg Pincus, the private equity company that is the main owner of Bausch + Lomb. For the past 10+ years I've been doing similar work to transform companies into high performance, starting with Pharmacia & Upjohn, then Pharmacia Corp., and then Schering-Plough Corp.—all in health care so far. I live on the lower east side in Manhattan where my partner, Tony Powe, owns a restaurant, a bar, and a speakeasy!
Kenbanta3@gmail.com

LARRY BARRETT

My time at TIME ended in November 1997 after nearly 32years. The last five of which my status was "contributor"—full time initially, then tapering down allowing time to teach at American University and freelance to several publications. That became tedious. So, after a wonderful trip to China, I went to work for two of my former White House play partners, Jody Powell and Sheila Tate.

Their PR firm included several newsies and I thought it might be amusing for a year or two. I stayed for seven. To the surprise of many (including Powell and Tate, who thought I was too snarky to deal with clients,) I developed a certain knack for the consulting biz. By 2005, I was a senior vice president and the firm billed suckers—I mean clients—$325 for an hour of my time. Incredibly, they paid. But the firm became ensnared in M & A gambits, and changed management so at 70 I decided to try retirement again. That is my present status, but I make no pledges as to future activity or, more likely, inactivity. We travel some, I write occasional nostalgia pieces, and still find outlets for competitive juices in poker and tennis. Only singles where the latter is concerned: I'm too young for doubles and golf.

4701 Willard Avenue, Apt. 1435. Chevy Chase, *MD 20815, patbar@ verizon.net*

JONATHAN BEATY

I moved to the A-spear ranch, in remote south-west New Mexico, after leaving TIME some 15 years ago, because of a small health problem, and Linda and I are still there. We raise cattle and horses on this 26,000-acre spread, and partners include Nancy Stone, from the *Chi Trib*; Steve Northup, veteran Time & Life photographer; and Dick Duncan. I manage the ranch and am on the Board of Directors of a non-profit New Mexico foundation that produces medical marijuana under state license.

A-Spear Ranch, PO Box 896, Williamsburg, NM 87942, phone: 575 740-1384 *jonathancrockettbeaty@gmail.com*

LISA BEYER

After leaving TIME in 2007, I joined the International AIDS Vaccine Initiative, an NGO dedicated to accelerating the development of an AIDS vaccine, where I have served as the senior vice president for public affairs. I have very much enjoyed this work, which, among other things, has given me the opportunity to travel to and around India and sub-Saharan Africa. I have just accepted an offer to join Bloomberg View, a new on-line commentary platform at Bloomberg, LP, as a writer-editor and a member of the editorial board. I start April 25th. I am divorced from Zev. Our children, Coby, 15, and Annie, 14 are interesting young people, and can be a handful.

Pelham, NY 10803, cell: 917 520-2734, email: *lisaabeyer@gmail. com*

ANN BLACKMAN

Ann Blackman has had the same magnificent husband for 37 years, seen both kids employed and married, gained and lost 25 pounds several times despite and thanks to hauling two more Golden retrievers around the block, written three biographies (one with Elaine Shannon) and is finishing a fourth. Best of all: twin grandbabies, girls, soon to be two years old! Heaven.

Ablackman1@aol.com

HANNAH BLOCH

I traded Pakistan for Palo Alto back in the fall of 2002, when I got a Knight Fellowship at Stanford University. In 2004, I packed up my stuff and drove cross-country to DC, where I've been ever since. I work at the National Geographic, where I helped launch and then produce a weekly public radio program before moving to a newly created writer/editor job at the yellow-border magazine three years ago. I'm gearing up now for a story that will take me to Easter Island in June.

hannahbloch@hotmail.com, Phone: 650 380-1358

GISELA BOLTE

After I left TIME, I worked for a few years as a public relations manager at Albert Uster Imports, Inc., an importer of fine Swiss foods, and I ate a lot of Swiss chocolate while I was there. More recently, I am studying Spanish at George Mason University. I take piano lessons. I sing in a church choir which led to an invitation for me to sing "The Armed Man; a Mass for Peace" by British composer Karl Jenkins with a 200 plus choir at Avery Fisher Hall, Lincoln Center, in January of 2010. What time is left between cramming for Spanish and rehearsing, playing and singing music is spent with my husband and our poodle, Lance. I also have four stepchildren and a step-granddaughter whom I like to stay close to. Keeping busy! *Cho.Bolte@verizon.net*

JORDAN BONFANTE

After retiring in 2000, I stayed in Berlin and freelanced, mainly articles about art for *Time Europe*, *Time.com*, and art and travel magazines. Then in 2009 I relocated to Connecticut, but I still travel back and fourth to Europe. Current address: 16 Halsey Drive, Old Greenwich, CT 06870, Phone: 203-344-2031. *jbonfante@aol.com*

CATHY BOOTH THOMAS

Formerly fabulous reporter reduced to wicked-stepmom-dom and discovers her dark side. That's it in a nutshell. Still writing trash for American Airlines in-flight magazine. Edit MAYBORN, the literary rag I started at UNT (*www.themayborn.com*) and Denton Live. Let me know if you have nonfiction books coming out! UNT pays authors to speak at The Mayborn Literary Nonfiction Conference. *cathybooththomas@gmail.com*

JOHN BORRELL

After covering the collapse of Communism in Eastern Europe, I left TIME to build a luxury lodge in the Koszubian Lake district of Poland and start a wine importing and distribution business. Award-winning Kania Lodge (*www.kanialodge.com*) is now in its 18th year and Wine Express Ltd. (*www.wine-express.pl*) is one of Poland's leading specialist wine merchants. I also produce and export my own Vestal brand of artisanal vodkas (*vestalvodka.com*) that can be found in top stores, restaurants and clubs in London and elsewhere in Britan. I was also the owner and publisher of a small weekly Polish-language newspaper, *Express Kaszubski*, which I launched to fight corruption in local politics. After a cleanout of city hall I sold the paper to the staff. I am now working on another book about my nearly two decades in Poland.

john@wine-express.com

JOE BOYCE

Retired in 1998 after 11 years as a senior editor with *The Wall Street Journal*.: Adjunct, Columbia J School. 1999 moved to Indianapolis. Adjunct, Indiana University/Purdue University at Indianapolis. Occasional consultant with WSJ.

boycevibe@aol.com, 1370 East 106 St., Indianapolis, IN 46280, Phone: 317 908-8098

JAY BRANEGAN

I left TIME in the 2001 buyout and taught journalism for a few years as an adjunct to Georgetown Medill's Washington program, and a DC high school. In 2003 I landed a job on the Senate Foreign Relations committee, working for Dick Lugar, a now-endangered Republican. I do a lot of writing for the Committee (but not press relations) and tend to get a couple of foreign trips a year, mostly to Asia, (Tibet most recently, after Indochina, China, Philippines) plus London, Qatar, Ukraine, Central America and West Africa. Issues I work on include corruption, energy, foreign aid reform, and agricultural assistance. I, and my wife, Stefania Pittaluga, who still works at National Cancer Institute, have gotten into birding, and we defied our age by going trekking in Bhutan.
branegan@aol.com

SCOTT BROWN

After Time, I spent a few years at the LA Times, and then settled into teaching journalism more or less full-time at Cal State Northridge. I've also been traveling, writing fiction (my first novel, *"Far Afield"* was published a few years ago and I'm most ways through a second) and playing punk rock, currently with my band Finland Station (that's our non-hit, "Worst President Ever" that you definitely did not hear on the radio.) The biggest accomplishment, though, is my daughter, Pilar, who's doing well and finishing up her first year at Brown. Lastly, in a few years, I'm looking to move overseas—destination unknown but mostly likely Asia somewhere. To do what, I'm not exactly sure.
bulldogbrown@juno.com

ROSEMARY BYRNES DOYLE

First and foremost, my husband and I finally paid our last tuition bill for our two children's university and professional degrees. Second, our hobby is having 30+ Arabian breeding mares and stallions at our ranch in Bend, Oregon and writing articles for Arabian horse publications. To pay for all of this, we have had a family business in China for 28 years. Yes, we still have our house in DC, just in case we can afford to retire to that lovely city.

October to April email: *rb@doylepacific.com* April to October email: *rosemary@doylearabians.com*

SHEILA GREENE CHARNEY

I am one of the remaining News Service holdouts at TIME magazine, currently working as editorial office manager. My daughter Melissa is 15 years old and has entered high school.

sheila_charney@timemagazine.com, nycmom530@aol.com, Phone: 917 359-0361

HOWARD CHUA-EOAN

Howard Chua-Eoan joined TIME in 1983 as a one-day-a-week secretary, filling in for Judith Stoler on her days off and on Saturday. His job description: making coffee, answering the phone and buying cigarettes for George Church. It has been downhill ever since. He has been a fact-checker, writer, reporter, editor and since August 2000, TIME's News Director.

Howard_chua-eoan@timemagazine.com, Phone: 212 522-5647, cell: 917 359-0704

STAN CLOUD

Since taking early retirement from TIME on December 31, 1993, I've co-written two non-fiction books with Lynne—*The Murrow Boys* and *A Question of Honor*. In addition, I've written two plays and am currently at work on a novel. Somewhere in there, I also spent a year as executive director of the Citizens Election Project, a national operation under the auspices of the Pew Center for Civic Journalism, and managed, through no effort of my own other than getting old, to acquire a couple of grandchildren. Lynne and I still live in DC at the address below.

stancloud@mac.com or *stancloud@earthlink.net*
3142 Q Street, NW, Washington, DC 20007, phone: 202 337-6213

SUZANNE DAVIS

I retired in 2001. Worried I would be bored, I signed up for all kinds of activities including serving for eight years on the board of an all girls' high school in Manhattan. I have finally extricated myself from most everything. Now I'm working on my addictions to Travelocity and my Kindle.

suzannedavisnyc@gmail.com phone: 917 282-3525

DAVID DEVOSS

David DeVoss, a former TLNS bureau chief in Bangkok and Mexico City, is communications Director for a U.S. Agency for International Development provincial economic growth program in Iraq. Prior to going to Iraq two years ago, he was director of Monitoring and Communication for a USAID development program in Northern Afghanistan. He also directed print media development projects for USAID in East Timor and Bosnia. When not overseas DeVoss writes for the East-West News Service from his home in California.

4159 Stansbury Avenue, Sherman Oaks, CA 91423,
EastWestNewsServ@aol.com or *DavidDeVoss@sbcglobal.net*

SALLY DONNELLY

Now Director of Washington Office for General Jim Mattis, head of US Central Command (the Middle East including Afghanistan and Iraq) after three years as Special Assistant to the Chairman of the Joint Chiefs of Staff. Husband Eugene is National Intelligence Officer for Russia. So together we got the military intelligence complex covered. Kids (Jackson 14 and Anna 12) are cool, and actually like school (father's influence.) And yes, I am still a Redskins fan.
sallydonnelly@gmail.com

DICK DUNCAN

Following my tour as Chief of Correspondents, I spent ten years as assistant managing editor and then executive editor of TIME, and another five years creating online content for Time Warner. Broadband content was just beginning to overtake Dialup, so we built a broadband service for TW Cable, and then for various components of Time Inc.'s "Pathfinder" service, not the least of which was an 18/7 TIME Online news site. I retired in 2000, just after the AOL takeover and just before it turned into a catastrophe. For a pro bono year I taught journalism at Queens College, and then when our children, Alex and Jessie, had completed high school and had gone to college, Cherie and I moved to Nantucket. That soon felt like a very small island, especially in the winter, so in 2005 we headed west to Taos, NM, where I edit history books, garden, ski, fish and complain sporadically about the current state of journalism.

329 Santistevan Lane, Taos, NM 87571, phone: 575 758-4418, cell: 917 648-3631 *rldunc@gmail.com*

ELAINE DUTKA

After several years as TIME's West Coast Show Business Correspondent, I headed across town to cover film—and later, the arts, for the *LA Times*. I was part of a team reaching the Pulitzer finals and won a LA Press Club award for a piece on Hollywood ethics. For the past five years, I've been freelancing, writing for the *NY Times* and *LA Times*, blogging on politics for *The Huffington Post*. I'm a "contributing reporter" at NPR's KUSC—honing new muscles in this print-challenged age. Traveling also part of the mix—to spots such as Russia, South Africa, Australia, Thailand and, each summer to San Miguel de Allende.

447 1Ž2 South Maple Drive, Beverly Hills, CA 90212, Phone: 310 274-1002, cell: 213 810-4447, *edutka@roadrunner.com*

TAMELA (TAMMY) EDWARDS

Me in thumbnail: Living in Philadelphia, married to a great guy (a five-star pastry chef!), mother of a deliciously cute 20-month old son, anchoring the news for the ABC affiliate. MY time at TIME will always be a wonder, in large part because of you amazing people. I wish that I could be there but have a good time and I hope to be back in touch with everyone. If you're in Philly, call—cheesesteaks on me!

tamalae@aol.com, Phone: 917 747-4330, or "Tam Edwards" on Facebook.

CHARLES EISENDRATH

The second thing I did after leaving the TLNS was to design and implement The Livingston Awards for Young Journalists, "a sort of Pulitzer Prize for the young," as described by Dick Clurman, my boss at TLNS and the director of the Mollie Parnis Livingston Foundation who invited me into the world of journalism prizes. That was in 1980. When Dick died, we added The Richard M. Clurman Award for the lifelong on-the-job mentors to honor him in a program otherwise restricted to journalist's under-35.

The first thing I'd done post-Time Inc. was become a professor at the University of Michigan, where the Livingstons are administered and where I also direct the Knight-Wallace Journalism Fellowships. Participants, Time Incers among them, spend an academic year of mid-career studying in Ann Arbor and are able to do some international traveling partially underwritten by a TLNS Travel Fund and from Time Warner. So in ways important to my professional life, I never wholly left the TLNS.

drath@umich.edu

JAIME FLORCRUZ

FlorCruz has studied, worked and traveled in China for nearly 40 years, and reported extensively on the country as a journalist since 1980, when he started his career at Newsweek. In 1982, he joined TIME magazine's Beijing bureau, and served as bureau chief from 1990 to 2000. He left TIME in 2000 and spent a year in NY as the Edward R. Murrow Press Fellow at the Council on Foreign Relations. In July 2001, he returned to Beijing as CNN Beijing bureau chief. Jaimie has reported on most of the significant events of China's past three decades, including the country's economic and social reforms, the crackdown on Tiananmen protests and the death of Den Xiaoping as well as the 1997 Hong Kong handover. In addition to his on-air reporting, FlorCruz has contributed to *CNN.com* and is the writer of a weekly online column "Jaime's China. He is married to Ana Segovia FlorCruz and they have two children.

Jianwai Gongyu 4-2-162, Beijing 100600, Phone: +86106532 4521, Office: +86106532, *jaime.florcruz@cnn.com*

JOHN FLOWERS

John Flowers is a writer living in Brooklyn. Then again, who isn't these days? He is currently writing a TV show for NBC News. Before that he was writing a TV show for CNBC. Before that, he was writing wire stories for Dow Jones; before that, there was TIME magazine (but you already knew that part.)
johnfflowers@gmail.com

ED GOODPASTER

". . . Since leaving the News Service?" Good Lord. Bought a weekly newspaper in Wisconsin, sold a weekly newspaper in Wisconsin, worked for (in succession) the *Washington Post*, Jimmy Carter, The Wilderness Society and ran a company called Grit. Finally, back to my roots and daily newspapering, *The Baltimore Sun*, and its city that I have made my home.

100 W. University Parkway, Apt. 7-A, Baltimore, MD 21210, Phone: 410 243-9233,
edgood1@verizon.net

JAMES (JAMIE) GRAFF

After the Paris bureau chief gig evaporated in July 2007, I was a senior editor in London for two years until that job was eliminated too. After installing my family in Ottawa—there is a high school there where my son could finish in style—I took a job as foreign editor of AOL News. (Yes, I appreciate the irony.) Last November, when there were only inklings of that enterprise's subsequent collapse, I was approached by *The Week*, a sprightly publication that thrives on editorial principles not unlike those of TIME before *any of us* were in the picture. I was named managing editor and was promoted last month to executive editor.

Jamesgraff1@gmail.com

SAM GWYNNE

I left TIME's Austin bureau in 2000 to become executive editor of the *Texas Monthly*, also in Austin, where I worked for most of the next decade writing feature stories. I also taught courses in the journalism school of the University of Texas. During this time my wife Katie and I were living in the Westlake area in Austin raising our daughter Maisie (born in 1993.) Last year I took a new job as a senior writer at the *Dallas Morning News*, and also published a book, "*Empire of the Summer Moon*," which became a bestseller.

sgynne@dallasnews.com, office phone: 214 977-8486, cell: 512 413-8131

DAVID (DUDU) HALEVY

Since I left the TLNS I wrote and published a book: "Inside the PLO" (William Morrow, NY) and worked as a contributor and editor for PBS, the Washingtonian, and other American and European television networks. Soon I joined the business world representing major American corporations (specializing in energy) in their endeavors in Israel and the Middle East. At the beginning of the 21st century I moved into commodities trading. The new venue has allowed me to travel throughout the world (Asia, Europe, North America and Africa) while trading in raw materials, with an emphasis on rough diamonds. I continue to do this to this day and enjoy every minute of travel, trade, meetings and business.

71 Kedoshe Hashoa Street, Herzliyah-Pittuach, 46854, Israel. *david.halevy@gmail.com*

BARRY HILLENBRAND

Since returning to the US in 1999 from all those cushy overseas assignments—Saigon (!!??), Rio (!!!), Tokyo (!!!), London (!!!!), Bahrain (???)—Nga and I have been living in Washington, and since 2001 in retirement. I've busied myself with a bit of writing and editing (but not too much), a bit of speaking overseas for the State Department, and a lot of concert going and work around the garden. As always, I buy a lot of books and now I even manage to read some of them.

3344 Upland Terrace NW, Washington, DC, 20015, Phone: 202 237-5566. *barryhillenbrand@mac.com*

RICK HORNIK

I left Time Inc. at the end of 2001 when the geniuses at AOL shut down *Asiaweek*, where I had been executive editor for a year. In 2003 I spent four months training journalists in Cambodia and Vietnam and returned for more training stints in Hanoi and Saigon until 2008, when someone in the Politburo realized that wasn't great for potential stability. In 2007 I began teaching at the new J School at Stony Brook where we have developed a news literacy course for all undergrads that is now taught in about 20 colleges in the US. The closest I've gotten to actual journalism in the past decade—and the most fun—came in 2009 when I spent three months helping Adi Ignatius reorganize and redesign the *Harvard Business Review*, where I remain a contributing editor *rhornik@gmail.com*, Phone: 631-379-0816

WALTER ISSACSON

I left TIME to go to CNN in early 2001, and decided I liked print a whole lot better. In 2003, I became President of the Aspen Institute, a think tank in Washington. I've written a few books since Evan Thomas and I co-conspired on *The Wise Men* while we were at TIME. These include biographies of Henry Kissinger, Benjamin Franklin, and Albert Einstein. (Editor's note: And in case you missed it, Steven Jobs.)

The Aspen Institute, One Dupont Circle, Washington, DC20036, Phone: 202 736-5840

DAVID JACKSON

After 23 great years with TIME, I moved to Washington, DC at the end of August 2001. Since then, I created and ran a website for the Defense Department after 9/11; director of the Voice of America; communications advisor and speechwriter in the State Dept.; director of Defense Media Activity (the Defense Dept. agency responsible for TV, radio and online operations.) Currently: Consulting for Burson-Marsteller.
davidjacksonmail@verizon.net

JAMES JACKSON

After retiring in 2001 I got divorced, got poor, got remarried, got rich. On a trip back to my beloved hometown of Santa Fe, I reconnected with a girl I've known since grade school and we married in 2002. Since then we've bought, built and sold more houses than John McCain, plus one boat (n/b Symposium, my home in London), in the process becoming a plumber, a tile-setter, floor installer and landscaper. We're now in a big old adobe with a charming guesthouse and all old TLNS veterans are welcome to visit. Chris Ogden's slept in it. Ask him.
Jojackson05@q.com

JOE KANE

Upon retiring, I worked with the inevitable PR firm who stole my ideas and fired me. I then took up with an outfit that drives little old ladies to their doctors before securing speakers for a men's organization. Wrote a lengthy bio for sons instead of the reliable book authorship. Did the usual traveling to Hong Kong, Thailand and the Baltic rim. Mediterranean next. Have four grandchildren. Last February traveled to the slums of Kingston, Jamaica for a week encountering the poorest of the poor. Kingston boasts it is the Murder Capitol of the World. *josephkane@bellsouth.net*

ANN KING

After working with Jim Kelly when he was ME at TIME and up on the 34th floor when he was corporate editor, I retired a year and a half ago when he stepped down. And now that I have gotten into the rhythm of retirement am thoroughly enjoying the freedom to travel a bit more (just back from a trip to London and Prague) and to do a little volunteer work at my neighborhood soup kitchen. *anking1271@gmail.com*

MICHAEL KRAMER

After TIME I joined Steve Brill to edit the short-lived CONTENT magazine. From there I hooked up with Ed Kosner as managing editor/columnist at the Daily News. Then my second wife, Anne Dyson, died of cancer and I determined to quit journalism and pursue the writing projects I'd put on hold—several books owed to publishers and play that I had been itching to write. Now, "Divine Rivalry," based on a real-life competition between Leonardo and Michelangelo overseen by Machiavelli, has had a tweaking run at Hartford Stage. The Shubert Organization is producing and it will be on Broadway next year. I can be reached mostly easily via email: *michaelkramer@earthlink.net*

CHRISTY LAIDLAW

Christy Laidlaw has gone back to arts and is currently the membership coordinator for both the Japanese Art Society of America based in NYC and the Cahoon Museum of American Art based in Cape Cod. She moved to Harwich, MA in 2009 and is loving it. Anyone who wants to say hi, please contact her at: *christylaidlaw@gmail.com*

ELAINE LAVERTY

"Joined Irish Times of Dublin for four years of covering conflicts in Middle East, Pakistan, Afghanistan. Features editor, More magazine. Was Editor-in-Chief of Ms. Magazine, and led magazine to its first National Magazine Awards nomination in 17 years. Now writing/editing, and owning The Old Mill Inn, a circa 1830 waterfront restaurant near the Hampton's, NY. Best training for running a successful business *elainelafferty05@aol.com*

LANS LAMONT

I left the News Service in 1975 after 15 years in Washington, London, and Ottawa and as UN correspondent. I have since published six more books, the last (2008) a memoir of my years with Time, *You Must Remember This* (Beaufort Books.) I got lucky with my first book *Day of Trinity* (Athenaeum 1965) that became an international bestseller. During the 1980's, I directed a public affairs program on US-Canada issues for David Rockefeller's Americas Society. Subsequently, I joined the board of the American Trust for the British Library where I am currently chairman.
lanslamont@verizon.net

JONATHAN LARSEN

After leaving Time in 1973, I became the editor of the New Times in '74 and remained its editor until its demise in 1979. Following a Nieman Fellowship, I joined LIFE from 1980 to 1982, then freelanced for six years for New York Magazine, ManhattanInc., then edited the Village Voice from 1989 until 1994. Since then, I have written book reviews and essays on journalism for the Columbia Journalism Review.

565 West End Avenue, Apt. 11-A, NYC, NY 10024, Phone: 212 595-4088, also 71 Demas Road, Waterbury, VT 05676, Phone: 802 229-0706

ELIZABETH LEA

It took several years to get used to the sense of amputation brought on by retirement. Travel helped—annual trips to Africa to see my mother (now 101), and a visit to New Zealand where my brother lives. My three granddaughters (12, 8, 3) light up my life. I'm lucky. I can't tell you how sorry I am not to be able to join you but would love to hear from you.

99 High Street, Netheravon, Salisbury, Wiltshire, England, SP4 9PJ, Phone: +44 1980 670561, *elizabeth_lea@btinternet.com*,

MARLIN LEVIN

I am enjoying my retirement by going to the doctor and dentist regularly, paying bills, attending concerts, watching films, eating three tasty meals daily, sleeping 8 hours nightly, swimming in our pool, keeping in touch with friends on the computer, entertaining guests and generally having fun in our wonderful residence for citizens in peaceful Jerusalem.
8/413 Avizohar Street, Jerusalem, Israel, email: *betmar@bezeqint.net*

LINA LOFARO

Lina Lofaro has recently left TIME after 20 happy years. She is in the process of discovering what she'll do for Act II! She'd love to be in touch and can be reached at:
serenissima13@aol.com

LAURA LOPEZ

Since 1997 I have been at ECLAC, which is the UN's Economic Commission for Latin America and the Caribbean, based in Santiago, Chile, a country no longer best known for being the longest-lasting dictatorship at the edge of the Andes, but rather for massive earthquakes and industrious miners trapped far beneath the ground. Oh yeah. The wine is pretty good too. Fortified by some of the best vintages the new world has produced, I have held three different posts here: Chief of Information Services, Director of Documents and Publications, and for the past three years, Secretary of the Commission. *laura.lopez@cepal.org*

MELISSA LUDTKE

Left Time in the fall of 1991 when I was a Nieman Fellow and combined my severance with a book contract and wrote *"On Our Own: Unmarried Motherhood in America"* (Random House, 1997.) Then, I became an unmarried mom when I went to China and adopted my nine-month old daughter Maya Xia Ludtke, now 14 years old and a 9th grader at Cambridge Rindge and Latin High School, the public school in Cambridge, MA, where we live. Since 1998 I have been the editor of Nieman Reports (www.niemanreports. org), a magazine about journalism. I've found enormous pleasure in mentoring Maya and her friends in community activities as members of a Roots & Shoots group called The Sprouts of Hope as they engage in environmental activism. I like staying connected to journalism and last year taught an introductory course, "Discovering Journalism," to first-year students at Emerson University in Boston. Loving life as

Maya's mom; she keep me young, or at least feeling younger than my age tells me I am.

D30 Buena Vista Park, Cambridge, MA 02140, home/work phone: 617 354-1728 *melissa.ludtke@gmail.com*

SCOTT MACLEOD

I am Professor of Practice in School of Global Affairs and Public Policy at the American University in Cairo. Also founding managing editor of a new quarterly journal published by the university, The Cairo Review of Global Affairs. Wife Susan Hack remains a contributing editor at Conde Nast Traveler, and our daughter Sophie is a freshman at Cornell University.

P.O. Box 9640 Erie, PA 16505, cell: 20 12 317 2477 *zmacleodz@aol. com*

JEREMY MAIN

Jeremy Main joined the news service in 1958 and was assigned to TIME's Washington bureau, where he covered the early space efforts and the Defense Department. In 1961, after an assignment to Guantanamo during the Bay of Pigs fiasco, he joined the Paris bureau and reported on NATO and diplomacy, and made many reporting trips to Spain and Portugal. After four-plus glorious years in Paris, he came home to New York to write in the Business section (ugh!). He soon left to become a writer at Fortune and then after a spell with the Ford Foundation, joined the Money staff. In 1980 he went back to Fortune and remained happily until he retired in 1991.

jeremain@snet.net

LAWRENCE MALKIN

After I retired, I ascended to Time Correspondent's heaven. For six years as the US Correspondent for the International Herald Tribune, I filed front-page stories from New York and Washington. Meanwhile I developed a sideline "collaborating" on memoirs—a term of art for ghostwriting, book-doctoring, or editing—with Paul Volcker of the Fed; Anatoly Dobrynin, the Soviet ambassador to Washington for a quarter of a century, and Markus Wolf, the infamous (and utterly charming) East German sypmaster known as the Man Without a Face. My own book, "Krueger's Men" is the story of the greatest counterfeit in history and inspired the Oscar-winning film "The Counterfeiters." My financial thriller "Dancing with Madmen," a story of Wall Street malfeasance resulting in a world-wide financial crash has been sent to more than a dozen publishers starting in 2002 and is still making the rounds. "Very hard to believe" said one rejection letter. I'm working now on a post-crash set of biographical essays with the working title, "Pillars of Capitalism."

www.lawrencemalkin.com, malkinlit@msn.com, work phone and fax: 212 213-0045

PENNY MARSHALL MALLORY

Since "leaving" Time Inc. and moving to New Orleans in 1975, I continued to work for the company part-time. Time-Life Books Division's Garden Series; pinch hitting for Emily Friedrich in the Washington bureau in summers when she was away; and for Cassie Furgurson, Sidey's researcher, when she was on sabbatical. My husband and I moved back to DC in 1979, had a child (now working in NYC), and I continued on my "new" career path—selling residential real estate—which I began while living in New Orleans. *Pmallory17@gmail.com*, Phone 301-654-7902

LARA MARLOWE

I left Time's Beirut bureau in the fall of 1996 to become the Paris correspondent for The Irish Times, the main daily newspaper in Ireland. Over the next 13 years, I covered Chirac, Sarkozy, the death of Princess Diana and the Concorde crash. I continued covering wars, including Afghanistan 2001, Iraq 2003 and thereafter, Lebanon 2006, Georgia2008 and Gaza 2009. In August 2009, I moved to Washington, as US correspondent. In 2010, I published *"The Things I've Seen; Nine Lives of a Foreign Correspondent.*

1517 30th Street, NW, Apt C-32, Washington, DC 20007, phone: 202 525-5140
lmarlowe@irishtimes.com

BILL MARMON

I left the LA bureau in 1977, to go to UVA law school. "Why on earth would he do that," I often heard. Turned out great. I clerked for a wonderful judge and went with a DC firm, and then to MCI telecommunications/Verizon, in house, where I was at last an insider. 23 years later, including 3 1/2 years in Singapore, I "retired." Currently affiliated with European Institute, where Joelle Attinger is President. *WMarmon@gmail.com*, phone: 301 654-7893, cell: 301 503-6103

WAITS MAY

I started at *Money.com* in the fall of 1997, which merged with *CNNfn. com* in 1999 (to become CNNmoney.com.) I moved with *CNNmoney. com* to the AOL Time Warner bldg. in the summer of 2000. We were background props for the CNN New York studios. I left the Time Inc. family in the fall of 2007 to develop and fill the new position of Web Guy at Hackley School in Tarrytown, NY where my two daughters go to school. It's a blast!
wmay@hackleyschool.org

JEF MCALLISTER

I left TIME in 2007 and have been practicing law in London with my wife, Ann Olivarius (*www.mcolaw.com*). We handle a variety of transatlantic business and corporate matters, employment discrimination, nonprofit governance and general litigation, both in the US and UK. Our firm now has 25 employees and is growing;

running a small business definitely exercises different muscles from reporting, in a good way. I miss the buzz of politics but have really enjoyed the law too. Casey and Kathryn are now through college, Jack goes next year, already three inches taller than his dad. I still have an itch to write history—probably in retirement, whenever that may happen. We're surprised still to be in London but love it. Our office is between Heathrow and downtown, on the Thames, next to a fabulous Tuscan restaurant, and the welcome mat is always out for News Service vets.

Home phone: +44 (0) 208749 9600, Office: +44 (0) 20 7386 1055, cell: +44 (0) 7711 95 75 65, USA cell: 203 444-4566
jefmca@gmail.com

JACKIE MCCONNELL

From 1980 to 1989 I worked at the News Desk in New York. A few months after having my daughter we moved to Florida to be near my sister, where I took a "long weekend" of two years to cook for a country club, restaurants and a catering operation. When a writing job at my town's community newspaper opened up I took it and after a couple of years became editor. After another couple of years we moved to Tampa where I joined the Tampa Bay Business Journal as a writer and its research director, moving up to managing editor about 10 years ago. Great times and the skills honed at the TLNLS prepped me very well for a great career so far.
jackiemcconnell@ymail.com

FRANK MCCULLOCH

Spring Lake Village, 5555 Montgomery Drive, Unit L-2, Santa Rosa, CA 95409, Phone: 707579-6858

JACK MCDONALD

Since leaving in 1991, I moved into documentary filmmaking, working with PBS, BBC, National Geographic Television, Discovery and other channels and outlets. From the mid-90's I was based in Rome and then Amsterdam, eventually moved to Boston, where I was a producer for the PBS/WGBH science series NOVA. In recent years I've focused on independent documentary; often with advocacy groups and aid organizations. For over 10 years I have been a story consultant to TV stations and production companies around the country, and have conducted annual workshops on writing and story development in the US and Europe. Recently I returned to New York, and live now in Brooklyn.
mcjackdonald@gmail.com, cell: 617 828-7484

JOHANNA MCGEARY

So, where was I? Oh yes, during stint in London (2005 to'06) sold our apartment in NYC and took a buyout. Loved TIME, my job, but glad I retired: new journalism has its points but I'm too old school. Rather work for a brand than be a brand. Rather report than opine.

We went to live in our house in Italy for a year, as long anticipated; got interrupted by family illness in CA, which led to buying a house by the beach in Orange County. Now that four generations of our family all live on the left coast, we were the lone holdouts in the East. Currently, we spend the summer in Italy and winter in Corona del Mar, CA. Huge change of lifestyle but we miss New York a lot. Getting to like CA. We're official, biologically incorrect grandparents to our four great-nieces/nephews which is a huge treat. Traveling a lot, cooking a lot, growing stuff—a 250-tree olive grove has come into our lives. And before everyone asks—NO am not writing anything, not books, not pieces, not blog, not tweet. Have traded in verbal arts for visual: doing this and that with photography/painting. Jonathan is grand too.

435 Carnation, Corona del Mar, CA 92625, Phone: 949 706-2198, cell: 917 379-2444
Tuscany, Phone: +39 0575 44 81 25, mobile: +39 339 146 8454
jpmcgeary@hotmail.com

JASON MCMANUS

Deborah and I are migratory birds between SoHo (Manhattan version), Garrison, NY and the Cap d'Antibes. She is busier with the diverse causes and boards and choirs then when an architect; daughter Sophie is a fiction writer and newly married to an artist; I write a lot (of checks). Thanks to everyone for putting this on; it is work. Next time I will send you my press accreditation from the French Service de Presse 1962.
jdmcmanus@aol.com

KATIE MCNEVIN

After retiring when the 2001 package was offered, I sat on the couch and watched reruns of "Murder, She Wrote", and once I started watching the same episode at 11 am and again at 4 pm, I realized I had better dream up something else to do. I went to New York School of Interior Design with the vague notion of working in that field but when I was asked to work on a woman's magazine being launched by Time Inc., I jumped at the chance. That was six years and a second 401-K ago.

215 West 91st Street, NYC 10024, phone: 917441-9252, cell: 917 941-6877
katie_mcnevin@allyou.com or *katiemcnevin@aol.com*

JEFF MELVOIN

After serving as a correspondent in the New York, Boston and LA bureaus, I left the News Service in 1982 to work as a writer and producer in one-hour television. I'm currently executive producer of the Lifetime dramatic series *Army Wives*, which is in its fifth season. Prior credits include *Alias*, *Picket Fences*, *Northern Exposure*, *Hill Street Blues*, and *Remington Steele*. I have been married forever to Martha Hartnett Melvoin, a former photographer for the LA Times, and we have two sons. Nick's going to law school after serving three years with Teach for America; Charlie's finishing up a masters in Chinese Development Studies at Jesus College, Cambridge. I've taught screenwriting at USC and UCLA, have been a Visiting Lecturer in Dramatic Arts at Harvard, and look forward to doing more teaching in the years ahead.

jeffreymelvoin@mac.com

JOHN MOODY

Said Moody: "I left Time in 1996 to become the vice president, News Editorial, at Fox News." Continued the former New York, Rome, and Latin American bureau chief: "After being part of that cable news phenomenon for 13 years, I was named CEO of NewsCore, a business unit of Fox's parent company, News Corporation." Concluded he: "Two post-Time books: a 1996 biography of Pope John Paul II, and, in 2010, *"Kiss it Good-bye: The Mystery, the Mormon and the Moral of the 1960 Pittsburgh Pirates."*

stday.nicholas@gmail.com

MICHAEL MORITZ

Has been a Member of Sequoia Capital since 1986.

moritz@sequoiacap.com

HENRY MULLER

Ten years ago I moved to Switzerland, where I live with my wife Christina Ferrari and our son Sacha, age 7. I've done some writing and consulting for Swiss magazines, but mostly try to stay clear of commitments that feel like work.

Route de Cully 18, 1091 Grandvaux, Switzerland, phone: 41 21 799 2038, cell: 41 79 625 0420, email: *henrymuller@bluerwin.ch*

ANN MOFFETT

7706 Elba Road, Alexandria, VA 22306, email: *moffmoe2@aol.com*

DON NEFF

After living in Washington for a number of years Don is now back in his hometown of York, PA. He says he doesn't travel too much any more and is sorry that he can't make the reunion. He would like to hear all about it.
hanfbook@aol.com,

BRUCE NELAN

I retired in May 1999 and then had a one-year contract with Time Europe. I worked for seven months with the former captain of the USS Cole on a book detailing the ship's attack by al Qaeda in Yemen, but he decided for personal reasons not to complete the project. I'm on the board and two committees of the Washington Institute of Foreign Affairs and serve as chairman of the Book and Author Dinner committee at the Cosmos Club in Washington.

5963 Valerian Lane, Rockville, MD 20852 *bnelan523@aol.com*

PAT LAMBERT NEWMAN

After leaving TLNS San Francisco bureau in 1979, I worked as a stringer for People, Time, Life, and T-L Books. I then went into hospital public relations, working at Mt. Zion Medical Center up to and after its merger with the University of CA, San Francisco. I started my own healthcare marketing communications business in 1991; primary clients were Kaiser Permanente and UCSF School of Nursing. I retired in 2008 and am enjoying the quiet of an over-55 condo community in beautiful Marin County, CA. *newmancom@comcast.net*

HERMAN NICKEL

To avoid any conflict of interest, I took a leave of absence from Fortune in 1981, when my name was put forward as a candidate for nomination as Reagan's ambassador to South Africa. That ended nearly 24 great years with Time Inc., all but three spent with the TLNS, including the bureau chief positions in Bonn, Tokyo and London, as well as a stint as senior diplomatic correspondent in Washington. On my return from South Africa late in1986, I decided not to go back through the revolving door to Time Inc., but to accept an appointment as a Senior Fellow at the US Institute of Peace. Subsequently, I served as Vice President of Global Business Access, a consulting group of retired Foreign Service officers. In 2000, we pulled up stakes in Washington to move to our new home in Tucson, AZ, our final foreign assignment. Sadly, I lost my wife Phyllis in 2003, but I decided to carry on here. *nickel-hw@att.net*

CHRIS OGDEN

Left the News Service in 1992, but continued on contract through 2000, mostly writing the View from Washington column for International. Wrote several biographies, got fit, lost weight, traveled extensively, often lecturing on long-haul cruise ships—not bad fallback for The Land Beyond Expense Account. Long marriage blew up at the end of the 20th century. Met fabulous woman—Linda Fuselier—early in 21st, married same on game reserve in South Africa in April 2010. Have abandoned non-fiction, trying a novel and missing my Time colleagues, an astonishing collection of smart, caring and hugely fun folk. I feel very fortunate to have known and worked with you. Almost all of you. Almost always. *cheno@comcast.com*

PRISCILLA PAINTON

I left Time four years ago to go to Simon & Schuster as executive editor with a mission to acquire non-fiction. My office is right across the street from the T & L bldg., so it wasn't much of a geographical stretch. I have many Time Incers on my list of authors, several of whom I am sure are on their way to the bestseller list.

1230 Avenue of the Americas, NYC, NY 10020, *priscilla.painton@ simonandschuster.com*

CHRISTOPHER (CHRIS) PORTERFIELD

I left the News Service way back in 1972, then spent several decades with TIME Edit as a senior editor, assistant ME and executive editor. My one foray outside of Time Inc. was from 1974 to 1980, when I wrote and produced TV shows for my old Yale roommate, Dick Cavett. I also co-wrote a couple of books with Dick. And then back in the fold.

Since retiring in 2005, I've done some free-lancing mostly for TIME—arts features, obits, books and CD reviews and occasional editing chores. I edited *Time: 85 years of Great Writing* (Time Books) and last year I was a consultant on *Time: The Illustrated History of the World's Most Influential Magazine*, by Norberto Angeletti and Alberto Oliva (Rizzoli).

Otherwise, Stevie and I are enjoying the life of retirees in Manhattan, grand-parenting, traveling etc. Still hanging on at 315 Central Park West, Apt. 11-S, NYC, NY 10025, Phone: 212 724-0948
cporterfie@aol.com

CURT PRENDERGAST

I was hired as a correspondent for TIME in 1950 during the Korean war and served subsequently as a bureau chief for TIME in Tokyo, Johannesburg, Paris, London and the United Nations in New York. While representing Time Inc. on the newly formed World Press Freedom Committee, I helped Frank White, my predecessor in the Paris bureau, organize the TLAS and served after him as its president. During those years, I also did considerable edit work for Time Life Books, and for

Time Inc. including the third and last volume of the corporate history (published by Atheneum in 1986.) My last writing for TIME was a piece on my Korean War experiences published in July 2000.

ANDREW PURVIS

I am dividing my time, with the help of sleeping medication, between Geneva and San Francisco. I spent the past month in Libya, Tunisia and Egypt in a multi-media whirl as a video producer and writer . . .. still breathing sand. I am running something called the storytelling project at the UN Refugee Agency, UNHCR. We are producing video and still photo profiles of refugees and former refugees in and out of conflict zones around the world, from Congo to Afghanistan. The idea is to create a place where refugees can tell their stories in their own voice on the web, mobile and Al Jazeera.

I was a Knight fellow at Stanford, where I developed an online project to link editors and producers in the US with local reporters around the world. My professional heart is overseas but the rest of my heart is in San Francisco where Gretchen and Emily are, and I plan to move there shortly.

andrewcpurvis@googlemail.com, or *apurvis0264@aol.com,* phone: +41 79 263 3429

BILL RADEMAEKERS

Bill Rademaekers, 80. Retired July 17, 1985, continued as consultant for another decade. Alive & well (?) and living in England, with forays to our place in France and the USA to see our six children. Tractor gone, but still huge organic farmer. *wimrad@aol.com*

RUDOLPH (RU) RAUCH

I left the News Service in 1980 to accept the Edward R. Murrow Fellowship at the Council on Foreign Relations. I returned to the Company in 1981 and held a number of positions, the final one in Magazine Development. After leaving Time Inc., I joined Andrew Heiskell in an attempt to launch a magazine on real estate. Edited *Constitution*, a quarterly developed by former TIME Publisher, Jack Meyers and Time Promotion veteran Alan Martin. Was Managing Director of the Metropolitan Opera Guild from 1994 to 2003 and editor of Opera News from 1998 until 2003. Retired in 2003 and live chiefly in Cold Spring, NY. I serve on two land trust boards and contribute occasionally to Opera News.

PO Box 117, Cold Spring, NY 10516, Phone: 646 285-2843email: *rauchru@aol.com*

CHRIS REDMAN

My first attempt to write an entry for the yearbook was sent back from New York for a re-write. So not much has changed. I'm just finishing up a screenplay and hope for better treatment from Hollywood. Jan and I divide our time between London and a house in the part of France that is loosely called Gascony—the Southwest not too far from the Pyrenees. If you are in the vicinity, please look us up.

43 Colehill Lane, London SW6 5EF, UK; Phone: +44 (0) 207
736-2285, Petre, 32410Castera-Verduzan, France, Phone: +33 (0) 5
62 28 81 31

redmancj@gmail.com

ED REINGOLD

I retired in 1992 in LA and finished two books before joining the
faculty at the University of Southern CA J-school and took over the
running of its degree-granting program in international journalism.
When that ended, I, with the late Leo Janos, a fellow music lover,
established a website called 'bestclassicalcds' in which we vented
our approvals and petty hatreds on defenseless longhairs. We never
expected to make any money at it, and we were proved correct. I
eventually managed to convince my wife Ellen, to give up her thriving
corporate Pilates practice and move with me to Portland. We saw LA
recede in the rearview mirror with some relief in 2004. Since then
I have done some pieces for local publications, light work for the
advisory board of the Center for Japanese Studies at Portland State
U, and am teasing out a family memoir for my grandchildren—who
may be old enough to recognize the hyperbole by the time I finish.
emreingold1@msn.com

MARGOT ROOSEVELT

Margot Roosevelt (ex-Hornblower) is an environmental reporter at the
LA Times, based in LA . . . and loving it! Covering mostly climate change
and air pollution. Occasional forays overseas to write about Brazilian

rain forests and climate negotiations in Copenhagen and Cancun. *margot. roosevelt@latimes.com* or Facebook.

ERIC ROSTON

I left Time's Washington bureau in 2006 to write a popular science book called *"the Carbon Age."* And most recently worked on the staff of the National Oil Spill. My wife Karen Yourish and I live in Bethesda with our three-year-old daughter, Madeline. *roston.eric@gmail.com*, phone: 202 253-5723

ROY ROWAN

After leaving the TLNS in 1977 I joined Fortune as a senior writer, turning out some 60 articles before retiring in 1985. I continued freelancing for *Fortune*, the monthly *Life*, *People* and *Smithsonian* while concentrating on writing books on intuition, war, fishing, and baseball. A China memoir, *Chasing the Dragon* has been optioned by Universal Pictures. My ninth book, *Never Too Late: a 90-year-old's Pursuit of a Whirlwind Life*, has just been published. *Rowanroy1@aol.com.* www.royrowan.com

JEANNE SADDLER

After several years as a TIME correspondent, beginning in New York and then as part of the Washington bureau, I joined the Wall Street Journal where I spent almost 12 years. My last two positions have been as a government communications/public affairs director—first in the Clinton administration and currently with the Metropolitan Washington Council of Governments. Along the way, I was blessed with a wonder husband, Warren Leary, a science correspondent who recently retired from The New York Times, and our two sons, Dana and Devon.

Director, Office of Public Affairs Metropolitan Washington, Council of Governments, 777 N. Capitol St., NE, Washington, DC 20002, Phone: office: 212 962-3250

jsaddler@mwcog.org

CAMILLE CASSATA SANABRIA

After 35 years, I retired in November 2009. Currently I am the business and finance manager for Mount Sinai Hospital. My son Andrew is just finishing up his second year of college and hopes to complete his studies in Emergency Medicine, and this year Rene and I celebrated our 26th wedding anniversary.

4801 Stonehedge Road, Edison NJ 08820, cell: 908 705-4270

csanabria1104@aol.com

TOM SANCTON

Time has indeed flown in the 10 years since I left the magazine. After the 2001 buyout, I stayed in Paris and wrote two books, *Song for My Fathers* (a New Orleans memoir), and *The Armageddon Project* (political thriller.) I moved back to my hometown of NO in 2007 with my wife Sylvaine. Currently teaching creative writing at Tulane, freelancing for Vanity Fair et al., playing a lot of music and looking after my 96-year-old dad.

4849A Magazine Street, New Orleans, LA 70115, phone: 504 218-5371, cell: 504 451-0990, email: *tomsancton@yahoo.com*, blog: *tomsancton.blogspot.com*)

BARRY SEAMAN

Not long after "The Night of the Living Dead" party at which those of us who "took the package" celebrated our freedom in the summer of 2001, I launched into research for a book about contemporary college life. After two years of living on 12 different campuses, I wrote *Binge: Campus Life in an Age of Disconnection and Excess* published by Wiley on 2005. Since then, I've done a fair amount of speaking on the subject. I also joined forces with John McCardell, the former president of Middlebury College, now president of Sewanee, to form an organization called Choose Responsibility. Our goal is to spur a re-examination of the minimum drinking age, which we believe (as I wrote in an essay for TIME) that the drinking age is part of the problem, not the solution to dangerous drinking so prevalent among college students these days. When McCardell left, I succeeded him as president.

The other main thing I do is sing with the University Glee Club of New York City, an all male chorus founded in 1894. We do two main concerts a year at Lincoln Center as well as some benefit concerts and the occasional trip. Singers, I find are a lot like correspondents: gregarious and prone to drink. Phone:914-591-8114 *absea@aol. com*,

CLAIRE SENARD

Soon after mid-2008 when I had to leave the TIME's Paris bureau, where I spent 32 great years, I joined my friend Judy Fayard (formerly of both TIME and LIFE) at France Today magazine, a monthly for Americans who love France (it's full of good stories: *www.francetoday. com.*—or better yet, subscribe!) When I'm not in Paris, I try to keep my family home in Alox Corton, in Burgundy, from falling down. Please come and visit. And lately, my husband Gerard Charlier, and I have also been traveling quite a lot—most recently to Syria, Turkey, Israel and Rome.

6 Rue de Mezieres, 7500 Paris, Phone: 33 1 45 44 89 23, cell: 33 6 13 09 48 97
claire.senard@gmail.com

ANN M. SIMMONS

I left TIME magazine in 1997 to become Nairobi Bureau Chief for the LA Times covering East, Central and West Africa. During my three-year assignment, I reported on stories from more than 30

African nations, interviewing soldiers on the frontlines of conflicts, including the Congo, Sierra Leone and Liberia; documenting the transformation of military dictatorships to civilian democracies, such as Nigeria; and highlighting the hardships—and hopes—of ordinary Africans. Additionally, I was bureau chief in Johannesburg and covered Zimbabwe from there as well. I won a Nieman Fellowship at Harvard University; served a couple of temporary assignments in Iraq, where I survived a suicide bomb attack; became the LA Times' primary correspondent based in New Orleans following Hurricane Katrina; and now cover local news in LA County.

annmsimmons@yahoo.com

WENDY SKINNER

I Left the Washington bureau of TIME in 1998 to move back to New England and be with my (now) husband Don. I fell into writing for higher education fund raising (mostly in the sciences) at Brown University, then the Marine Biological Lab (MBL) and now for the University of Massachusetts. I also do freelance writing, consulting and teaching on fund raising in academia and with local, direct service non-profits. I am on my town's Conservation Commission (a thankless job) and am involved in land conservation efforts. Don and I live in our 330-year-old house (yup, King Philip's War) in Rehoboth, MA with seven misfit cats and a bunch of RI Red hens.

wendykskinner@gmail.com

MARTHA SMILGIS

After I left TIME, I was a producer on 'Extra' for two years. After TV, I wrote a biz column for the SF Examiner called "Outraged Investor" (survival following the tech debacle, etc. Nieman Reports did a nice piece on my column.) When the Examiner expired, I was hired at Santa Barbara Newspress where I wrote a popular social and political column called "The Dish." Since then, I have been trading stock, half-heartedly writing a book on the joy of aging, and traveling.

82 Olive Mill Road, Montecito, CA 93108, Phone: 805 969-1223, *msmilgis.@aol.com*

JOHN STACKS

I retired, just in time, in 2001, having been at the magazine for 35 years, more or less. After retirement, I managed to finish my fourth book, *Scotty, The Rise and Fall of American Journalism.* Little, Brown published the book, before they were sent packing from Time Warner. The book was well reviewed, but I never had the nerve to ask for sales figures. The University of Nebraska Press published a paperback edition a few years ago. I still do a bit of travel and golf writing and am working fitfully on a sort of journalistic memoir. I have figured out the correct response for retirees when the question "what are you doing" is posed. My answer now is "whatever I want."
stacks@aol.com

WILLIAM (BILL) STEWART

At the moment, I am a columnist for "The Sante Fe New Mexican" (which bills itself as the oldest paper in the West), writing weekly on foreign affairs and politics. I also teach courses in the spring and fall on foreign affairs and the history of the Middle East for Renesan, an extended learning service. I also do a weekly talk radio program on current events (foreign, national and local) with two or three other participants. And then I'm still toiling away on a personal memoir, which I hope to finish in a couple of months. *wstewarttesuque@aol.com*

ROD STODGHILL

I Left New York in 2004 and now live in Charlotte, NC, with my wife Robyn and three sons. Since then, I've worked as a senior editor for Fortune Small Business, business writer for The New York Times, and today as the business columnist for the Charlotte Observer newspaper. I also wrote a nonfiction book Redbone—Money, Malice and Murder in Atlanta; HarperCollins, 2007 and am currently working on other books/documentary projects.

3015 Symphony Woods Drive, Charlotte, NC 28269, Phone: 704 598-6239, cell: 704 778-6390
ronstodghill@aol.com

JUDITH STOLER

After 32 years with TIME in New York and Washington, DC, I packed up my things and headed for the beauty and peace of Ottawa, Canada, where Peter and I once lived and where the dear friends we made were awaiting my arrival. Moving here was the best present I have ever given myself. Since my arrival in 2008, I have busied myself with charitable work of all kinds with a particular passion for my seat on the Board of Directors for the Ottawa Peace Foundation which, among other things, brings Arab and Jewish young women, from Israel to Ottawa each summer to live and work together while participating in a conflict resolution course administered by St. Paul University.

judithstoler@mac.com

ROGER STONE

Following TLNS postings (1961-1968) as a correspondent and new bureau chief in San Francisco and Rio de Janeiro as well as acting bureau chief in Paris, I returned to New York and the corporate side as assistant to then Time Inc. President Jim Linen. I left Time Inc. to become successively vice president for international communications at the Chase Manhattan Bank, president of the Center for Inter-American Relations in NY, and vice president of the World Wildlife Fund in NY and Washington.

As my focus sharpened on environmental issues, I returned to writing and now have five published books and many articles and editing gigs on environmental-economic connections. Viking/Penguin published the first book, Dreams of Amazonia, in 1985. In 1n 1994 I left WWF to launch the nonprofit Sustainable Development Institute as a vehicle for print, film and web environmental communications project. Am currently working on a book about the Hudson Valley environment. My wife Flo meanwhile launched the environmental Film Festival in the Nation's Capital, the largest of its kind. Life is good.

1527 30th Street, NW, Washington, DC 20007, Home phone: 202 337-6286, office phone: 202 338-1017, email: *susdev@igc.org*

GEORGE TABER

After spending 21 years as a correspondent and editor at TIME, I left in 1988 to start a weekly business newspaper in New Jersey, where I lived. It was a rip-off of others like "Crain's New York Business" and the Washington Business Journal". Thanks to my inadequacies as a manager, it took a long time to make a profit forcing me to work odd weeks and odd hours at TIME doing everything short of greasing the presses.

The business weekly finally made it financially and I sold it in 2005. While at the paper, I had been working on a book about a story I did for TIME. It's gone into wine history as the Judgment of Paris, which was the headline on the ModLiv story that ran in 1976. The story was only four paragraphs about a blind tasting of California, French Cabernet Sauvignon and Chardonnay with top French judges who picked the California wines as best in class. I was the only journalist there. All other reporters presumed the French wines were going to win, so there would be no story. That TIME story put Napa Valley on the map.

The Judgment of Paris came out in 2005 and was the basis for a movie "Bottle Shock" followed in 2008. I had nothing to do with the movie, certainly not picking the guy who played me. The book, though, opened the road to my third career in writing wine books and I went on to write three more.

My wife and I split our retirement life between summers on Block Island, RI and winters in Vero Beach, FL. We call it our endless summer. *george@georgemtaber.com*

PHIL TAUBMAN

Since I left Time in 1977, I have worked as a roving editor (read sports editor) at Esquire during the Clay Felker reign and then thirty years as a correspondent and editor at The New York Times. My postings at The Times included Moscow bureau chief and Washington bureau chief and a run as an editorial board member and deputy editorial page editor. Since 2008, I have been based at Stanford University as a consulting professor. I have written two books, one on the development of spy satellites during the Eisenhower administration and the other, published in 2012, on nuclear threats (The Partnership: Five Cold Warriors and Their Quest to Ban the Bomb). Felicity Barringer and I celebrated our 40th anniversary in 2011. She remains at The Times as a national environment correspondent. We live not far from Stanford, realizing a dream to settle in Northern California that dates back to our days as Stanford undergraduates.

DICK THOMPSON

I left TIME in 2001, and went to work for the World Health Organization in Geneva, Switzerland. At WHO, I led WHO's communications on SARS, developed the WHO Outbreak Communications Guidelines, helped to train officials from 120 governments in outbreak communications, and worked with Ministries of Health in several countries during high profile outbreaks. My last job at WHO was as the Director-General's communication adviser. During our eight years in Switzerland, Kristin and I developed a great affection for Swiss mountains, French cheeses and Italian wine. After Obama's election, I came home to work at the FDA for a year, and am now the senior global editor at the policy journal Health Affairs.

305 North Lincoln Street, Arlington, VA 22201, cell: 202 642-3133. *dickthompson1@gmail.com*

DIANA TOLLERSON

My parting gift from TIME in 2001, when I took the early retirement package, stated: "Diana Tollerson . . . Retires, Spends 401(k), Joins Tennis Circuit." The only item they didn't predict was my involvement in the community. I spend the time between playing tennis and spending my money on travel and gadgets, doing volunteer work as a Pink Lady at the local hospital, writing the neighborhood newsletter, delivering Meals on Wheels, or driving as a Medical Expert Transporter for the elderly (who are more feeble than I). I also joined a local church and work on the Pastor's Aid Committee. My former colleagues are cringing now over that long sentence—but I managed to get it all in three sentences. My last one will be: "Sorry, I can't be with you all in May, but do keep in touch."

2115 Brookview Drive, NW, Atlanta, GA 30318, Phone: 404 355-4307 *drtollerson@bellsouth.net*

KAREN TUMULTY

I left TIME in April 2010 and am now national political correspondent at the Washington Post. Phone: 202-334-9576.*tumultyk@washpost.com*

MIA TURNER

After bouncing around the world working in crises and disasters as a spokesperson for the U.N. World Food Programme, I joined the UN Environment Programme's headquarters in Nairobi, Kenya, almost two years ago to work on covering the news angle of environmental protection, climate change and natural resources(to help understand all those year of conflict and disasters) as well as China's role in the climate debate, on renewables and environmental conservation.

Phone: +254 (0) 20 762-5211, cell: +254 (0) 710620495 *miaantoniaturner@gmail.com,*

DOUG WALLER

Doug is the author of Wild Bill Donovan: The Spymaster Who Created the OSS and Modern American Espionage (published by Free Press.)

He is also working at the moment as a defense analyst/editor at Bloomberg Government in its Washington bureau. Phone: 703 256-4063, cell: 202 253-0515
dcwaller@aol.com

DRURY WELLFORD

Since I left TIME 16 years ago, I have lived in Mexico, Argentina and Florida (ugh,) finally landing back in my hometown of Richmond, VA in 2003 (double ugh.) I earned my MLS from Pratt Institute and have worked variously as a university librarian, high school librarian, assistant archivist at Virginia's Department of Historic Resources and am currently Photo Archivist at the Museum of Confederacy.

My only true achievement has been the raising of two of the loveliest and wittiest young ladies you'd ever want to meet, my daughters Maria (19) and Rosie (16.)

8041 Whittington Drive, Richmond, VA 23235, Phone: 804272-3734, cell: 804 334 7502. *drurywellford@gmail.com*

GREG WIERZYNSKI

I left TIME in 1983 for government work, first as a special assistant in the office of the secretary of defense, followed by a stint as director of Radio Free Europe in Munich. I had a brief life as a private consultant after the fall of the Berlin wall, helping American companies become acquainted with the new post-communist governments in Eastern Europe. When they no longer needed my advice to get around, I embarked on a congressional career as staff director of a special commission on U.N. policy, then at the House Committee on Banking and Financial Services in charge of investigations (Whitewater) and capital markets and, finally, as the chief of staff for Congressman Jim Leach, a moderate Iowa Republican and an old friend. I retired in 2007 when he lost his seat.

4426 Klingel Street, NW, Washington, DC 20016, *gregor@wierzynski. com*

JIM WILLWERTH

I retired in 2000 to continue to write books and found the fast-changing publishing industry resistant to the quasi-journalistic books I'd done before. Next came a painful divorce, followed, blessedly, by marriage to Uli, whom I met on a hiking trail in Spain. I've begun a family memoir about something that has gnawed at my insides for a long time, and my agent is encouraging. Lastly, I've taught writing as a volunteer for 10 years to people recovering from serious mental illnesses.

3360 N. Glenrose Avenue, Altadena, CA 91001, Phone: 626 529-3726
jimwillwerth@gmail.com

DON WINBUSH

TV detective Jim Rockford's lifestyle (Rockford Files) held a certain fascination when I left TIME in 1992, ostensibly to pursue freelance journalism at an unhurried pace. A couple of captivating marketing-related assignments with the Atlanta Braves and the National Black Arts Festival led me to commercial copywriting—corporate speeches, video scripts, marketing materials, crisis training, and such. That's been the gig ever since, while wife Georgia and I pushed and guided our son Omari and daughter Sigele through college (amazingly, my daughter found herself in a class taught by Jack White, at Hampton University in Virginia). Home is College Park, GA, in the shadow—but not the flight path—of the world's busiest airport, and where my labor of love is leading a business organization in a community in economic revitalization. As for the Jim Rockford thing, I got over it.

2280 Wexford Drive, College Park, GA 30349, Phone: 770 907-4571
dwinbush@mindspring.com

PAUL WITTEMAN

Since getting the hook from S.I. in 2001 (well-deserved,) I have done as little as possible. I'm married to the former TIME writer and editor Ellie McGrath, and we divide our time between New York and

Tenants Harbor, ME, where I do even less. Our daughter, Kate, will be going to college this September. Our Jack Russell terrier, Tucker, will not.

110 Riverside Drive, Apt. 1-A, NYC, NY 10024, Phone: 212 595-4161
pwitteman@aol.com

JACK E. WHITE

Has taught journalism students at Hampton, Virginia Commonwealth and Howard Universities, and contributed freelance pieces to *TheRoot.com*. He now lives in Richmond, VA, with his wife, Gayle Jessup White, whose sister, Janice, was the wife of the late TLNS correspondent Wally Terry. *blackdogdc@gmail.com*

JEAN WHITE

My husband and I left New York (not certain why even now) and moved to a small town—a very small town—in Western PA (Ligonier.) We bought a very old house with a huge backyard and restored, and renovated the house and planted grass and flowers etc. It was very pretty but I still had to wonder why I was there. Robert died and I had to think of some place else to go and something to do. I travel mostly to the bay area of California and northern New Mexico. And, I take my first elder hostel trip this summer!
Jeanw9@hotmail.com

DICK WOODBURY

Returned to campus for some of the stuff I never learned the first time or long ago forgot. Enrolled at Metro State in Denver, where I am advancing my Spanish and brushing up on philosophy and religion. Dabbling in other humanities courses through various senior programs . . . Earlier stints in language camps in Quito and Cuernavaca . . . Writer for Latino Suave magazine and other bilingual publication in the West . . . Travel writing for assorted dailies. *rwdenver@aol.com*, Phone: 303 355-1782

MARY WORMLEY

3012 Homewood Pkway, Kensington, MD 20895, Phone: 301 933-2140, cell: 301 233-2004 *mwormley@aol.com*

JOHN YANG

I left the TLNS in 1985 because I missed the adrenaline-rush of daily journalism. I covered the collapse of the savings and loan industry and, later, Congress for the Wall Street Journal. In 1990, I moved to the Washington Post where I covered Congress, the George H.W. Bush White House, was economic policy editor in the Business section and oversaw political features in the Style section. A television project for The Post turned into a job as a correspondent for ABC News in 1999. After 9/11, I spent about three years as the Middle East Correspondent based in Jerusalem, shuttling in and out of Iraq after the fall of Saddam Hussein. I moved to the NBC at the beginning of 2007. I was White

House correspondent for the final year of the Bush administration and moved to Chicago in 2009. From there I've done two coverage tours in Afghanistan and write this from post-earthquake and tsunami Japan.

yang.john.e@gmail.com

MARVIN ZIM

I left TIME in 1978 after putting 17 years with the News Service, mostly in Washington, but also as the bureau chief for South Asia, based in New Delhi. I subsequently worked for Union Pacific Corp. as Director of Corporate Communications and retired in 1994. Since then I have been writing magazine articles, and have been a consultant to the Center for Strategic and International Studies (CSIS.) I also enjoy playing tennis and bridge and am active in the Princeton Alumni Association. (Editor's note: Marvin Zim died in 2011)

CPSIA information can be obtained at www.ICGtesting.com
Printed in the USA
BVOW070013140912

300245BV00002B/12/P